Jawan
to
General

Attention Authors

We Convert Fighters into Writers'. That's the motto of Manas Publications since more than four decades. Our message to the world is that India can win the battle not only by the bullet but also by the pen. There is no dearth of intellectuals in our country, but their knowledge is confined to them only. No sincere effort has been made by any other publisher to channelise their knowledge in national interest. That is why the talent of a large number of intellectuals remains latent. An author transforms his knowledge into a manuscript, and it is our job to spread his/her knowledge by converting it into a beautiful book. For over four decades, Manas has been motivating the intellectuals by publishing their manuscripts and would like to publish your manuscript too. If you or your colleagues have any manuscript ready for publication or are working on it, kindly contact us with detailed synopsis and list of contents. We will transform your work into a valuable publication. If you wish, we can also suggest you the suitable subjects for writing the books related to your area of expertise. Manas is known for its publishing quality and commitments. We take utmost care in production and give wide publicity to the book as well as its author through our national and international distribution network.

Jawan to General

Lt Gen Sushil Kumar, PVSM (Retd)

Manas Publications
(We Convert Fighters into Writers)
New Delhi-110002 (INDIA)

Manas Publications
(We Convert Fighters into Writers)
(Publishers, Library Suppliers, Importers & Exporters)
4402/5-A, Ansari Road (Opp. HDFC Bank)
Darya Ganj, New Delhi-110 002 (India)
Phones: Off.: 011-23260783, 23265523, Res.: 011-23842660
E-mail: manaspublications@gmail.com
manaspublications@yahoo.com
Website: www.manaspublications.in

ISBN: 978-81-7049-484-3
₹ 795/-

Designed at
Manas Publications

Printed in India at
Printways, Delhi
and published by **Mrs Suman Lata for**
Manas Publications, **4402/5-A, Ansari Road,**
Darya Ganj, **New Delhi-110002 (INDIA)**

Contents

Foreword

Lt Gen Sushil Kumar has written a highly readable autobiography. Lt. Gen Sushil Kumar has written, in a way, an inspirational autobiography. The inspirational aspect is derived primarily from the fact that despite a difficult childhood, being denied opportunity for completing higher education and joining the Army in the ranks, he rose to the penultimate rank in the Army. I have not known of another Army officer in our Army who has attained such success, despite initial handicaps. I recall when I graduated from Patna University in 1943, Dr. Radhakrishnan, one of our great philosophers, then Vice Chancellor of Banaras Hindu University, delivered the Convocation address to us. The subject he chose was Life is a Game of Chance. His theme was that chance comes to everyone in life, one should grab the opportunity and through hard and dedicated work, achieve success. Those who do not make use of opportunity that comes their way, fail to succeed. Fortune favours the brave only. Dedication and hard work are essential for achieving success in life. Sushil Kumar's life story vindicates, what the great philosopher Dr Radhakrishnan, who later became President of India, told us at the convocation. There is much in common, between the author and me. We are of the same age. We served in the Army for forty years, joining and retiring at about the same time. Having been commissioned, directly as an officer, I was three years senior to him in the Army. Both of us had Police connections. My father and grandfather had served as senior officers, during the British regime. His maternal uncle was in Sikar State Police and after independence, served with UP Police. He influenced his career and encouraged him to join the Army. He had the opportunity to get close to three civil officials, who were either from Bihar or from Bihar Cadre. They knew my grandfather and father very well. Thus, I too was close to them. They were Governor L. P. Singh, former Chief Secretary P. K. J. Menon and a young Police officer B. P. N. Sahi, who had served under my father. Sushil followed me in various appointments as a junior staff officer in Military Operations Directorate, as an Instructor in Tactics at Mhow and in combating insurgency in the Northeast and so on. In 1961-62, we were both Majors serving in London. I was a student on a course and he on a diplomatic assignment in the staff of the Indian High Commission there. Our families got close to each other. When we went to Paris for a holiday for three or four days, we left our children in the care of his wife and him. We served as staff officers at Army Headquarters together, he in a key appointment as Director Staff Duties in the rank of Maj General, while I was Adjutant General in the rank of Lt General and finally, when I was Army Commander, he was my Chief of Staff and was of great assistance to me. Sushil has made generous reference to me in this book at various places.

While going through his book I felt nostalgic sharing with him my memories of our common bygone days. He has graphically recalled events of the past and mentioned individuals, whom I had also known well. It was my own past life and old memories that kept coming back to me. After thirty years, of his retirement from the Army, he has faithfully narrated in his various incidents and his interaction with various individuals in detail. This is rare for a person of our age. During each of his appointment, in the Army, he made significant contributions.

Apart from his life story being inspirational for the young generation of Army officers, this book is significant in providing a glimpse of the way of life in previous era. Today, the study of history has additional dimensions but in the past the history books confined themselves to the story of Kings, Conquerors, Leaders and Great Achievers. The new trend now is also to know how in the past common men in various walks of life lived and what the social conditions and values of the past were like. As a case in point, the author has given a glimpse how joint extended Indian family functioned and helped each other. Today, the emphasis is on a nuclear family and the extended family and its values have become a thing of past.

Normally a person retiring, after serving for forty years in his chosen profession, feels he has reached the end of his career. Few venture out actively in other fields and continue to lead a purposeful life. The author chose to work in different fields and as a family man helped his children settle in life and at the same time discharged his responsibility to his mother, to whom he owed so much as he has mentioned in this book. All these qualities of head and heart are worth emulating.

I recommend this book particularly to the present generation in the Army. It is not only inspiring, but it also enriches one's knowledge of the past.

Lt Gen (Retd) SK Sinha

New Delhi

Dedication

To My Late Mother
Smt. Krishna Devi Gour

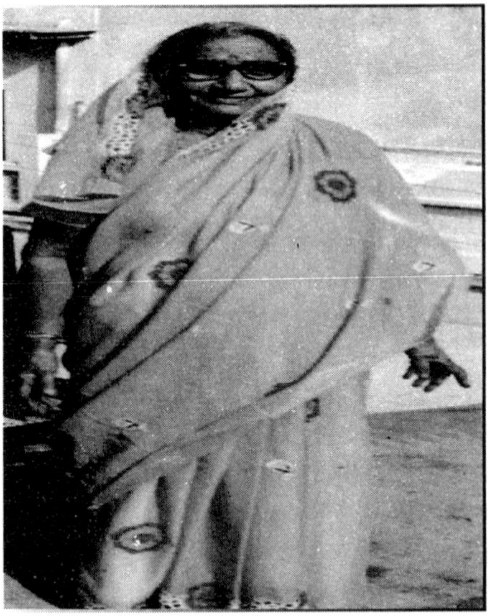

Who laid the foundation of
my character and thereby
my DESTINY

Preface

As I pen this preface for my autobiography, it has been a thirty years since I retired from the Indian Army in 1983 and now I am in the 89th year of my life. The world around me, as well as in the Army, has undergone tremendous changes in the intervening period. It has been said that I should have undertaken the task of writing this account of my life much earlier, at a time when the work would have been more relevant to the context of a fast changing world. This was never intended to be a book on military strategy or its history. I was fortunate to have been inducted into the Army in the year the Nation gained its independence. I feel that the story of my life as seen through my eyes in an era most of the younger readers would be unfamiliar with, is a time capsule waiting to be opened. The message of sustained hard work, unshakable integrity and a bit of luck propelling one to achieve, what seemed an impossible dream is timeless and forever relevant.

In accomplishing this autobiography, I fulfill a longstanding debt to my mother. She had been the fountain of inspiration in the early stages of my life. In the most trying of circumstances, she never ceased to encourage me. From a modest traditional Brahmin family, with limited resources and as a young man, unfamiliar, with the ways of the defence services, it has been an unbelievably exciting and breathtaking journey for me. I look back to it with a sense of wonder and satisfaction. I wish to share this account of my life with others for the sake of posterity.

Having led a long, active, robust and fulfilling life, which continues to be a work in progress, I immersed myself in and enjoyed the journey, all the way. From a 17-year-old boy with a dream, begining as a Havildar and rising to become a senior commander in the rank of Lt. General in one of the world's finest professional armies, has been a roller coaster of a ride. Along the way, I have had the privilege of meeting and traveling with many extraordinary people. Many of them inspired me: some became lifelong friends; others were instructors, teachers and beacons. Even those, whom I had the privilege to command were a source of education and inspiration. It would be impossible for me to thank all those who made my journey in the Army possible but I acknowledge them all as integral to my steady progress. Many, whom I served with are legends, who laid the foundations of the modern Indian Army. It was a privilege to walk the course with them.

I avail this opportunity to thank my Regiment, the 11 Gorkha and all the officers and men, who were and continue to be like family to me. To Col Gautam Dass(retd.), an author of repute, who felt I must share my life story with others, especially with young officers, who could draw some inspiration from it. My sincere thanks are due to my editor Tapan K. Ghosh, who spent many days painstakingly editing the draft and offered innumerable suggestions to make these memoirs readable; to my wife Neeru, who lovingly supported me in every possible way, along this journey; my children, who insisted I get this work published, and finally, to Ashu, my younger son, who patiently and cheerfully assisted me in completing this endeavour.

Lt Gen Sushil Kumar

Abbreviations and Acronyms

Appointment:

Pl Cdr	Platoon Commander
Coy Cdr	Company Commander
Adjt	Adjutant
QM	Quarter Master
Bn Cdr	Battalion Commander
Bde Cdr	Brigade Commander
Div Cdr	Division Commander
Corps Cdr	Corps Commander
Army Cdr	Army Commander
GOC	General Officer Commanding
GOC-in-C	General Officer Commanding in Chief
2IC	Second in Command
CO	Commanding Officer
BM	Brigade Major
GSO 1	General Staff Officer Grade 1
GSO 2	General Staff Officer Grade 2
GSO 3	General Staff Officer Grade 3
DAA&QMG	Deputy Assistant & Quarter General
Col GS	Colonel General
AA&QMG	Assistant Adjutant & Quarter Master General
BGS	Brigadier General
Brig i/c Adm	Brigadier In-charge Administration
MGGS	Major General General Staff
MG Adm	Major General InchargeAdministration
COS	Chief of Staff
DSD	Director Staff Duties
VCOAS	Vice Chief of Army Staff

COAS	Chief of Army Staff
CISC	Chief of Integrated Defence Staff to COSC
NSA	National Security Adviser

Arms & Service:

Armd Corps	Armoured Corps
Inf	Infantry
Arty	Artillery
Engrs	Corps of Engineers
Corps of Signals	Corps of Signals
ASC	Army Service Corps
EME	Corps of Electrical & Mechanical Engineers
AOC	Army Ordnance Corps
MES	Military Engineering Service
GR	Gorkha Rifles
AR	Assam Rifles
DGAR	Director General Assam Rifles
IGAR	Inspector General Assam Rifles
DIG	Deputy Inspector General
Comdt	Commandant
Dy Comdt	Deputy Commandant
Asst Comdt	Assistant Commandant

Air Force:

AOC in C	Air Officer Commanding in Chief
SASO	Senior Air Staff Officer
AM	Air Marshal
AVM	Air Vice Marshal
Gp Capt	Group Captain
Wing Comdr	Wing Commander
Sqn Ldr	Squadron Leader
Flt Lt	Flight Lieutenant
GL	Ground Liaison

Unit/Formation:

Sec	Section
Pl	Platoon
Coy	Company
Bn	Battalion
Bde	Brigade
Div	Division
Comd	Command
GRRC	Gorkha Rifles Regimental Centre
MO Dte	Military Operations Directorate

Decorations:

AC	Ashok Chakra
PVC	Param Vir Chakra
PVSM	Param Vishisht Seva Medal
AVSM	Ati Vishisht Seva Medal
VSM	Vishisht Seva Medal
SM	Sena Medal
MVC	Maha Vir Chakra
SC	Shaurya Chakra
KC	Kirti Chakra
VrC	Vir Chakra

British Decorations:

VC	Victoria Cross
KC	Kings Cross
DSO	Distinguished Service Order
MC	Military Cross
GM	George Medal
IDSM	Indian Distinguished Service Medal
OBE	Order of British Empire
OBI	Order of British India

Others:

INA	Indian National Army
PARA	Parachute
Cdo	Commando
IMA	Indian Military Academy
NDA	National Defence Academy
TA	Territorial Army
OTS	Officers Training School
Air OP	Air Observation Post
FOO	Forward Observation Officer
HQ	Headquarters
POK	Pakistan Occupied Kashmir
POW	Prisoner of War
CFL	Cease Fire Line
LOC	Line of Control
GPT Co.	General Purpose Transport Co. (Army)
BSF	Border Security Force
ITBP	Indo-Tibetan Border Police
CRPF	Central Reserve Police Force
MOD	Ministry of Defence
UPPAC	UP Provincial Armed Constabulory

NCC	National Cadet Corps
IAS	Indian Administrative Service
ICS	Indian Civil Service

Ranks:

Sep/OR	Sepoy/other rank
Rfn	Rifleman
L/Nk	Lance Naik
Nk	Naik
L/Hav	Lance Havildar
Hav	Havildar
Hav Maj	Havildar Major
NCEs	Non-Combatants Enrolled
JCO	Junior Commissioned Officer
VCO	Viceroy Commissioned Officer
Nb Sub	Naib Subedar
Sub	Subedar
Sub Maj	Subedar Major
Hon Lt/Capt	Honorary Lieutenant/Captain
2/Lt	Second Lieutenant
Lt	Lieutenant
Capt	Captain
Maj	Major
Lt Col	Lieutenant Colonel
Col	Colonel
Brig	Brigadier
Maj Gen	Major General
Lt Gen	Lieutenant General
Gen	General
FM	Field Marshal

Comittees :

DCC	Defence Committee of Cabinet
DMC	Defence Minister's Committee
COSC	Chiefs of Staff Committee
JIC	Joint Intelligence Committee
JPC	Joint Planning Committee
CCS	Cabinet Committee on Security

Guru of Author, Sri Sri Sitaramdas Omkarnath Ji Maharaj

Parents of Author, Shri Damodar Das Gour and Smt Krishna Devi

Raj Rishi College, Alwar (Raj) Alma Mater of the Author

COAS Gen Carriappa with officers of 11 GRRC, 1948
(Author as 2 Lt in back row, 3rd from right)

COAS Maharaj Rajender Sinhji with officers of A Garrison and 11 GR, Kargil.(Author as Capt. standing on the right)

COAS Gen Thapar and Lt Gen Kaul with staff of Military Advisor at India House, London 1962. (Author second from left behind Gen Kaul)

Handing over Command of 5/11 GR to Lt Col L S Rawat
at Dharamshala 1967

Col Sushil Kumar with Maj Gen Inder Gill, GOC 17 Mountain Div
(Sikkim 1967)

Brig Sushil Kumar with RM Babu Jagjivan Ram at Ladakh 1970

Chogyal of Sikkim awarded highest honour of state to Capt Ganju Lama VC of 11GR, 1968 (Author is 3rd from left, Ganju is 5th and Chogyal 6th)

Author as Brigadier
with Maj Gen SP Malhotra, GOC 3 Inf Div, at Leh 1971.

COAS Sam Manekshaw on his visit to Bde in Suratgarh before 1971 War. (Brig Sushil Kumar on left)

Author with Lalthanhawla (currently CM of Mizoram) presenting GOC Hockey Cup

RM Bansi Lal amongst troops with Maj Gen Sushil Kumar at Aizawl.

Lt Gen Sushil Kumar as DG, Assam Rifles with Naga Guards at Tuensang

Actg President Shri B D Jatti presenting PVSM to Author, April 1977

Maj Gen Sushil Kumar (DSD Army HQ) with King of Bhutan, 1978

Author and Mrs Sushil Kumar with Naga Guards at Tuensang 1980

HM Gyani Zail Singh with Author (DGAR) at AR Mela, Shillong 1980.

Shri B B Lyngdoh, CM Meghalaya releasing Ist day cover of Assam Rifles 1980 (Lt Gen Sushil Kumar on right)

Assam Rifles Public School, Shillong. Founded by Author 1980

Lt Gen K Sunderji (GOC-in-C Western Command) along with his wife, bids us farewell on my retirement, Shimla Ist May 1983

Mountaineering Legends (seated Maurice Herzog, Sir Edmund Hillary); standing from left—Author, Toshiba, Reinhold Messner Junko Tabei, Capt M S Kohli, Sushil Gupta.

With Lt Gen Rawlley GOC 11 Corps and Maj Gen Ram Singh GOC F Sector at Suratgarh 1971

Lt Gen and Mrs Sushil Kumar with immediate family members, Shimla 2010

Shiv Mandir at Etawah, constructed by Great grandfather of Author and still maintained by family

Shri H C Joshi, SP-Sikar, Maternal Uncle of Author

1

Childhood

Etawah in Uttar Pradesh, the city of my birth, literally means a place meant for burning of bricks (brick kilns) and there were many around town. It is located on the bank of the river Yamuna. The Northern Railway's Main Line Delhi-Kolkata and the National Highway 2 (Grand Trunk Road) passes through it.

The history of this region goes back to the days of the Mahabharata, when it was ruled by the Panchals, who were close to the Kurus. Much later, during the first war of independence of 1857, the area provided a staging post for freedom fighters as well as for the British troops. It threw up a number of local leaders, who became the rallying point for the fight against the British. Interestingly, Alan O. Hume was the District Commisioner of the area at that time. He handled the situation delicately and effectively. He later came to be known for his pro-Indian attitude and has gone down in history, as the man, who founded the Indian National Congress. During the freedom movement, the people of Etawah were politically conscious and organised rallies, hartals (strikes) and boycott of British goods.

However, during my childhood, Etawah was a peaceful town. It had a mixed population, like other towns, with Yadavs being in a majority. It was known for good breed of buffaloes and goats. It therefore produced a substantial quantity of milk and its product of 'khoya' was sent to many towns of North India. Localities had narrow paved streets and were provided with in and out gates and entry of motor vehicles was barred. Crime was unheard of. Relations and interaction amongst the families living in my locality were friendly and harmonious. Etawah has today developed into a bustling modern town and is also the headquarters of the district of the same name.

I was born in 1925, into a traditional Brahmin family. My ancestors were pundits and simple people of limited means. My forefather, Prithvi Nath (1801-1871) migrated from Narnaul (now in Haryana) to Etawah and started living in Katra Seva Kali. Later, his son Mohan Lal built a double-storey house and right opposite this house, he constructed a temple of Lord Shiva. Mohan Lal's son was Jagan Nath, who had two sons–Puttu Lal (my paternal grandfather) and Lal Man and a daughter named Bitto. Puttu Lal had two sons including Damodar Dass, my father and a daughter.

Puttu Lal had gone to a local English medium school. He got a job in the Irrigation Department. Later, one Dada Bhai Piston Ji, a Parsee came in contact with him. Piston Ji was so impressed by my grandfather's honesty and dedication that he urged him to leave the Government job and join his firm as a Head Clerk. Subsequently, Piston Ji made Puttu Lal, the executive head of his entire business and also included him as an equal partner. Business consisted of a flour mill, a brick kiln, a cinema and a construction firm.

Puttu Lal was good at his work and generated huge profits. He had a brick kiln spread over a large area and produced bricks marked with letters 'PL', which he used in the construction of buildings contracted to him. He also acquired another house, adjacent to the one in which his family was living. Both houses were interlinked. The family of his younger brother Lal Man lived in the second house. This house had a well which met the water requirement of the two families. There was no piped water supply in those days.

When I was 10 years old, I used to see buildings with markings of PL with great pride, which had been constructed by my paternal grandfather. Sanatan Dharma High School was one such building (now known as Sanatan Dharma Inter College, near Kotwali). Unfortunately, my grandfather expired before my parents married. He bequeathed considerable accumulated wealth to them.

My mother, Krishna Devi, who was married at the age of 13, came from a well-known respected Joshi family of Alwar, then a state in Rajputana and now a district in Rajasthan. Her father Anandi Lal Joshi was a learned man, had thorough knowledge of Persian and had written many books which can still be seen in the Alwar Museum. The State was ruled by Jay Singh. His full title was Colonel, Raj Rishi, Sawai Maharaj, and Sir Jay Singh Virendera Shiromani Dev Bharat Dharm Prabhakar of Alwar. Jay Singh was a nationalist and did not conceal his dislike for British rule. There are numerous stories about how he treated British officials. A popular tale relates that after shaking hands with senior British officials, he would turn around and wash his hands in their presence. He was an eccentric, but erudite and generous. He made a handsome donation to Madan Mohan Malviya for Benaras Hindu Universty and Hindu religious leaders honoured him with the title of 'Raj Rishi'. He bought a Lanchester 40 HP motor vehicle from England with its rear part modelled as a royal coronation coach–the only unique version in the world. The British found Jay Singh 'sinister' and a trouble maker. The British Government held an enquiry into his various alleged misdeeds and maladministration of the State and found Jay Singh 'guilty'. He was exiled and prohibited from entering the State. Jay Singh moved to France and died after 4 years at the age of 54. People from Alwar did not believe the news of his death. His body was then brought to Alwar and taken in a procession in a sitting posture in his Lanchester. I witnessed this as a 12 year old boy.

Jay Singh used to respect Anandi Lal (my maternal grandfather) a great deal and often sought his advice in important State matters. After all, Anandi Lal had served four generations of Maharajas. He was provided with a big house by the State. He had a flowing grey beard and an imposing personality. He was a known ready wit like the legendary Birbal, the renowned Minister of Akbar the Great, who had a ready answer for everything. One story has it that one day, the Maharaja called Anandi Lal for some advice. Anandi Lal approached the palace riding piggyback on another man, which was seen by the Maharaja. The Maharaja asked Anandi Lal 'Joshi Ji, why are you using this unorthodox means of transport as your personal conveyance. It is below human dignity'. Anandi Lal, replied, 'Huzoor, I am an old man and feel tired walking and hence resorted to this unconventional means of transport.' Maharaja understood the implied meaning and immediately sanctioned a *rath* (bullock drawn cart). On another occasion the Maharaja, who had an aversion to beards, asked Anandi Lal 'Why do you keep a long beard, don't you feel hot and irritable?' Anandi Lal replied, 'Huzoor, on the contrary, when wet it serves the purpose of air cooling, while during winter it provides warmth'. Maharaja had a hearty laugh and did not raise the subject again. There was no electricity in Alwar in those days. My mother had nine brothers and five sisters. There was no family planning then. Cost of living was cheap and there being no economic pressure, large families were a normal trend.

As mentioned earlier, Puttu Lal expired before my parents were married and his younger brother Lal Man, who had a limp in one leg and had a large roundish growth on one cheek, being the eldest in the family, had to make all the arrangements for the wedding. My paternal grandmother (Meneka) was a responsible and strict lady and ran the house with a stern hand. Her elder brother Banshi Lall was the Royal Physician of Rewa State in Central India, a place famous for its white tigers. According to my mother, the brick kilns were still working and there were some ongoing construction contracts, when she came as a new bride. My father Damodar Dass was not interested in the business which was being looked after by my grand uncle Lal Man, who was uneducated. He was not able to complete contracts in time, which invited the wrath of a British engineer, who imposed heavy fines. The brick kilns also got flooded due to heavy rains and the entire produce was washed out. All this caused great financial loss. My father's younger brother Bhola Nath was also not interested in that business; his interest was in music and while teaching music to a young widow, by the name of Atta, in the neighbourhood, he fell in love with her and thereafter never got married. It was rumored that he had fathered a girl named, Kamla. In fact I met Bhola Nath a few times in Lucknow and he had introduced me to Kamla. He was very much attached to Kamla but I got no news about her mother. Later, Bhola Nath expired and despite my best efforts, I was unable to trace Kamla or the circumstances about my uncle's death.

As a young child I was locked after by a full time servant called Munia and my paternal grandmother Meneka was all the time doting on me. We were still living in the two-storeyed house. The temple next to our house which housed the deity of Lord Shiva was an important religious and cultural centre for the local community. The entire locality would worship in the temple and once a year, during the month of Bhadrapad–Krishna paksh, sixth day (Chhat), there would be a procession in which the deity of Lord Shiva, known as Dilligi Maharaj (God known for Cracking Jokes) was taken to the banks of the Yamuna, about 5-6 km away. It invariably rained on the festival day. This used to be a major attraction and was well attended by the local people. The locality had a complete holiday and all shops were closed. We also used to host a lunch for the Brahmin community. Since the temple was constructed by my grandfather, it was our family's responsibility to maintain and look after it and also organise the annual festival.

My admission to the local primary school and writing the first word was a great occasion for the family. When I was in class IV, I stood first in the class and got a story book as prize. My grandmother was so overjoyed by this event that she distributed sweets to all the families, of the locality. Our joy and happiness was shortlived as my grandmother soon fell seriously ill and expired. This was a tragic blow to my mother, who was quite dependent on her mother-in-law. Meanwhile, the fortunes of the family were dwindling fast as the business was not generating any income. My father still showed no interest and made no effort to revive the business. There was some accumulated wealth, however, which helped. Banking was not popular in those days and cash, gold and ornaments used to be hoarded in various concealed places in the house.

My mother's main worry was to get my aunt Jagdamba (my father's sister) married. She was able to successfully do this. Her second worry was my education. My grand uncle Lal Man (Puttu Lal's brother) had three sons. They were also not well educated. The atmosphere in the house was not conducive to a balanced development and satisfactory growth of children. By this time I had two younger sisters, Sarla and Madhuri (aged six and one). My mother had great perseverance and was not one to accept defeat in adversity. She decided to visit one of her elder brothers, Vishnu Chandra Joshi at Karoli (Rajasthan). He was the Chief Justice and also in charge of prisons. I recollect, for sometime he was also acting Dewan. He had a big sprawling bungalow and I often used to see many prisoners with fetters around their ankles working in the garden. Vishnu Chandra was the first M.A., LL.B from Alwar and was an introvert and also very proud. He was a man of few words and lacked communication with family members. He married four times and had four sons and two daughters, but never paid any attention towards their education and balanced development. Consequently, they all went astray and wasted their lives. When he was studying, Vishnu Chandra was supported financially by Maharaja Jay Singh of Alwar, but after completion of his education he decided to take up a job outside Alwar. This displeased the Maharaja, who considered it an act of disloyalty. My mother had a rude shock, when Vishnu Chandra flatly refused to help in my further education. My maternal grandmother (Baji) happened to visit Karoli and listening to the woes of my mother, offered to take us to Alwar.

To Alwar and Anand Bhawan

On arrival at Alwar, we lived with Baji (maternal grandmother) in her portion of the house and made arrangements for cooking with the resources provided by Baji, who herself used to have food with one of my maternal uncles Ramesh Chandra. It was a big house, gifted to my maternal grandfather (Anandi Lal) by the Maharaja of Alwar and there were many spacious rooms and large verandahs. After some time, Vishnu Chandra suddenly landed at Alwar with bag and baggage and appeared to be mentally disturbed; all the time he was apprehending a police raid. No one in the family knew the reason for this paranoia. He tried to start his legal practice at Alwar but was a miserable failure. During this period he was an object of much pity in the family.

The house in Alwar was known as Anand Bhawan. Opposite this house was a Mission Primary School and nearby there was a big garden, Munshi Bagh. Two maternal uncles were also living with their families in Anand Bhawan. They were Suresh Chandra, who worked as a Customs Inspector with four sons and two daughters and Ramesh Chandra, who was incharge of State Royal Library, with five sons and two daughters. Ramesh Chandra tried to get me admitted in the local school. The Headmaster was an Anglo-Indian by the name, Tom who used to put on a sola hat and was a strict but kind fellow. Since, it was the middle of the session, he did not admit me, but allowed me to attend the class informally and later permitted me to appear for the examination of Class V. When the result was declared, I had passed but all the children of my uncles Ramesh and Suresh had failed! This created a furor in the house. There was even talk of how my mother's music practice and story telling sessions had distracted the children from studies! My mother was indeed a gifted lady and was often surrounded by the children of the house. Obviously, no one had noticed how I remained focused on my studies despite the many distractions and festive occasions normal in a large extended family. I had now become a regular student of Class VI and my mother played her part as my mentor goading me to work hard and excel in my studies. The school then (in 1936) was in the present building of Town Hall of Alwar and subsequently shifted to a place outside Malakhera Gate.

Another maternal uncle, Mahesh Chandra was also in Alwar, holding a good position in the State Administrative Service and was living in a separate house, though he had a share in Anand Bhawan. The eldest maternal uncle, Kanti Chandra was living close to Anand Bhawan in a separate house. He ran a printing press and also published a local newspaper. He had two sons and one daughter and was popularly known as 'Press Wale'.

My mother wrote several letters to my father in Etawah but got no response. It was a very worrying and humiliating situation. I must say that all the maternal uncles had a soft corner for my mother and were ever willing to help her. Press Wale uncle suggested that his son-in-law Nand Kishore, who was a teacher by profession, but was starting a flour mill (*atta chakki*) could do with a partner and mother should put in some money in the business and generate some income to support the household. Mother disposed off some ornaments and gave money to (Press Wale) uncle and requested that her share in the mill should be in my name. I do not know if any legal papers were ever prepared. The third partner was one Ram Kishore. The mill started outside Malakhera Gate. Nand Kishore also gave tuitions to me occasionally. I used to go to the flour mill daily after coming back from school and bring flour and the day's earnings for domestic consumption.

There were two other maternal uncles, Sansar Chand, who was elder to my mother and worked in the Customs, while Harish Chandra was younger to my mother. Harish Chandra was brilliant, with an impressive personality and modern thinking. He had a special affection for me. He had undergone police training at Moradabad and was appointed Superintendent of Police in Sikar (Rajasthan). He had one son and one daughter. His wife came from Gharonda (Haryana) and was soft spoken and charming, but semi-literate. She soon became quite close to my mother and me. Her father was a railway contractor and had earned considerable wealth. She had great affection for me and often trusted me to escort her to Gharonda.

Harish Chandra was my role model and he inspired me to become either a Police or Army officer. However, his own life story was a tragic one. He was full of enthusiasm and willing to take risks. One day Rao Raja Kalyan Singh (1922-67) of Sikar mentioned to him 'SP Sahib, we have a horse, which is uncontrollable. We do not know what to do with this wild animal.' Harish replied 'Sir, with your permission, let me try to see if the horse can be controlled.' In his bravado, Harish jumped on the saddle of the horse, but the horse got out of control and he was thrown off atop a cannon, located at one of the main city gates. He broke both his wrists and also suffered some head injuries. He took a long time to recover. Mr Freddie Young*, the popular Inspector General Police of Jaipur, was fond of him and through his recommendation Harish got the appointment of Principal in Police Training School, Gwalior. However, due to head injury his brain was somewhat affected, which reflected in his erratic behaviour. He never fully recovered from his head injury. After Independence and due to merger of states he lost his job in Gwalior. Subsequently, he accepted jobs of Deputy Superintendant in Central Reserve Police Force (CRPF) and United Province, Provincial Armed Police (PAC) for some time. CRPF at that time was known as Crown Representative Police Force and had just one unit, located in Neemuch (presently CRPF has many a units, deployed all over India).

---

* He was known for his close association with the legendary Sultana Daku. He participated in the capture of the dacoit, but kept his promise to look after Sultana's son after the dacoit was hanged.

This was a serious setback for Harish Chandra and his family. Finally, he gave up. In mysterious circumstances he was detained near the Viceroy's House in New Delhi and sent to Mental Hospital in Lahore. This was in the end of 1947, when I was under training at the Indian Military Academy. I learnt this when I visited Alwar, during a break and found that no one—not even Avinash, son of Ramesh (maternal uncle), who had become an Inspector of Police, was willing to go to Lahore to fetch him as the country was already divided between India and Pakistan and riots were taking place all over. I offered to go to Lahore. As an IMA cadet I got all the help from the military, deployed in Amritsar. At Lahore I was put up by the Deputy High Commissioner for two nights. I visited Harish in the Mental Hospital and found him to be nearly normal. I told him that I had come to take him to Alwar, He was delighted and next day I brought new clothes for him, including a tie which he wore. He said to me, 'Batan (my pet name) you are an Army Officer and I should be properly dressed, while accompanying you'. I had to clear the dues of the Hospital. I ran short of money but the Deputy High Commissioner lent me the amount, which I paid back later. From Amritsar to Delhi, we travelled in First Class and I had no problem with him. At Delhi, suddenly he flatly refused to travel to Alwar in First Class and we had to travel in Class III. On arrival at Alwar he again got agitated and refused to go to the house. He preferred to stay in a *dharamshala* (community guest house). To cut the story short, he never fully recovered. Later, his son Mahender (Manne) got married to my wife's younger sister Usha and thus our relationship was further strengthened. Manne served in Indian AirLines and had great regard for my mother and me.

Etawah Re-Visited: Fighting Adversity

Sometime in 1937 my mother had decided to visit Etawah and see for herself the conditions there, particularly, how my father was doing. I accompanied her. The condition of our family shocked and saddened us. Both houses were already sold for a pittance and most of the household goods were also disposed off. My grand uncle Lal Man had expired and his children were also in a bad economic state. News came that my aunt Jagdamba had expired. Under such circumstances, my mother immediately decided that the only alternative to this condition of doom was to take her husband to Alwar. My uncle Bhola Nath refused to shift to Alwar, as he was too attached to his beloved Atta, the widow. My parents thus moved to Alwar, abandoning their ancestral place with great sadness. Father meanwhile had taken to opium and was also gambling on numbers. He seemed to have no urge to do anything though, he was educated up to X class and had a beautiful handwriting, both in Hindi and English. With the arrival of my father at Alwar, we rented a separate house and took up residence there.

With the help of my maternal uncle, Mahesh Chandra, a senior Administrative Officer in the Alwar State, my father started taking small construction contracts. Funds were again raised by disposing off some of my mother's ornaments. However, the new business was not profitable and did not last long. Meanwhile, there was some cheating and siphoning of funds in the flour mill by other partners and my share had to be disposed off. My father then got a temporary job but the income was not adequate to run the family comfortably. Later, with the help of one of my uncles, my father got a Government job in Rehabilitation Department, which dealt with the refugees from Pakistan and held this position till retirement. The family had grown and my four younger brothers, Bal Krishen, Gopal Krishen, Prakash Krishen and Daya Krishen were born. This added to the economic woes of the family.

Sometime in 1939, I took part in a drama staged by a

local organization named Abhaya Samaj headed by Pundit Nand Kishore. The play was 'Ganga Vatran' (Descent of Sacred Ganga to Earth). This was staged in the City Palace and the Chief Guest was Maharaja Tej Singh of Alwar who had succeeded Jay Singh as the latter had no sons, Tej Singh hailed from a small principality, Thana. I was assigned the role of Ganga. It went off so well that I was awarded the His Highness Gold Medal for acting. I was only 14 then and very influenced by my mother's sacrifices for the family and especially for me. The medal was of pure gold. Since my mother had disposed off nearly all her ornaments to support the family, I insisted that the medal be converted into some ornament for her as a token of my love and gratitude to her. This she accepted with great reluctance.

My mother's younger sister was married in the Pujari family in Raipur (Madhya Pradesh). Her father-in-law Badri Prashad was awarded the title of Rai Sahib by the British for his loyalty. He owned 17 villages and was a respectable big zamindar (landlord) of the area. Rai Sahib happened to visit Alwar and was shocked to learn from uncle Mahesh Chandra about our family condition. He was aware of the past position of our family in Etawah and could not believe that our fortunes had dwindled to such a low level. He offered to assist in my education by assigning the monthly rent of one of his houses at Jaipur, a princely sum of Rs. 13 per month. It was a handsome amount in those days and was a great help to me in buying books, stationery and also a cycle to commute to school. I visited Raipur at the time of the wedding of my cousin sister (daughter of my younger maternal aunt) and was well looked after. Later, after my retirement and at the time of death of Gopal Pujari (mother's sister's husband), I visited Raipur and stayed there for a few days. I availed of this opportunity to express my gratitude to the Pujari family, for the help rendered to me by their late grandfather. My aunt (mother's sister) had already expired and their son Kishnoo showed me respect and treated me like an elder brother.

I often thought of giving up my studies and taking up a job to help the family, but I was too young. Finally, I took up a part time jcb with the Alwar Chamber of Commerce; after coming from school I would work in their office in the evening for a couple of hours. After Class X, during summer vacation, I also worked as a sorter in the Census Office for two months which also brought some income for the family. In class XI I opted for Commerce and joined the Raj Rishi College, the only college in Alwar. This was only upto Class XII. There were no facilities for further education in Alwar and students, aspiring for higher education generally used to go to Agra. The Raj Rishi College was an imposing building near Moti Doongri and was named after the late His Highness Jay Singh. The Principal of the College was Mr Pai with a degree from the UK and the English teacher was Mr Jaimen while commerce was taught by Mr Awasthi. All the teachers were quite dedicated to their profession.

During the first year of my college I made some good friends and specially remember Bala Prashad, who later joined the State Forces which subsequently merged with the Indian Army and retired as Colonel. Ram Singh Nadheria was a good friend and we became very close. Nadheria owned vast property and had numerous business interests. He was quite portly and often had to fend off the good natured jibes by fellow students aimed at his corpulence. He was a very sincere and honest friend. Then there was Prahalad Bhargav, a diminutive person like me, who later became a CA and settled in Kanpur. Chhottu Singh was another person, who was hefty but named Chhotu (small). He was a happy-go-lucky person and was from a business family. Later, he entered politics and on a Congress ticket became a member of the Legislative Assembly of Rajasthan. He ran a Women's college at Alwar and my sister-in-law

Kamla Sharma was the Principal and later Director of the College. I met Chhotu sometime in 2005/6 when he was recovering from a stroke. He was delighted to meet me and introduced me to all members of his family and we talked about old times.

By 1942, I had passed the First Year at college in the Commerce Stream (equivalent to XI class today). The Second World War was raging and Field Marshal Rommel was giving a tough time to the British troops in Africa. The Germans had scored major victories over the Allies in the West, while the Japanese had struck in the East and had advanced up to the eastern frontier of India, after capturing Malaya, Singapore, Indonesia and Burma. A large number of British troops along with Indian troops had surrendered in Singapore, thus demolishing the pride of British Empire where the "Sun never sets"! The Quit India resolution was passed in 1942 by the Indian National Congress and independence movement in India was at its peak. All the Congress leaders, including Mahatma Gandhi and Pandit Nehru were in jail. The whole of India was in turmoil and the atmosphere in the country was tense.

At that time, an Army Unit-73 General Purpose Transport (GPT) Company was being raised at Alwar, where I found a temporary clerical job during my summer vacations for two months. I did not know much about the Army. My friend B.P. Sharma had earlier joined Alwar State Jay Paltan as an officer and this provided some inspiration to me. The head clerk of the unit, Anand Dutta Saxena became friendly with me and advised me to get enrolled as Havildar Clerk. I was told this could at a later stage offer an opportunity to become an officer in the Indian Army and thus realise my aspirations. The Commanding Officer had the authority to recruit directly up to Havildar. I was 17 years and 4 months old but the age factor was overlooked by the Unit. I decided to accept this offer and was enrolled on 1 August 1942, as a sepoy and promoted the same day as a Havildar (Sergeant) Clerk. My family was very upset and my maternal uncles were quite annoyed, but the die had been cast. My mother's brothers even remarked that my future had been sacrificed for the sake of the family. Nevertheless, this did not change my resolve. During this period, my younger sister Sarla was married to Kashi Nath Gour of Lucknow, who was a cashier in the Punjab National Bank. All our relations helped in the marriage, particularly my uncle Pandit Narottam Lal Ji of Vrindaban, to whom my mother's elder sister Durga was married. Pandit Narottam Lal was a reputed astrologer and Acharya of Vrindaban. He and his wife had great affection for me. I developed good friendly relations with all their five sons, who also became quite fond of me.

2

My Days in the Ranks

Till August 1942 I was a temporary civilian clerk. On enrolment, I had to live in the lines. I was issued with uniform and equipment. Strangely, I received no military training on enrolment, as is normal, probably due to shortage of time. All officers were British and the Commanding Officer was one Major G. T. Dinsmore. He was often in an inebriated state. The senior Viceroy Commissioned Officer (VCO), now redesignated as Junior Commissioned Officer (JCO) was Sub. Chandgi Ram. He was like an Adjutant and Subedar Major of an infantry battalion rolled into one. I had tremendous difficulty in adapting myself to the Army way of life but with the help of Anand Dutta, the head clerk, I was able to gradually adjust to the hard life. I was not used to sleeping on the ground or improvised bamboo beds, which was the norm in camp life. Anand Datta was very fond of non-vegetarian food, which at that time, I disliked. I had to gradually get used to it. We rarely went to eat in the men's cook house as Datta, himself cooked in the tent. This was overlooked by Sub. Chandgi Ram. I had to adapt to using deep trench latrines and bathing in the open.I also had to carry my baggage during shifting which I found difficult as I was diminutive and not very fit.

I found that the British officers were not regulars and were mostly civil executives commissioned to meet the war emergency. They did not know Hindi and had difficulty in conversing with the Jawans. Chandgi Ram did not know much English and could converse only in faulty English. Hence, Anand Dutta became the key link between officers and VCOs/men. Chandgi Ram turned a blind eye to the activities of Anand Dutta like staying out late, while visiting the city and cooking food in his tent.

I did not notice any effort on the part of officers to mix with men or to initiate measures to weld them into a cohesive unit. They remained aloof. Perhaps they thought, it was not necessary as it was not a fighting unit. However, later some young Indian Emergency Commissioned Officers joined the Unit; notably Prakash Krishen (he later joined the Indian Administrative Service) and Muthanna, whom I remember. They were not treated well by British officers and felt isolated and neglected. They often came to our place to chat and also enjoy Indian food, which they badly missed in the officer's mess. They were not allowed to listen to news on radio in the Mess as there was widespread agitation in the country by the Congress call for Independence and British officers apprehended that this might affect the loyalty of Indian officers. British apprehension was compounded by the activities of Netaji Subhash Chandra Bose and his direct appeal to Indian soldiers to join the Indian National Army created by him.

The frustration of Indian officers was understandable. This was the period when the Cripps Mission had failed and the Indian Congress Leaders including Mahatma Gandhi had given the call for the British to quit the country. Since Alwar was a State in Rajputana (now Rajasthan), the All India political agitation did not much affect the State even though all the political leaders were arrested. Large scale sabotage and violence had also broken out in rest of India. Despite the turmoil all over India, Alwar remained comparatively peaceful.

My First Experience on the War Front

The Unit was ready for mobilisation and moved out on Diwali Day, sometime in November 1942. It was ordered to move to Dimapore. There was a hue and cry at home, as I was leaving the house for the first time and that too for the war front in the East during Diwali festival. The British had met with crushing defeats in Africa and had now stabilised their defences at Al Alamein, West of Cairo. In the East, the Japanese had humbled the British pride and were knocking at the door of India. Netaji Subhash Chandra Bose had already raised the Indian National Army (INA) from the Indian prisoners captured by Japan in Singapore-Malaya and had given the two famous slogans–'Dilli Chalo' and 'Jai Hind'. Netaji had earlier made a daring escape from British custody in India and journeyed through Afghanistan to Germany and thereafter to Japan. The INA was fighting along with the Japanese soldiers against the British and the Indian Army on the Indo-Burma Border. Though we were serving the British our feelings against their rule were so strong that we secretly celebrated the capture of Burma by the Japanese and Rommel's victory in North Africa even as we travelled in the train from Alwar to Dimapur. There was no bridge over Brahmputra and trains used to be ferried across to Guwahati in steamers. On reaching Dimapur I experienced the first real hardship of army life when I had to carry the heavy kit bag myself, which I was not used to [approx 70 Kg]. Our destination was 87.5 Mile Stone on Dimapur-Imphal Road. To feed the 14th Army commanded by Gen Bill Slim (later Field Marshal) a Line of Communication (L of C) system was introduced in place of the convoy system. This involved establishing several service stations along the Dimapore-Imphal Highway, where loaded vehicles were serviced, refuelled and drivers replaced but the same vehicles continued right up to their destination for delivering their load. This reduced the turn a round time considerably. The system had one major drawback though, in that the officers were completely divorced from the supervision over the work of their men which led to lack of contact with men. Men merely came to sleep and rest in the unit till their turn came to take over a vehicle at a service station. It was bound to lead to numerous cases of indiscipline. We were living in tents and life was dull. Very soon the Japanese were knocking at the door of Imphal. We were quickly organised to defend the perimeter of the camp and immediately put on the job of digging trenches.

I learnt the use of the .303 rifle and often manned the trenches at night. On the slightest noise there would be alarm in the camp. Rumours were afloat about Japanese bravery and how the British were not able to capture any Japanese prisoners, as they were highly motivated and committed *harakari* (suicide) if capture was imminent. We had a sneaking admiration for the Japanese bravery. The Japanese mounted a right flanking attack by a very difficult long approach march through arduous jungles and hills on Kohima and were soon ready to cut the main road, the Dimapore-Imphal Road at Kohima, the lifeline for British troops deployed on Indo-Burma Border in Manipur region. The task was brilliantly executed by Lt Gen Sato commanding 31 Jap Division. This was the toughest task and the Division laid seige of Kohima by March 1944. Dimapur, which was being developed as a base by Gen. Slim for launching his 14th Army into Burma now lay undefended and he had to rush a British Division from central India to augment the defence of Dimapur and subsequently lift the siege of Kohima. The epic battle of Kohima saw many acts of unmatched gallantry by Brtitish and Indian troops, as also the Japanese troops.

However, the road from our location to Imphal was still open. It was feared that this may be cut by the Japanese at any moment. Our unit was therefore, moved to Imphal where it was to ply vehicles up to Tambu on the Burma border. In addition, our jawans were to defend a portion of inner perimeter after the siege of Imphal commenced. Shortly after our move to Imphal, Dimapur-Imphal Highway was cut by the Japanese Army at Marram where a big Ordnance Depot was located. The task was carried out by the Japanese 15 Division under the command of Lt Gen Yamauchi. Besides 33 Jap Division, commanded by Lt Gen Yanagida, and well armed and equipped was also used in the assault on Imphal. On our side, we had 4 Corps commanded by Lt Gen Scoones, comprised 17 Division, 20 Division and 23 Division, with a large number of administrative troops.

The battles of Imphal and Kohima were most gruelling, and the testing ground for management of logistics and generalship on the part of the British. In fact, very recently the British have accepted this event as one of the most critical battles of the British army*.

---

* Recently in April 2013 in a contest held at National War Museum, London, the battle of Kohima and Imphal against the Japanese in WW-II was rated by a select group of people as No.1 in terms of importance for the British Army among many actions fought by them since the 18th century. The Normandy invasion or D-Day took the second spot, confirming the view of many historians that the invasion of Europe unfairly took the limelight away from this critical battle against the Japanese.

The British had complete superiority in the air. This allowed Slim to move the entire fifth division by air to Imphal to boost the defences and consequently lift the siege. Soon the siege of Imphal and Kohima were lifted. The Japs had overshot their bolt and were on disastrous retreat. Slim was a Gorkha Officer, who had deliberately planned to fight the Japs, keeping the interior lines of communications short and easy to maintain, while the Japanese forces were on extended lines of communication and had no roads or air supply to maintain them. The Japs had banked on capture of British/Indian supply depots in Imphal/Kohima, which failed. The moment the Dimaport-Imphal road was opened, it was decided to evacuate all the administrative troops besieged in Imphal, in order to lessen the logistic load and prepare for a big push to Burma. Consequently, our unit was moved out to Shillong for rest.

Out of the Battle Zone

It was a welcome change. Shillong is now the capital of Meghalaya. It was my first visit to this beautiful hill station. People in Shillong follow the matriarchal system, in which the inheritance goes from mother to daughter and not from father to son. Hence, women play a dominant role in society.

After a few months of rest, our unit was moved to Chittagong (now in BanglaDesh), not far from the sea. We relaxed on the seashore and sometimes accompanied Capt Prakash Krishen on snipe shoots. The new Commanding Officer of the Unit was Maj. A.S. Rudge. With the dropping of atom bombs on Hiroshima and Nagasaki on 6th and 8th August 1945 by the Americans, destroying both the cities and causing thousands of casualties, War in the East also came to an end. The Japanese finally surrendered. This also put an end to Emergency in India. The Government now set the demobilisation plans of the British Indian Army in motion, which due to war had grown considerably, in fact to about 25 lakh.

Post-War: Opportunities and Challenges

During my entire service in 73 GT Co, I had assigned my complete salary as family allotment to my mother for support of the family. My brothers, Bal Krishen, Gopal Krishen, Daya Krishen and Prakash Krishen were growing and studying and so was my sister Madhuri. Mother therefore, needed the funds for running the household. In any case, I did not need any money during the War.

The Government decided to commence regular permanent commission courses at the Indian Military Academy, Dehradun, which was conducting short courses for Emergency Commissions during the War. Army cadets were also allowed to compete for the admission into the IMA, provided they were 21 years of age on the date of entry into IMA and had passed Class X. Initial screening was to be done by the Sub Area/Brigade Commander and thereafter the candidate had to appear before the Services Selection Board. There were strict instructions from the Army HQ that no application would be held back by any Commanding Officer at unit level. The first course was to start in February 1946. However, due to remoteness of the area and difficult communications, our unit did not get the intimation for the First Course. The Second Course was to start in August 1946. The instructions for the Second Course were received by the unit and this had a provision that those, who were eligible for the First Course and could not apply due to non-receipt of instructions and had thus become overage for the Second Course, were also to be permitted to apply. Anand Dutta, the Head Clerk advised me to immediately apply for this course and also pressed the Commanding Officer to forward the application to the Sub-Area, Chittagong. I was interviewed by the Sub Area Commander in the presence of the Commanding Officer Maj Rudge. I was asked some very elementary questions regarding my family background, education, past military service among others. These I answered satisfactorily. The Sub Area Commander informed me that he was recommending my case for interview by the Selection Board, Jamshedpur. I was naturally elated having crossed the first hurdle. Rudge rebuked me and remarked: 'wipe that smile off your face! It is too early to celebrate; you have a long way to go.' After a couple of weeks I got a call for interview by the Services Selection Board at Jamshedpur. I requested that I be allowed one month's leave after my interview as I had not visited my parents for two years. The leave was sanctioned. The interview at the Selection Board lasted three days. There were group discussions and we had to write an essay on a subject of our choice. We were also put through an obstacle course to test physical endurance and finally the interviews were conducted. While I did not fare well in group discussions, I did well in the obstacle course. In the essay I chose to write on my experience during the 1939-45 War. In the interview I felt I had done fairly well. The competition was indeed tough as most of the boys were from public schools and most were graduates. This gave me some inferiority complex but at the same time inspired me to do my best. I then reached Alwar and my family was delighted to meet me after a long period of absence. My brothers had grown and were school - going. I had little hope of being selected for the IMA and started planning for release from the Army and taking up my studies again. However, Almighty God had different plans for me. While having tea one fine morning a telegram from the unit arrived. This stated 'you are selected for the Second Course IMA commencing on 8 August 1946. You are required to return to the Unit immediately'. Our joy knew no bounds and there were celebrations in the family. I had joined the Army on 1 August 1942 as a Havildar Clerk and had served on the Burma front for 4 years. This was a tremendous jump in my career. No one in the family had ever joined the Defence Services or the All India Administrative Services in the officer cadre. The family and relations were therefore rightly proud of this achievement. On return to the Unit, I was given a grand farewell by the officers (including Maj Rudge), VCOs and Clerks. The Unit as whole was proud that they had produced a person, who would be commissioned from the IMA as a permanent regular officer in the Indian Army. Thus, ended an important phase in my life, which was very significant in grooming me for future.

Anand Dutta had acted like a real elder brother and adviser throughout and I owe a great deal to his support. Later, when I was a Captain in Military Operations Directorate, Army Headquarters in 1955 and was selected for Defence Services Staff College Wellington, I met Anand Dutta at Gwalior Railway Station en route to Wellington in December 1955. It was a very emotional meeting and we hugged each other and cried. He had become a Subedar and had brought tea and snacks for us. Years later I tried to get in touch and made efforts to track down his address but failed. I believe he expired early in life, after retirement. He was a heavy drinker and this could have hastened his end.

3

At the Indian Military Academy

I joined IMA on 8 August, 1946. I was looking forward to a new phase in my life as Gentleman Cadet (GC 215) with enthusiasm. I was assigned B Company housed in Kingsley Block. My neighbours were R.P. Singh (GC 216) and Vijit Singh Raje Gaekwar from Baroda Royal family (GC 217). RP was from Calcutta, a short, plump and cheerful person and we immediately took a liking to each other. We became good friends and continued this friendship, during the service and after retirement. Gaekwar was a flamboyant person, with plenty of money to flaunt around and had a car, which he used for visiting his friends in town. He was a friendly sort but did not take much interest in training. He later died in a car crash.

During the first week, we were taken around the

Academy and shown drill square, physical training area, weapon training area and the sports ground. When we entered the main hall of the Chetwode Building, we were struck by the motto, written in gold letters on the front face of the entrance stairs;

> ***The safety, honour and welfare of your country come first, always and everytime,***
>
> ***The honour, welfare and the comfort of the men you command come next,***
>
> ***Your own ease, comfort and safety come last, always and every time.***

Interestingly, this stirring credo was extracted from the inaugural address of the British Field Marshal Sir Philip W. Chetwode BT GCB KCMG DSO, the then Commander-in-Chief of India, to the First Course (40 cadets) on 10 Dec, 1932 (FM Sam Manekshaw was also from this course) This was to be the guiding principle, throughout our careers; and every officer commissioned from the IMA follows this CREDO with pride, throughout his service.

One evening we were called by the seniors to line up. We were all in our night dress and chappals, while seniors were in physical training dress. We were taken out for a long road walk and run and at the end we were all thoroughly exhausted. This was our introduction to the IMA life. I learnt later that freshers in other companies faced a much rougher treatment at the hands of their seniors.

RP and I always went out together. Once, while visiting Sahastradhara (hot springs), we bumped into a Sikh family, which owned a shoe shop in the town. There was a pretty girl by the name Santosh. It appeared that between RP and Santosh, it was love at first sight. We used to visit Santosh's family together and RP and Santosh continued their correspondence. After commissioning, I am happy that they finally got married. I used to visit a relative Mr Bharadwaj, whose sister was married to Mahesh, my maternal uncle. Bharadwaj was an officer in the Forest Department and was often away on duty. They had five sons. I might have been an inspiration to them as the fact was that two of them joined the Army. During my visits to their house, they always looked after me well. As cadets, we were financially well off as we were getting the salary of a British Sergeant. There used to be a bar in every Company ante room and we were allowed some beer and cigarettes as weekly rations. However, this practice was given up after our course.

The IMA Commandant was Brig. A. B. Baltrop OBE MC, popularly known as 'Groppi'. He had played a sterling role in transforming IMA from wartime Officers Training School, into a peacetime military institution, as it existed prior to 1939-45 war. Lt Col Thakur Mahadeo Singh DSO was head of the Training Team. He later took over command of IMA, as Brigader from Baltrop and assiduously reorganised the IMA with Indian officers and JCOs/NCOs, after the departure of British consequent to our Independence. The Adjutant was Maj A. J. Wilson MC, (Jim) who later opted for the Pakistan Army and became Military Secretary to their Chief of the Army Staff, Gen Gracy. As part of the national policy to gradually replace British by Indian officers after Independence, Maj Wilson was replaced by Lt Col S. P. Malhotra (Smoky) from the Guards. I, later served under him as a Brigade Commander in 1970-71, when he was General Officer Commanding third Infantry Division in Ladakh. IMA Regimental Sergeant Major was Mcgurite from the Irish Guard, who was feared on the parade ground. Cadets were organised into a battalion, namely 'Auchinleck' which was commanded by Lt Col L.T. Fairbanks OBE, a physical fitness fanatic. The Battalion had four companies; A Company was commanded by Maj A.C. Ayappa, from Signals, who had been a prisoner of war under the Japanese.

B Company was commanded by Maj T.R. Johnson from the Frontier Force Regt. Maj K. Zorawar Singh, from Central India Horse commanded C Company and D Company was commanded by Maj M.A. Rahman MC from Frontier Force Rifles. Our Platoon Commander was Capt G.S. Mehdi, who was known as the 'Killer', as he was physically very tough and was a hard taskmaster. Since I was not from a public school, I was a bit shy and an introvert and found the going difficult. Due to lack of proficiency in English I could not take part in group discussions and was reticent. I had not studied literature and was totally at loss during some of the academic periods. I overcame these handicaps by studying extra time in the excellent IMA library. Moreover, I was not physically strong and I had not played any organised team games e.g. football, hockey or cricket. I therefore, could not take active part in these company games except in a limited manner in hockey, where my platoon commander could assess my qualities of agility, skill and team spirit. Nevertheless, I took to squash with gusto and acquired a certain proficiency at it. In the first term my performance was below average and I was cautioned by Mehdi. I put in real hard work thereafter, and used to spend a lot of time in the library to improve my academics, particularly English language. At the end of the second term, I was complimented by Mehdi for remarkable improvement. Mehdi told me 'Sushil, you have turned the corner and I am pleased with your performance. Keep it up.' I took to squash playing and also learnt swimming, which was mandatory for all cadets. I remember I had to box for three minutes in an inter-company competition.

After our second term, the Third Course Cadets joined us in February 1947, and a new Company was formed by the name Meiktila and I was posted to this Company. It was housed in temporary huts near Dhobi Ghat. The new Company Commander was Maj Beal and Platoon

Commander was Maj P.S. Gill from the Corps of Signals. All the instructors were outstanding officers. I particularly remember Col Gould (Academics), Col. Steal, and Capt Tikka Khan, who later became Commander in Chief of Pakistan Army and presided over the defeat of his Army in 1971, Indo-Pak war! I met Col Steal in London in 1961, when I was posted there on the staff of Military Adviser to the Indian High Commission. Col Steal was reemployed after retirement in the War Office and I had a lot of interaction with him. Maj Zorawar Singh was married to a pretty Greek girl. He used to keep a strict vigil on her, as he felt that other officers and some senior cadets were attracted to her. Much later in 1968, I and my wife met Zorawar Singh in Sikkim on the eve of his retirement at a party hosted by the Chohgyal of Sikkim. I was Colonel (General Staff) 17 Mountain Division, while Zorawar was commanding 27 Infantry Division. After the death of Zorawar, Mrs Zorawar Singh (Anar) continued to meet us during the annual gatherings of Second Course officers and once she even stayed with us for three four days as she had become a good friend of my wife Neeru. Capt. Inder Singh Gill was an ex-British Army Engineer, who later joined Parachute Regiment. He later retired as Army Commander. He was very bold, a dare devil and admired by the cadets. Once we were watching a game of squash, in which Maj Beal's sister was taking part. After the game was over, Inder wished to play with the young lady and instead of approaching the court through the door, he jumped from the spectator gallery and broke his ankles! This was talked about for a long time. Later in service, I served as his Colonel General Staff, when he was General Officer Commanding, 17 Mountain Division in Sikkim. Inder Gill was used to hard drinking and his mind worked better after a few drinks. He rose to be Army Commander before retirement. He was a very effective Director of Military Operations at Army HQ during the Indo-Pak War of 1971. Maj M.A. Rahman was popular amongst cadets. He migrated to Pakistan and retired as Lt General. He visited India several times, as his brother had stayed back after partition and was in the Indian Foreign Service. During these visits, he always made it a point to meet some of us from the IMA Second Course. There were also Maj. Thapan and Maj Nakai, who later retired as Army Commanders. The thing to note is that instructors in IMA were all outstanding officers and most of them reached the peak of their profession before retirement.

The toughest part of our training was the 'Chindit Initiative'. We had to cover 100 miles in five days, walking in full battle order through the Shiwaliks! At that time (1946-47) the Shiwaliks were teaming with games of all variety and there was little habitation. We were allowed one bottle of water a day for drinking, cooking and ablutions. My platoon commander Mehdi 'The Killer' also walked with us in full battle order, setting a personal example. An interesting episode was related by one of my fellow cadets, who saw Mehdi scolding a cadet for a minor lapse. This was also observed by a village woman, who upbraided the Captain and screamed: 'Stop it. You will kill these poor boys!' An apoplectic Mehdi tried to chase the woman with his stick, while the villagers cheered.

Two episodes are worth mentioning during the life at the Second Course. At the declaration of Independence of India and Pakistan on 15 August, 1947, communal riots broke out all over India and Dehradun could not escape from the mad communal massacre. We were all issued with rifles and ammunition and formed into squads to patrol the affected areas. I was given the responsibility to patrol Forest Research Institute, adjacent to the IMA. After our patrolling duty, we used to rest in the verandah of the house of the Director Mr. Chengappa, Mrs Chengappa would ply us with hot coffee throughout the night.

The other notable episode was the departure of Pakistani

cadets, officers and staff with their families for Pakistan. On the evening of 14 October, 1947 i.e. two months after Independence Day (15th August), we were informed by our Company Commander at the Ante Room procedure that all Pakistani cadets would leave early morning by Royal Air Force aircraft ex Saharanpur. Earlier, we had been informed that at the time of partition of India and Pakistan, all Muslim cadets would complete their training with us and leave for Pakistan after commissioning on 21 December 1947. However, they were now to leave at 03.00 hrs on 15 October, 1947. The other cadets helped them to pack and get ready for departure. Some of us had tearful faces at their send off. There were 45 of them and soon after their arrival at Chaklala they were informed on 20 October, 1947 that they should consider themselves as 'commissioned'. They were, thereafter, sent off to their respective Regiments. Soon after, all the Muslim officers and staff, with their families also departed for Pakistan. We faced some of them from opposite side, during the wars of 1965 and 1971.

Notwithstanding sour relations between the two countries and the Kashmir problem, we continued to meet some of our Pakistani colleagues, during our gettogether at our passing out Golden Jubilee and Diamond Jubilee. Only some of them were able to attend these functions at IMA, where they showed considerable cordiality and goodwill. Later, when Parvez Mushrraf was the President of Pakistan, they invited the entire Second Course officers, with families to Pakistan in 2007 and made elaborate arrangements for the visit. The visit had the official sponsorship of Pakistan Government. On our side, the visit was supported by Army Headquarters, External Affairs Ministry, and Ministry of Civil Aviation. We were provided with complimentary air tickets for officers with their wives to Lahore and back. Chief of the Army Staff, Gen J. J. Singh generously sanctioned a financial grant of Rs 50,000 for a trophy to be presented to Pakistan Military Academy, Kakul. Our Pakistani colleagues had made an elaborate programme for our visit, which included reception at Wagah, travel to Islamabad along their Express Highway, stay for one night at Murree, with an official Second Course get together, visit to Pakistan Military Academy at Kakul, stay at Lahore and visit places of interest, before returning back home.

There was tremendous enthusiasm among our colleagues and their families about our visit to Pakistan, but unfortunately, the serial blasts in Bombay in 2007 executed by terrorists based in Pakistan derailed the relations between India and Pakistan. This vitiated the whole atmosphere and the trip had to be cancelled.

Incidentally, later in 2011, it was close to the Pakistan Military Academy at Kakul that the notorious terrorist Bin Laden was living for years, obviously under the patronage of Pakistan Army. His place was raided by US Navy Seals, in a dare devil commando operation at night and Laden was killed. His body with some prisoners and documents was taken away by US commandos. The entire operation was carried out in the heart of Pakistan, which caused great embarrassment to Pakistan and its Army.

There were rumours that our course would be shortened as operations in J&K had commenced against the Pak infiltrators, but ultimately we were commissioned as scheduled on 21 December, 1947. The salute on passing out parade was taken by India's Defence Minister Sardar Baldev Singh. This was the first and the last time that a politician took the salute at the passing out parade of the Academy.

Prior to commissioning, we were asked for our choice of Arm/Service/Regiment, in which, we wished to be commissioned. No one advised me about this, though we had discussion amongst ourselves. Since my parents choice was Army Service Corps, I decided to opt for it. However, later, when I had wider interaction with colleagues and officers I realised that I had made a mistake as the career progression in the Infantry was much better. I resolved to rectify this mistake at the earliest opportunity.

After Independence a need arose to decide on the future of Gorkha regiments in the Indian Army. As a result of tripartite agreement between India, Nepal and Britain, six out of the ten Gorkha regiments stayed with the Indian Army. These regiments were exclusively headed by British officers. A large number of officers were, therefore, transferred from Indian regiments to these Gorkha regiments to replace the British officers who were moving out. Besides, some selected officers from our course were also posted to Gorkha Regiments taken over by India. A new Gorkha regiment was also under raising, for which officers were required. I therefore, immediately applied to the Military Secretary for transfer to a Gorkha regiment.

After commissioning, we were given two weeks leave to visit home and thereafter report to Small Arms School Saugor (now known as Sager in Madhya Pradesh) for training. It was during our training at Saugor that a great tragedy struck the nation on 30 January 1948 when the Father of the Nation, Mahatma Gandhi was shot, during a prayer meeting at Delhi. Unprecedented gloom descended on the School and many of us cried unabashedly. After training at Saugor, the entire course proceeded to Mhow for Junior Leaders Course at the Infantry School (now College of Combat). There I met Maj Tappy Raina, who was commanding our company. We found Raina to be an outstanding officer and a great patriot, who was greatly admired by all of us. Later, I was fortunate to have him as my instructor in the Defence College Wellington. He later rose to be the Chief of Army Staff.

After the Course at Mhow, I reported to ASC School Bareilly.

When I had just joined the Army Service Corps School Bareilly, for Young Officers course, I got the orders for my transfer to 11 Gorkha Regiment, Palampur. This was a new regiment raised from non-optees, who had refused to join Her Majesty Government Gorkhas. Nothing was known about this regiment. However, I immediately left for Palampur, where 11 Gorkha Rifles Regimental Centre (11GRRC) was located and reported for duty on 23 February, 1948. I have never regretted this decision.

Later on 30 May, 1948 Second Lieutenant Rajendra Nath Pandit, from my IMA Course also joined the Centre from Artillery School. He had a similar problem and had applied for change of arm. I was delighted to get the company of an old course-mate and we forged a lifelong friendship.

4

The Gorkhas

Gorkha Regiments were unique as the British exclusively commanded them before Indian Independence and spread a baseless rumour that the Gorkhas did not like Indian officers. It is pertinent to recall here the history of the Gorkhas in the Army, during British rule. It may be mentioned that the literal meaning of the word 'gorkha' is the protectorof cows. However, all Nepalis in their Army were known by the term 'Gorkha'. In early nineteenth century, Nepal had extended its rule in the west, up to Simla, Garhwal, Kumaon Hills and in the East, up to Sikkim, under their able commander Amar Singh Thapa. Interestingly, during this period, Amar Singh visited the holy place of Gangotri and constructed a temple. Further, Nepal had raided Terai area and annexed a large chunk of its territory. This threatened British rule in India and therefore after an ultimatum to Nepal, which remained unanswered, a coordinated multi-pronged attack was launched by the British on Nepal occupied areas. This included an attack from the Terai plains towards Kathmandu, a force to capture Simla Hills and the third force was launched towards Dehradun-Srinagar (Garhwal). The Gorkhas were equipped with fusil (musket), bows and arrows and kukris. They relied on arms and ammunition, captured from the British and their kukri in close combat. The kukri is a curved knife which was used in close combat, with skill and deftness. Later, when the Gorkhas formed part of Indian Army under the British, the kukri became a personal equipment of a Gorkha soldier.

The Gorkhas main defence were the hills and jungles, which they used skillfully in a defensive battle. The British strength was nearly 100 percent more than the Gorkhas and comprised cavalry, artillery with six pounder guns and infantry, with fusil. But the British soldiers were not used to mountain and jungle warfare. After a bitter and fierce fight on all fronts, the Treaty of Segauli was signed on 4 March, 1816 between the British and Nepal. The British realised that Gorkhas were tough and brave fighters and any attempt to attack Nepal would result in prolonged war, causing heavy casualties. It was, therefore prudent to have Nepal as an ally and a source to provide good fighting material for their Army in India. As a result of the aforementioned treaty, Nepal ceded Simla, Garhwal, and the Kumaon Hills in the West and Sikkim in the East as also the Terai area. The British recognised the raw courage and bravery of the Gorkhas and in an unprecedented gesture erected a monument in Kalanga (Dehradun) as a tribute to their gallant adversary Balbhadra Singh, who had commanded the Gorkha troops. The British were allowed to recruit Gorkhas in their army in India.

During the first war of independence in 1857, Jung

Bahadur Kunwar, the Prime Minister of Nepal offered services of Nepali troops to the British and even led a force of 6000 troops personally. Gorkha troops fought along with British infantry in their attack on Delhi and also helped the British in lifting the siege at Lucknow Residency. In recognition of Nepal's help, British restored the Terai tracts to them. Jung Bahadur was bestowed the title of Rana by the King of Nepal.

During the Indian independence movement, it may be recalled, the British used Gorkha troops to fire at the protesters at Jallianwala Bagh. However, the Indian leaders did not blame the Gorkha troops as they were merely carrying out the orders of their Commander Brig R.E.H. Dyer.

Gorkhas in the Indian Army Post-Independence

By the time Second World War started, British had ten gorkha regiments, numbered from 1 to 10. At the end of Second World War in 1945, it was apparent to the British that India will gain Independence in near future. A problem arose as to what was to be the future of Gorkha Regiments in independent India? British could not absorb all the regiments in the British Army, as their economy was in tatters and their empire in the East was shrinking. As far as India was concerned, though enough material was available in India to meet the requirement of the Army, considering political, strategic, geographical importance of Nepal and historical cultural ties with her, it was decided by Nehru Government to keep the Gorkha Regiments as part of Indian Army, if Nepal Government agreed. Nepal was amenable to the idea of Gorkhas serving in the Indian Army as their remittances to home and their pensions were a great economy booster. The question of Indians not being allowed to command the Grokha units did not arise. As a result of a series of high level discussions, a tripartite agreement was signed between India, Britain and Nepal on 9 November, 1947, according to which it was decided that of the ten Gorkha Regiments, four would go to the British and six would be retained by India. After considerable deliberations, the British selected 2, 6, 7 and 10 Gorkha Regiments to be transferred to the British Army, while 1, 3, 4, 5, 8, 9 Gorkha Regiments stayed with India. 2nd and 6th Gorkha Regiments recruited men from West Nepal, who were mostly Magars, Gurungs, while 7th and 10th recruited Rais and Limbus from East Nepal. Gurungs and Magars are cheerful, kind hearted, physically tough, and amenable to discipline and can be relied upon when things are going wrong in war. They are proud and very particular about self-respect. Any act which appears to be unfair or insulting to them would deeply hurt their pride and may provoke them to indulge in indisciplinary acts. Rais and Limbus were not recruited by the British till 1907. They are good in an offensive action in war, though they require good leadership and tactful handling. Any indiscreet language or act which may hurt their self-esteem would infuriate them and may result in undesirable retaliation.

There was a provision in the agreement that men of the four regiments selected by the British will be given several options:

(a) They could stay on in a unit going to the British;

(b) Seek transfer to a unit of the Indian Army;

(c) Go home on pension.

Referendum in units of four regiments selected by the British was held under joint supervision of British and Indian officers. The results of this referendum were most shocking for the British, who expected most of the men to opt for them. For example, 2nd Battalion 6th Gorkha Rifles was on duty at Viceroy's Lodge; only 30-40 men from this unit opted for the British Army. Similarly, 1st Battalion of 6th Gorkha Rifles was on duty in Bombay, who had fought along with the British in siege of Delhi in 1857 and was awarded Queen's Truncheon. Referendum in this unit produced an unexpected result. This was particularly most embarrassing for General Sir Francis Tuker, who was the Colonel of the Regiment and at that moment was General Officer Commanding Eastern Command, Calcutta. A large number of optees from 2 and 6 Gorkha Rifles were absorbed by raising new battalions for 1, 3, 4, 5, and 8 Gorkha Rifles, as these regiments also recruited Magars and Gurungs, from West Nepal. 7 and 10 Gorkha Rifles had Rais and Limbus, from Eastern Nepal. A total of 1604 men from the battalions of theseregiments (1/7, 2/7.1/10,2/10 Gorkha Rifles) opted for India. Further, 1034 men from 7 Gorkha Rifles Regiment Centre (7 GRRC), located at Palampur and 780 men from 10 Gorkha Rifles Regimental Centre located at Alhilal opted for India. Only 215 men from 7 GRRC and 95 men from 10 GRRC opted to serve under the British. Thus, a total number of 3418 men from 7 and 10 Gorkha Rifles opted to serve in India. This necessitated the raising of 11 Gorkha Rifles.

The episode of 2/7 Gorkha Rifles, which was stationed at Ahmedabad, is the most interesting and must be related. Men of this unit had already made up their mind to opt for India, despite persuasion by British officers. This infuriated the British officers who imposed severe cuts on the heavy advances and leave applied by men. The men collectively protested against this arbitrary action of British Commanding Officer. Sub. Maj Ishwar Man Rai was blamed for this indiscipline and was arrested. Some men were also arrested. This was most embarrassing for the British, who termed the action of men of this battalion as mutiny. Brig D.S. Brar, Sub Area Commander, Bombay intervened in the matter and listened to men's grievances. The above action further alienated the men from the British. The unit was moved to Madh Island, where the referendum was held. As a result, the entire unit opted for India, except 53 men who were mostly officers' batmen, drivers and mess waiters; 664 non-optees were moved to Santa Cruz and attached with 3/5 Gorkha Rifles, till they were constituted into 3/11 Gorkha Rifles.

Why did Gorkha soldiers opt in such large numbers to stay back with the Indian Army, despite having served under the British for nearly 150 years? The British charge that Gorkha soldiers were influenced by Indian propaganda is not true. A Gorkha is intelligent, speaks less and is devoted to his family. He had not been home for the last five years, due to War and serving in the British Army would have further extended this period of staying away from home. He was keenly looking forward to leave and going home. Moreover, the service conditions under the British had not yet been announced. No Gorkha had yet been given commission, under the British, while there were many Gorkha commissioned officers in the Indian Army. Clerks in the Gorkha units were more educated and they opted for India, in large numbers. All this exploded the canard spread by the British that Gorkhas disliked Indians and did not want to be commanded by Indians.

Raising of 11 Gorkha Rifles

Maj H.S. Chauhan, Rajput Regiment, a product of Col Brown Public School, Dehradun, was ordered by the Army Headquarters to take over the non-optees of 7 and 10 Gorkha Rifles at Palampur. Maj Chauhan arrived at Palampur on 31 December, 1947. From 1 January onwards non-optees were referred to as 'Indian Gorkha Detachment.' Formal orders of raising the 11 Gorkha Rifles were issued by Army HQ on 27 January 1948, and Chauhan appointed as its Commandant in the rank of Lt Colonel. By the time I reported to the Centre on 23rd February 1948, 11 Gorkha Rifles was raised.

Maj M.M.S. Bakshi (later transferred to 8 Gorkha Rifles) had been the Second in Command and Capt D.E.M. Shannahan was the Adjutant. Maj N. Ghosh, also from Rajput Regiment was OC Training Battalion. Maj. S.D. Sawhney was Officer-In-Charge Records with Lt. K.S. Mehta as his deputy. Maj D.S. Khatri, who had joined the Centre a week before me was Officer Commanding 'A' Company. There were two outstanding ex JCOs (junior commissioned officers), Capt Gobind Singh Limbu, Sardar Bahadur, OBI and Capt M.B. Rai, MC, IDSM. When Gorkha Regiments got Indianised, selected senior JCOs were given commission in each unit with a view to assist and advise Indian officers in handling Gorkha soldiers.

Col Chauhan had a stupendous and a challenging task in moulding the non-optees of two regiments into a viable and functional regiment. I was informed that during raising there was some trouble between optees and non-optees of 10 GRRC at Alhilal. Chauhan took immediate action to speak to non-optees and had them moved to Palampur. Also, optees of 7 GRRC were moved from Palampur to Alhilal.

Col Chauhan related an incident to us, which demonstrated that Gorkha soldiers who opted for India, had completely switched their loyalty to India. During the New Year's dinner in 1947 in the 7 GRRC mess, as per custom, the Band Major was required to report to the Commanding Officer at the end of the dinner, but he reported to Col Chauhan. When Chauhan told him that he should report to the Commanding Officer of 7 GRRC, the Band Major replied 'Sir, I have opted to serve in the Indian Army and you are now our Commanding Officer.'

British officers had taken away all regimental funds contributed by the men, all the silver of officers' mess and even pots and pans of all the kitchens. Chauhan had to organise these locally and spent even personal funds where necessary so that the Centre could get going. In the Officers Mess, officers made personal contributions to build up silver gradually. The men were moving around in Palampur with 7/10 Gorkha Rifles badge on their caps. Officers were using badges of the Regiment they came from. Chauhan issued instructions that no badges would be used on uniform/caps, till a new 11 Gorkha badge was approved. Chauhan studied the badges of all the Gorkha Regiments and designed an 11 Gorkha badge with crossed kukris and eleven in roman in the centre, with Ashoka emblem mounted on top. However, Army Headquarters had some difficulty in producing the badge as mentioned above and therefore Chauhan accepted the design without the Ashoka emblem so that these could be produced by ordnance on a mass scale. As regards the Regimental flag, Chauhan got hold of a piece of green cloth on which he got stitched the proposed badge in white cloth. This was used by the Quarter Guard.

Col Chauhan was an upright officer. His honesty and integrity was beyond reproach. He was imbued with a high sense of dedication and discipline which often made him inflexible in handling problems. But he always believed in leadership by personal example and took full responsibility for his decisions. He was a teetotaler but an excellent host. He was meticulous in planning and did the new regiment proud in putting it on sound footing during its formative years. I personally owe him a lot for basic grounding and teaching us regimental customs, importance of discipline, art of management and command of troops. Officers dreaded to go into his office and I often saw senior captains and majors coming out with tears, after receiving a royal dressing down. His reserved nature and honesty perhaps affected his career prospects and he could only attain the rank of Colonel before retirement. The Regiment affectionately gave him the title of 'Father of the Regiment', as he was the one who raised it. It reflected all the honour and respect his men had for him.

Gobind Singh Limbu was a huge man, with tremendous experience, endowed with earthy intelligence, somewhat reserved and very soft spoken. He was highly respected in the Regiment. M.B. Rai MC IDSM was an extrovert, liked good things of life, spoke English, which facilitated his adaptation to officer life. MB was a gallant soldier who, later on while serving with Naga Village Guards, was awarded the highest gallantry award in peace i.e. Ashok Chakra.

I learnt a lot from both these officers about the idiosyncrasies and nature of Rais and Limbus. Major Ghosh, known as Dada Ghosh, was the Training Major. He was of cheerful demeanour and friendly nature, ever willing to teach young officers. He was a good instructor and team leader. Derrick Shannahan was a good sportsman, smart and well turned out. He presented an excellent example of a good officer. Dhaman Singh Khatri, a middle aged officer, who had risen from the ranks, was always smiling and brightened up the parties.

I and Rajendra Nath being from the same IMA course became very good friends which continued after our retirement. We used to spend a lot of time studying military history together. On Sundays, we often took a bottle of beer with packed lunch and climbed nearby hills covered with snow. He was physically tough and climbed like a mountain goat. I had great difficulty in keeping pace with him. He was given command of Boys Coy and appointed Physical Training Officer while I was given command of Training B Coy and also looked after weapon training and education. Ganju Lama, VC MM was my Education Havildar and was responsible for organising and assigning recruits to various classes under the Education JCO according to their competence. This association developed into a close personal bond which continued even after retirement. He retired as Honorary Capt. and ADC to the President of India (Gyani Zail Singh). He was made Vice-President of

VC Association which used to meet in London biannually and Ganju and his family always called on us on their way to UK and on return. Later in life he was afflicted by cancer and was in Delhi for treatment, accompanied by Health Minister of Sikkim. One day in the year 2000 he rang me up frantically to request me to be present with him during the visit of UK Defense Attaché. The British offered to fly him to the UK for treatment but the doctors after examining his documents declared him beyond treatment. He then flew back to Sikkim and lived a few more weeks till his life ebbed away. The Sikkim Government gave him a State funeral. 11 Gorkha Rifles Centre also sent a contingent to participate in his funeral. Gorkha Brigade and Army Headquarters at my request and through the efforts of Lt Gen J.B.S. Yadav had helped him financially in his treatment. It shocked us, when we learnt that he had donated his medals to his old Regiment 7 Gorkha Rifles (in the United Kingdom) who had promised to take care of his family financially. All this was done secretly and the Regiment had no inkling. The deal was clinched by an officer of 7 Gorkha Rifles who flew from London to Sikkim to negotiate the terms with Ganju. I wish he had mentioned his financial problems to one of us and the Regiment would have had no difficulty in giving this commitment of taking care of his family and children. After all he had come to the Regiment as a Rifleman and had risen to the rank of Honorary Capt. and ADC to the President!

Palampur Cantonment had a number of parade grounds, like terraces, officers mess and offices were at the lower level. We all had to walk up to the parade ground which was physically strenuous. The area was surrounded by tea gardens. We sometimes used to see a young lady on horse back trotting on the side of the top parade ground. Our senior JCOs told us that she was Raj Kumari and owned some tea garden. Rajender Nath and I decided to call on Raj Kumari who was living in a bungalow. After ringing the bell we were ushered into the drawing room and were asked by a 'gentleman' as to whom we would like to meet. We said, 'We have come to meet Raj Kumari and we are from 11 GRRC'. This person replied, 'I am Raj Kumari!' We had expected to meet a charming young lady but there was a middle aged woman with all the signs and mannerism of a man. She was known to keep two young girls who were referred to by locals as 'her wives'. We felt embarrassed and made a hasty retreat. This episode became a source of amusement for officers in the Mess and amongst the JCOs.

5/11 GR was under raising at the Centre. Its two companies were already in J & K engaged in active operations. Colonel M.L. Barua was the Commanding Officer and Maj. Daljeet Singh was the Second-in-Command. I and Rajendra Nath were keen to join this unit so that we could get a chance to get the feel of active operations. One day we decided to see the Commandant to present our request and were treated with his usual epithets of 'you wooden headed, pig headed so and so!' and had to beat a hasty retreat from his office. Thereafter, we dug our graves in front of our rooms to demonstrate that we would end our lives in the Centre! Chauhan of course saw these and laughed it away. One morning when we came for breakfast to the Mess, we were surprised to meet Maj Rana Jhalak Jung Bahadur of 5/11 Gorkha Rifles, having brandy along with breakfast. He was already a bit high. We were both amused and horrified as this was the first occasion to meet an alcoholic though not the last. Barua and Daljeet were hard drinkers but had to restrict it on dinner nights, which were observed strictly, though they continued their drinking sessions after dinner.

The country had just become independent and we all were imbued with a strong sense of nationalism. I and Rajendra decided to drop 'Gour' and 'Pandit' from our names respectively so that our caste remained unknown. This is how I became Sushil Kumar and he became Rajender

Nath. I had some problem with my bankers, who were suspicious initially and wanted to know the reasons for the change of name. After I explained the matter, they were satisfied and made the correction.

The first Subedar Major of the Centre was Nardhoj Rai, who retired on 8 March 1948. Subedar Major Chaturman Rai took over from Nardhoj. Chaturman had complete hold on the men. He used to speak very fast and also walked fast. The men had therefore nicknamed him 'Howrah' i.e. Howrah Mail, the express train that runs daily between Delhi and Kolkata. Being first from the post war IMA regular course other officers had high hopes from both of us and we both tried to live upto their expectations. My Company Subedar was Ram Dhan Limbu. He was soft spoken and well experienced in handling the men. I learnt a lot from him, in particular, how an officer was to conduct himself in the presence of jawans on or off the parade ground and at social Regimental functions. If he ever saw me going wrong, he would quietly whisper in my ears and I immediately made amends.

In May 1949, Chauhan was nominated for the Defence Services Staff College and left for Wellington after a very productive tenure, as first Commandant of the newly raised regiment. Maj Bakshi officiated till Col Yadav joined as the Commandant. General K.M. Carriappa, who had been appointed as the Commander-in-Chief, visited the Centre. He was accompanied by Lt Gen S.P.P. Thorat, the Army Commander and Maj Gen J C Katoch, the Area Commander. I was detailed as his Liaison Officer. The party was staying in Circuit House. In the evening the Chief got hold of me and spoke to the press and said 'Here is Second Lieutenant. Gour, a rare commodity. Where ever I go, I only meet senior officers. This was because most of the officers after the British left, had become too senior. We were informed that General Cariappa usually saw the

Regiment's ceremonial parade and therefore, we practised hard for the same. However, the General was late and could visit the Centre only in the evening. We were formed up on parade. On arrival, he mounted the saluting base and signaled all officers and JCOs to fall out and line up behind him. Thereafter, he motioned the entire parade under NCOs to come closer and form up in a hollow square. This is how he addressed the troops. He was pleased with the turn out and the disciplined manner in which troops formed the hollow square for which he complemented us in his usual British Hindi.

While at the Centre I did two Army courses; Unit Education Course at Pachmarhi and Quarter Master Course at Jabalpur. Pachmarhi is a beautiful hill station in Madhya Pradesh and I thoroughly enjoyed the course. At Jabalpur, the Army Ordnance Corps (AOC) School and Centre were located on a high ground called the Ridge. That was where I learnt cycle polo, which became popular among students. Jabalpur is famous for marble rocks on the Narmada river. It is indeed a beautiful site at night, during full moon.

Years later, after retirement, in 2009, I along with my wife and younger son Ashu with his family, were invited by Lt Gen G.M. Nair, the then Col 11 GR, who was commanding Nine corps in Yol, to spend some time with him. During my stay in Yol, I visited Palampur, the old site of 11 GRRC, which I had joned on commissioning in 1948. It was a nostalgic visit. A Division Headquarter was located there. Palampur had developed into a town centre with a number of institutions and developing its tourism potential. Roads had been constructed and one could drive to any location with ease. New buildings had come up in the old centre location. The only old buildings which were still intact were the Officers Mess (now Alfa Mess), Commandant's bungalow, (now being used as the residence of General Officer Commanding) and single officers quarters, including the rooms in which I and Rajendra Nath had stayed sixty years ago. It was a memorable visit down memory lane.

Tenure in 3/11 Gorkha Rifles

Soon after Chauhan left, Rajendra Nath was posted to 3/11 GR. I followed him soon after. The battalion was located in Dewa Batala and was commanded by Thakur Prithi Chand, MVC. He along with his cousin Kushal Chand, both from Dogra Regiment with a handful of soldiers had walked during winter in snow from Baltal to Leh and organised the local militia to defend Leh against Pak raiders. For this gallant action, both of them were awarded MVC. Col Prithvi Chand was fond of drinking and often after a few drinks talked incoherently and acted illogically. He was not exactly friendly with youngsters like us. Capt. Indradhoj Limbu, an ex JCO, invariably gave him company in those drinking sessions. Once in the mess, I had a heated argument with him and I was so infuriated that, but for Rajendra Nath, I would have resorted to unwarranted action. After this incident the CO did not come out of his tent for three days and remained under the influence of drinks.

One morning, he called me and ordered me to take my Company and occupy a feature on the Pak border as he apprehended an attack from Pakistan. I was given one hour to move. As regards logistics, I was informed that those would follow and I need not worry. Rajendra was given similar orders to occupy a feature on my flank. We did not get food and water for the next 24 hours. This was yet another example of his erratic behaviour. He retired as Colonel and settled down in Manali where he had an orchard. He was undoubtedly a hero of Leh, but was not destined for higher command. Later, my younger son Ashu and his wife Gauri, during a holiday in Manali called on him and the Colonel fondly remembered his association with me and offered excellent hospitality to them. Ashu noticed that the drive-way to Colonel's cottage was decorated on both sides with empty beer bottles turned upside down; a somewhat theatrical reminder of the Colonel's love for drinks! Some time in 1950 I was detailed to attend a Ground Liaison Officer Course with the Indian Air Force at Jammu. At the end of the course I was posted to 13 Ground Liaison Section located at Halwara near Ludhiana in Punjab, a new Air Force Station under development, based on a disused airfield of the Second World War. Meanwhile, there was reshuffling of officers in the Regiment and I and Rajender, being commissioned on the same date, could not be in the same Battalion and thus I was assigned to 5/11 Gorkha Rifles.

My Days with the Indian Air Force

In 1950 the Halwara Air Force Station was commanded by Wing Com. Moolgaukar, who later retired as Chief of the Air Staff. He was highly intelligent and a thorough professional. He was known as a good fighter pilot and this is how he typically behaved in the mess. Halwara was a disused airfield of Second World War period and was to be soon commissioned. There were no aircrafts. The only pastime Moolgaukar had was to hunt down barking deer from his running jeep on the air strip, which we used to share as a delicacy. There were also drinking bouts with bawdy English songs. There was no wild game act at that time. Moolgaukar disliked the Army and was particularly critical of Gen Carriappa, who had become the Chief of the Army Staff and held the designation of Commander-in-Chief. He disliked our presence in his mess parties and treated us as outsiders but had to bear with us. I met Moolgaukar again as a student of National Defence College, when he was the Commandant of the College and there was no mention of Halwara between us. Maj. Meharwan Singh Grewal was the OC 13 Ground Liaison (GL) Section. Grewal was a paratrooper who had long association with the Air Force. He was more of an Air Force man than the Army. He retired as a Colonel but remained in touch with me. He settled down in Maler Kotla. Our mess in Halwara was in a Canal Inspection Bungalow. We all were living in tents. One morning we found that our cots were floating in water due to floods; the canal had overflowed its banks! Many of us climbed the trees to escape the fury of the floods. Later, we had breakfast in the mess in our underwears!

In 1950 there was a severe earthquake in North East and Air Force was ordered to position a detachment at Jorhat for a supply dropping mission. I was detailed as a liaison officer with the detachment. I often went on the air drop mission myself. We dropped even opium for consumption of locals. The earthquake had led to massive landslides, blocking many streams/rivers and creating artificial lakes. The administration was worried that if the blockages were cleared the lower areas would be inundated. The detachment was commanded by Sqn Ldr Malse, a dare devil pilot, who later retired as Air Marshal. We were staying at the Circuit House and were entitled to free food. The local contractor was responsible for catering. Menu included chicken everyday and to ensure that there was no adulteration Malse always insisted that we should be served roast chicken; chicken curry was taboo, as it could easily conceal the nature of the bird!

Joining 5/11 Gorkha Rifles

In 1951 I was posted to 5/11 Gorkha Rifles, after a year and half in 13 G L Section. The Battalion had just returned from J & K and was located in Kanchrapara-Dharampur Camp, an old prisoner of war camp of Second World War vintage. The Commanding Officer was Lt Col I.S. Rana and Second in Command was Maj R.D. Hira (Rocky). The Adjutant was my old friend Capt M.B. Rai. I was asked to take over as Quarter Master of the Unit. I had earlier done the Quarter Master Course at Army Ordnance Corps School Jabalpur, while being posted at the 11 Gorkha Rifles Regimental Centre (11GRRC) . There were only two family quarters in the centre of the camp which were occupied by the Commanding Officer with his family and the Adjutant, with family respectively. I do not recollect the CO ever coming to the officer's mess. He remained completely aloof from the officers. The seniormost officer, who was member of the mess was Maj RD Hira (Rocky). We were accommodated in a barrack with a false ceiling; a portion of which was falling apart due to lack of maintenance and repair. The barrack was divided into cubicles with the help of wooden almirahs and we had to use community toilets, located at the end of the barrack. There were no entertainment facilities. Kanchrapara, being a prominent railway station, the railways had an officers club and we were made temporary members of the club. However, we could only visit on weekends, the mode of transport being cycle rickshaw. The unit had only one jeep which was used exclusively by the CO. There were no dinner nights in the mess and we spent evenings drinking and singing songs in English, often led by Rocky. It was a common practice to find minor faults with the dress of an officer and then compel him to order a round of drinks for all officers present. Rocky displayed tremendous team spirit and leadership qualities and officers looked up to him to lead, a quality which helped him in war, during 1965 and 1971, when he led his brigade and division gallantly and with distinction. Sometime at the end of 1951, the Battalion moved to Gopalpur on the banks of river Icshamti on the border of East Bengal, due to tensions between India and Pakistan. Officers were housed in a school building, which was in ruins. We spent most of the time training and playing games with the men. One of the most popular games amongst the men was a fancy dress football match between officers/JCOs and men which sent the men into rapturous laughter.

In November 1951 Maj A.S. Pannicker from Travancore State Forces joined us, followed by Lt Col Kushal Singh in January 1952 to relieve Col Rana. As Pannicker got his seniority from the State Forces he became senior to Rocky; consequently he was appointed Second in Command and Rocky got transferred to 3/11 Gorkha Rifles. The change of command of the unit led to complete transformation of the unit. The first thing Kushal did was to persuade the Brigade Commander to move the unit to Barrackpore, where we could live with families. We were allotted old British troops barracks. Kushal laid the real foundation of the Fighting Fifth. He infused a new spirit into all ranks and knit them into a well oiled machine with tremendous sense of pride. Not one aspect of the unit's life remained without the stamp of Kushal. Training was tough and well organised. All officers played games with men and standard of football reached a high, winning all competitions up to command level. Athletics were organised, which became the envy of the entire Brigade. The events included: 100 m, 200 m, 440 m relay races and marathon. Field events included long jump, high jump, pole vault, shot putt and javelin throw. I gave the running commentary wearing a felt hat and smoking a cigar keeping the spectators informed and entertained. It was Dada Ghosh, who gave me the nickname of 'Farouqh' the king of Egypt, who also used to smoke cigar. There was a lot of spit and polish employed in making the lines spick and span. In the officers mess dinner nights became a regular feature. There was hardly any silver in the mess and all officers pooled their resources and donated generously to create some admirable silver pieces, crafted by Bartons of Bangalore. Officers had their mess dress tailored by Phelps in Calcutta whose master cutter came to Barrackpore to fit for us. Mess was housed in the imposing Gwalior House on the banks of Hoogly. Married officers were required to dine in the mess once a month to give company to bachelors. A ladies night was held once a month when guests were also invited. On holidays, we often gathered in the mess to play bridge or to undertake a leisurely sailing trip in a steamer on the Hooghly, or if nothing else, we all went to Calcutta in a 3 ton vehicle (only one jeep was authorized in the unit) to witness free style wrestling by Dara Singh and King Kong, followed by dinner at Capri restaurant in Chowranghee. There were no exceptions and all officers with their wives joined in the outings. All these activities generated tremendous cohesiveness and team spirit.

One of the memorable evenings was the one when Brig Young of the British Gorkhas, along with his officers, was invited to our Dinner Night. He was obviously keen to see how the Indian officers were handling a Gorkha Regiment. In the mess they were subjected to 'martial games' after dinner, a Kushal specialty, and many of them departed without tunic buttons and ties but in a jovial mood.

A Gorkha soldier is generally identified by his Gorkha hat. The entitlement was only one hat per soldier, which was also in short supply, being an imported item. Kushal instructed me that he would like all men to be equipped with double Gorkha hats and he did not care what procedure I adopted. The Brigade Ordnance Officer came to our help and he condemned a large number of these hats as fair wear and tear for free replacement. In six months time the entire unit was fitted with double stitched Gorkha hats, while other Gorkha units were still using berets.

Under Kushal's leadership the Battalion made tremendous progress and was considered as the best unit in the Brigade. A number of senior officers from Army Headquarters visited the unit, among them Gen Choudhury the Adjutant General, (he later became COAS) to see how the young unit was shaping and were full of praise for the standards achieved.

The only major training event, before the Unit moved

to Kargil, was an exercise advance to contact with a squadron of light Stuart tanks of 8 Cavalry and a battery of 26 pounder guns. The tank squadron was commanded by Maj Jey Dalvi, whom I later met again at the Staff College Wellington and we became good friends. The exercise was along the Calcutta-Basirhat Road and I was assigned the role of Vanguard Commander, one who leads the Unit in battle formation. The exercise was run under General Officer Commanding (GOC) Bengal Area - Maj GenS.B.S. Roy and his General Staff Officer (GSO) I, Lt Col H.S. Chauhan, our first Centre Commandant. Our Brigade Commander (9 Infantry Brigade) was Ajit Guraya, whom we nicknamed as Ok Doc Brigadier as he was in the habit of saying 'Ok Doc' after every sentence. By evening there was a heavy downpour and the road and surrounding areas became slushy, with the result the tanks could not get off the road. Deployment of guns posed a problem and even infantry had difficulty in marching on slushy ground. The exercise, therefore, was called off and we returned to our camp. Guraya later commanded Assam Rifles as its Inspector General and on retirement, called on me when I was Director General Assam Rifles at Shillong in 1980. He wanted to visit Eastern Arunachal, where he had earmarked some land in the name of his son. The land was in a remote area in north east of Arunachal on the Burma border. It was sparsely populated by tribals and and was not connected by road. I arranged a helicopter in which Guraya got a lift to visit the area.

5

Battalion Moves to Kargil

In August 1953 my Battalion received orders to move to Kargil in J & K under Able Garrison commanded by Col. P.O. Dunn. The army did not have much experience of high altitudes at that time. We were therefore made to acclimatise at Gund (located on the road to Baltal-Zojila Pass.) The second stage of acclimatisation was at Baltal, at the base of Zojila Pass. We moved to Kargil by a narrow road in one-ton trucks whose upper structure had been removed to avoid overhanging cliffs. The widening of road was in progress. Acclimatisation has been now replaced by lasix tablets, known popularly as 'piss tablets'. Troops are now inducted directly to Leh and placed on lasix for a week. On arrival at Kargil I was asked to take over as Adjutant from DEM Shannahan, who was migrating to the UK. Maj Hem Raj Sharma was commanding A Coy in Leh and Maj (Dada) Ghosh was commanding B Coy in Gurgurdoo on the banks of the Indus. Col Dunn was later relieved by Col D.G.R. Rajwade, a very fine officer and a gentleman; I was later to serve under him, when he was Military Adviser in London.

Kargil was connected with Srinagar by a one ton road.There was no road from Kargil to Leh. Kargil was dominated by Pt 13620 which was in our occupation. It changed hands with Pakistan several times and in 1971; 2/11 Gorkha Rifles, under Col R B Gurung reoccupied this through a gallant action. The Battalion was awarded numerous gallantry awards and also battle honours as well as theatre honours. During winter, Kargil was cut off from Srinagar, due to heavy snowfall. There was a small airstrip and sometimes the entire garrison from Commander downwards would get involved in clearing the snow with the help of wooden planks. Very often, the strip was clear enough for Dakotas, but weather enroute from Srinagar was bad, which prevented aircrafts from flying. This made us frustrated after all the effort put in to clear the airstrip, especially as planes were the main source of receiving mail and fresh vegetables, during winter.

However, snow clearing was an enjoyable exercise. Even during winter we visited pickets. Kushal himself made sure that he visited Pt 13620, Gurgurdo and other pickets, during the time when the area was snowbound. He was invariably accompanied by me and Sub Maj (Bal Bdr Thapa) and at times by Quarter Master Capt Kulu Joshi. The unfortunate incident with 4/11 Gorkha Rifles, where the total neglect of men by officers resulted in disbandment of the unit, was fresh in our minds and we did not want to repeat past mistakes. In the officers' mess there was tremendous camaraderie and plenty of drinking and bridge sessions. Able Garrison Commander and his staff officers also dined in our mess and were a friendly lot. During the winter, not much training was possible except some patrolling and visiting pickets. There was an Advanced Dressing Station which was headed by Capt. R.N. Gour, who was our Regimental Medical Officer, when the unit was in Gopalpur and was well known to us. Men also had faith in him. He was not a full-fledged surgeon but he was known for carrying out some daring surgeries with meagre medical facilities successfully. We again met in Shillong, when I was DGAR and Gour was an Air Commodore Medical Officer with HQ Eastern Air Command.

The Battalion was visited by the Chief of Army Staff Gen Maharaj Rajendra Singh (in summer of 1954) who was quite pleased to see the young unit in high spirits. Later, we were visited by Lt Gen Kalwant Singh, the General Officer Commanding in Chief, accompanied by Maj. Gen. Jey Singh, General Officer Commanding 19 Infantry Division (located in Srinagar Valley). Their baggage train could not fetch up due to sudden snowfall and they were stranded for a couple of days. Gen Kalwant had a reputation of being a bully and terror, but we found him so pleasant in the mess. He would tell junior officers to go ahead and have a drink or play cards. After some time, Col. Kushal Singh after a memorable tenure was transferred to the Indian Military Academy and Panicker took over the command with the rank of Lt. Colonel.

In October 1954 I was detailed to attend the Junior Commander Course at Infantry School Mhow. Pannicker instructed me to move to our rear at Gund before Zojila closed due to snow and prepare for the course.

Prior to proceeding for the Junior Command Course at Mhow, I visited the Holy Cave of Amarnath, along with a section of our men from Gund. I took a short cut from Baltal along with a local guide. It was tough going over frozen rivulets, but we reached the Cave by 1100 hrs. We all had good *darshan* (view). The Shiv Ling was fully formed. I was intrigued to see an Indian gentleman with his foreign wife. The person was unwell and incapable of walking and so his wife had brought him in a palanquin for darshan of Holy Amarnath. It was clear they had tremendous faith in God which enabled them to undertake the arduous journey from Pahalgam to Amarnath. Our return journey was easier and I made it to Gund before it got dark. This route has now become a normal alternate yatra route to Amarnath.

Junior Commander Course at Infantry School, Mhow (Now Army War College)

My preparation for the course proved very beneficial. It was a three-month course. I worked hard for two months, averaging six hours a day. Conditions were harsh and minimal diversions were in fact ideal for my preparations. When the course result was declared, I found that I had secured 'A' grade and the remark 'fit to be instructor'. While on course, I got my posting as General Staff Officer Grade 3 Military Operations Directorate, Army HQ at New Delhi. Since Kargil and Srinagar-Kargil road was still snow bound, I was instructed not to return to the unit but report after the course to my new assignment. Thus ended my first tenure in the Battalion, which was most educative and instructive. Col Kushal was an outstanding commanding officer and my tenure under him as Quarter Master and Adjutant was a great learning experience. I learnt from him how to run a happy team and instill in the men a sense of pride. He taught us to lead from the front and to never neglect the requirements of men. This built up on what I had learnt from Col Chauhan at the Centre.

My First Tenure at Army HQ

On joining Army HQ, I was allotted married accommodation at 13, Sikandra Road Hutment. I immediately went to Alwar and fetched Nirmala (Neeru) my wife and children Pravin, Ranjana and Ashutosh and settled them in our quarters. Pravin and Ranjana, aged five and four years old respectively, were admitted to the American School on Bhagwan Dass Road. Our neighbours, Mrs and Mr Bhargava, who were childless then, helped Neeru a great deal in looking after Ashu, who was only 15 days old. The quarter had four rooms in a row. We invited our brother-in-law Bal Krishen and his wife Vidhya to stay with us. We soon acquired a second hand matchless Motor Cycle by taking a Government loan and became mobile. We often visited Bengali Market, Connaught Place and Chandni Chowk for meals and chaat. In Chandni Chowk, opposite Red Fort, there was a Vij Restaurant which used to serve two stuffed puries, with chhole and achar, costing only four annas, (25 paisa) which was most enjoyable. Bengali Market chat was also unforgettable.

In 1955, Military Operations Directorate was a small organisation headed by Brig Raj Bir Chopra of 4 Gorkha Rifles, with three sections; Military Operations 1 (MO1) and Military Operations 2 (MO2) headed by Lt. Col. R.S. Norona of Madras Regiment and Military Operations 3 (MO3) headed by Lt Col J.P. Dalvi of Guards. Major Kundan Singh, Rajputana Rifles was a General Staff Officer 2 (GSO2) in MO1 and Major H.N. Shingal of Garh Rif was GSO 2 in MO3. There were only two General Staff Officers in 3 (GSO3), one in MO1 and the other in MO3. I was to work under Maj Shingal. Dalvi later achieved fame as 7 Infantry Brigade Commander Namkachu/Towang during 1962 Indo-China War, where he was taken prisoner by Chinese Army and as the author of Himalayan Blunder, a masterpiece on the Indo-China conflict, with particular reference to NEFA

(North East Frontier Agency). Norona and Kundan Singh, both retired as Lt Generals, while Hari Shingal retired as Maj General. Brig Chopra was later posted to UK as Military Adviser to Indian High Commissioner but was recalled before he could assume the appointment. He took voluntary retirement and became a Director with Metal Box Ltd. He was a popular figure in Delhi Golf Club and used to write a regular column in the "Golfingly Yours" magazine. He was replaced by Brig Katoch, who later retired as Lt General. Life in Army HQ was comfortable and easy going as there were no major security problems facing the nation in 1955.

I was advised that this was an ideal place to prepare for Staff College examination. Hari Shingal was most helpful and relieved me from office responsibilities so that I could sit in Defence Ministry Library and study. Tactics B paper is always the bug bear of the Staff College Exam. Col. Dalvi offered to coach me in the subject and I used to go to his residence for guidance. He gave me questions and then corrected my answers. I am most grateful to them for this assistance. I was thus fully prepared for the exam. When the results were announced I had secured a competitive vacancy. One day I was rung up by Col Jenkins, the Deputy Military Secretary to come and see him. He informed me that I had done very well in the Order of Merit and deserved to go to Staff College Camberley in UK, but he had reservations about my financial capability to sustain my family of three children. His information was based on the fact that I had taken a loan from my Defence Service Officers Provident (DSOP) Fund recently for the wedding of my younger sister. I replied that I had done no wrong in drawing money from my DSOP Fund. I assured him that if selected for Camleerley Staff College, I would leave the children with my mother, who could take good care of them. He assured me that he would do his utmost to get me to a foreign staff college, failing which he wished me good luck for the Staff

College Wellington. I had no one in the Army to lobby for me. I therefore, missed the opportunity to do a course at Staff College Camberley. Once, while dining out with Norona, who was Officiating Director Military Operations he remarked that had he known about my merit position in the exam result he would have ensured that justice was done to me. MO Directorate gave me a farewell cocktail party at the National Sports Club of India. During the party Bhawani Singh of Jaipur also happened to be present. I was not used to much drinking and being a happy occasion I got a bit tipsy. Bhawani and some other officers came to drop me at my residence. Next morning I asked Neeru as to how I had reached my residence and who took off my shoes. I felt very embarrassed, when I got the answer particularly, as I found that the socks which I had put on the previous night had big holes!

We enjoyed our one and a half year stay in Delhi. Our neighbour Mr Bhargav, who was adviser to Planning Commission, was a thorough gentleman. His wife and sister-in-law were extremely friendly and wanted to take care of Ashu all the time. As stated earlier the Bhargavs did not have any children. Later, they were blessed with a son, whom they named Vijay and liked to believe that they were blessed with a child due to their association with Ashu. As far as I remember, Vijay grew up to become a pilot but we lost track of them.

During summer holidays we went to Alwar to spend some time with Neeru's parents and mine. During this period my elder brother-in-law Kiran Chand Sharma, who was married to Neeru's elder sister Vimla, came and stayed at our residence, as he was preparing a thesis for his doctorate and wanted a secluded area. Our servant Tej Bahadur, a young Gorkha, looked after him. On our return from Alwar, we were asked by our neighbours, whether we had given permission to Tej Bahadur to use our motor cycle, as they had seen him with his girl friend on it. We were naturally shocked to hear this and immediately dismissed him from service. Neeru's elder brother Bal Krishna was married into Ravi Brothers family. Due to some misunderstanding, they were staying separately; his wife Vidhya was staying with her parents, while Bal Krishna stayed with a friend in Daryaganj. Ravi Brothers were the leading furniture makers of Delhi, located in Kashmiri Gate. Ravi was the eldest son of Ram Chandra Ji, who had started his furniture business in a modest way by pawning the bangles of his wife and by sheer hard work, became the biggest furniture dealer in Delhi. He led a spartan life and often walked around his premises with a dhoti, wooden sandal (kharaun), sacred thread and bare body above the waist. He was already over 80 years old and still active. Whenever I visited his place he would talk to me about the Army and my experiences. Neeru and I were instrumental in bringing Bal Krishna (my brother-in-law) and Vidhya back together again and they came to live with us till we left for Wellington for the course.

My mother was worried about the marriage of my younger sister Madhuri, as I was soon to depart for Wellington for a year's course. My wife and I finally found a suitable groom for her and she was married at our residence. Being short of funds, my wife sold some personal ornaments to meet the impending expenditure. It was to her credit and sense of responsibility and loyalty to the family that she had herself offered that. I am indebted to her for the sacrifice. The marriage of Neeru's cousin Luxmi was also celebrated from my residence in New Delhi. She was the principal of a College and was married to a pilot.

I was the first officer from the Regiment to be posted in Delhi and many officers from the Regiment and the Battalion used to call on us. One day Lt. Umesh Saxena came to call on us. He had joined the 5/11 Gorkha Rifles in Kargil, when I was the Adjutant. He was just posted to the Centre. He admitted that he was already married when he joined the unit but did not have the courage to admit it at that time, as the rule was that an officer could not get married till he attained the age of 25 years. I advised him that a genuine mistake had been made, but now he should own up and I was sure that the Centre Commandant would forgive him. He followed my advice. He later rose to the rank of Brigadier and was also Military Assistant to Gen Bewoor, the COAS.

Defence Services Staff College, Wellington

Anand Dutta Saxena, my old friend from 73 GT Coy ASC days was now a Subedar and was posted at Gwalior. I informed him that I was proceeding to Wellington and that if convenient, he should meet us at the station. We could not break journey but he came to meet us at the station and we were delighted to meet each other after a long gap. It was a long journey and my first trip to South India. Journey by narrow gauge from Mettapalayam to Conoor was most memorable, due to the picturesque landscape.

We were well received by the staff of the College and the arrangements made were a reflection of the efficient staff training imparted at the premier defence institution. We were accommodated in Circle Quarters, It was a double storey block of four quarters and we were allotted ground floor. I found that I was the only one from 11 GR and Second Course IMA Capt. Pratap Singh from Artillery of the Second Course had the distinction of doing a Course earlier. It was 1956/57 Course and from my regiment, I was the first to secure a competitive vacancy. Col Chauhan the first Commandant of 11 Gorkha Rifles Regimental Centre had attended an earlier course as a nominated student. The aim of the Course was to train officers for higher staff and command in the Army. It was an Inter-Services Course in which officers from the Air Force and Navy also participated. Besides, there were some officers from Nepal, UK, Australia, Canada, Ceylon and some African countries. There were plenty of social activities in which we fully participated. We had an English speaking maid servant to look after the children. Local schools were good. During the course many VIPs visited us. Those were the days of Hindi-Russi Bhai Bhai. Bulganin and Khrushchev had come to visit us. There was a grand dinner in their honour.

The Commandant was Maj Gen P.S. Gyani from Artillery, an accomplished horse rider, known for his fondness for hunting. The College had horses and hounds. I also joined their Hunt Club and Neeru started learning riding. The Hunt Club used to go to Ooty Downs (at Ootacmund) for hunt on holidays and it was a great pleasure to participate in those meets. Gen Gyani knew the names of all the hounds, though they looked alike but often faltered while calling names of student officers. Gangadhar Bisht from Nepal and Krishen Malik of 5 Gorkha Rifles, from Alwar, became good friends. Bisht retired as Adjutant General of Nepal Army, while Malik retired as a Colonel and settled down in Alwar.

Among the instructors I fondly remember Deputy Commandant Bhagat VC (retired as Army Commander), Col Tappy Raina (retired as COAS), Col Bawa (retired as E-in-C), Col P. Choudhry (retired as Maj Gen; later I served under him as a Brigadier, when Chow was commanding 3 Div in Ladakh) and Col N.L. Kapoor (known as spitting Kapoor, as he used to spit while speaking) retired as Brigadier. They were so kind to me and a great help during the Course. I often met them in various capacities through my future career.

An important feature of the Course was an all India tour by a special train (in first class compartments) to acquaint us with the industrial progress in the country and also to visit various defence and civil institutions. This was most enjoyable as the whole Course batch moved together. During the tour, we visited Ambala, where Maj Gen. B.M. Kaul was commanding 4 Mountain Division. Army was short of accommodation for men and families and GenKaul had offered to construct the same with troop labour on the pattern of the Chinese and thus economise on funds by cutting out contractors. The Government accepted this offer. It was a unique experiment, but it adversely affected the training of the troops, with far reaching consequences. Kaul had also laid on a firepower demonstration which included an infantry battalion in attack, supported by artillery of the entire division and the Air Force. This was done in great style and a large number of politicians, diplomats, government officers and other VIPs attended this.

On the whole, the period spent at Wellington was most enjoyable and educative. Neeru and I often visited Ooty and Coonoor on motocyle, which we had brought from Delhi. We invariably went to Conoor on Sundays for a South Indian lunch. Here we also made many friends, who continued to be so during the rest of my career and beyond. At the end of the Course I was posted as GSO3 at HQ 19 Infantry Division at Srinagar. I had to dispose off my motorcycle as it was of no use in Srinagar. This was our first set of wheels and Neeru felt sad at its loss.

Sojourn in Srinagar and Valley

In Baramulla, 6/11 Gorkha Rifles was located under the command of Lieutenant Col Uttam Raj. On hearing that I was posted to HQ 19 Inf Div, he wrote a letter welcoming me to the Valley and suggested that I should come with family and he would make all the necessary arrangements for our stay. It was winter and I was not keen to take my family to the valley, till I had made necessary arrangements for their stay there. However, Neeru, having seen the letter from Uttam Raj insisted on accompanying me. From Pathankot, we travelled in a 3 ton vehicle. On reaching Bannihal, we were held up in the transit camp for three days, as the Bannihal tunnel was closed due to heavy snowfall. CaptM.L. Yadav of Ordnance Field Park, Srinagar was also held up and became our good friend. Yadav later retired as Lt. Gen. When the tunnel opened and the convoy started, Yadav took Pravin, my eldest son, in his vehicle. It was a slow journey through walls of snow on either side of the road. We reached Srinagar transit camp quite late at night. Yadav got separated in the journey and took Pravin with him to his own house. I could find no trace of Uttam Raj at Srinagar and there was no way to get in touch with him. It was extremely cold and the transit camp had no arrangements to put up families. I had no option but to ring up Maj Bajwa the GSO2 (operations) of the division. who very kindly consented to put us up in his house for the night. During our stay with Bajwa we found his wife cold and curt towards us.

After two days stay with the Bajwas, we moved out to a hotel and started looking for a house. My relations with Bajwa were formal and never friendly. Bajwa retired as a Colonel and was re-employed as Railway Transport Officer ,at Ranchi. He suddenly expired due to a heart attack. I was Chief of Staff Western Command when this happened, some time in 1982. I was approached by his brother-in-law to arrange to move his body to Delhi. This was a difficult task. But keeping in mind our past association I made special efforts and arranged to move the body by road to Calcutta and then by an Indian Airlines flight to Delhi.

We got a house, next to the Yadavs in Raj Bagh which belonged to the Badials of Jammu. The Badials were timber merchants from Jammu and were thorough gentlemen. The house was across Jhelum and in a low lying area. During rains we often had to wade through knee-deep water. The children were admitted in a convent, close by. Maj Gen

Suresh Misra was the GOC. He was fond of cigars, easy going, and a friendly sort. There were no major security problems in the Valley in 1957-58. During the summer of 1958, HQ of the Division was moved to Pahalgam under the pretext of an exercise but mainly to allow officers and their families to visit the Holy Amarnath Cave. We also availed the opportunity and equipped ourselves with an arctic tent and winter clothing from the Ordnance to undertake holy pilgrimage.

This was my second pilgrimage to the shrine. Not many people visited the shrine those days due to lack of basic infrastructure. We spent the first night at Sheshnag and were thrilled to see the beautiful Sheshnag Lake. The entire landscape, with snow-covered mountains inspired awe and spiritual emotions and one felt peace and tranquility of mind and body. We had carried an oil stove and rations and Neeru cooked the evening meal. We had hired a pony and Neeru occasionally took a ride, but I walked the entire distance of 26 kms. There were no food stalls at Sheshnag except one *dhaba*, run by a Sikh gentleman, who provided one vegetarian dish with bread to the needy. After crossing Panchtarni we had to walk on a glacier and by mid-day we had reached the Cave. We were so excited and spiritually inspired to have *darshan* of the Lingam which was fully formed. We were also lucky to observe the pair of legendary white pigeons. By night fall we were back at our tent at Sheshnag, thoroughly exhausted, but happy with the thought of having completed the difficult pilgrimage. Next morning we were back at Pahalgam. During this period, we had left the children under the care of the Badials. In fact they were instrumental in encouraging us to undertake this pilgrimage and we were deeply grateful to them for it. During this period we had some guests. Our cook was a Muslim and our guests would not take meals prepared by him. The Badials helped us out of the dilemma and provided the guests with meals.

Then, 3/11 GR moved to Guraiz, commanded by Col Chauhan, with Maj R. D. Hira (Rocky) as his 2IC. Rocky brought his wife Sajni and accommodated her in a house boat in Srinagar. We met them, whenever time permitted. One Second Lieutenant Shashi Sharma from Signals was attending Winter Warfare Course at Gulmarg; he turned out to be a relative and often visited us. We also discovered that Rama a relation of ours was married in a very rich and influential family of Bals in Srinagar. They owned the only movie theater in Srinagar. Rama was not well educated but was charming and became a socialite. Rohit Bal the famous fashion designer is Rama's nephew. Later, she came and stayed with Neeru in Pratap Chowk, Delhi, while I was commanding 57 Div in Mizoram. Life in Srinagar was quite peaceful and enjoyable and I along with the family visited Gulmarg, the Dal Lake, Shankaracharya temple and Shalimar Gardens. I also took an opportunity to visit the front area, specially Uri and Tithwal to learn about the layout of terrain and deployment of our own and Pak troops on the ground.

By this time my colleagues of Second Course IMA were picking up rank of Major and I also got my posting to Infantry School (now Army War College) Mhow, as Instructor Class B becoming Major in the Junior Command Course.

6

At Infantry School Mhow (Now War College)

On arrival at Mhow, I found many of my colleagues posted there as instructors. They were, Major Chiman Singh (retired as Army Commander), Maj Mohan Tuli (retired as Master General of Ordnance in the rank of Lt. Gen), Maj G.S. Rawat or Ganju, retired as Vice Chief of Army Staff in the rank of Lt Gen), Maj. Jasbir Khurana retired as Colonel and Maj Hari Kukarni retired as Major General. The School was commanded by Brig P.O. Dunn of 3 GR. Junior Commander Wing was commanded by Col. James of 5 GR. It had two wings. A wing was commanded by Col Sagat Singh 3 GR and B Wing was commanded by Col Sucha Singh VrC of PARA. I was assigned to B Wing. I made friends with many officers and had a wonderful opportunity to interact with a large number of officers of the Army, who came to attend various courses. Maj. Zoru Bakshi of 5 GR was in the training team and Zoru and I and also our wives, became good friends. I used to play squash with Zoru regularly and found him to be a thorough gentleman and professionally competent and I learnt a lot from him. Zoru earned fame in 1965, when he commanded 68 Inf Bde, and in a brilliant tactical action, captured Haji Pir Pass (in J&K). The final assault and capture of this Pass was executed by Maj R.S. Dayal (he retired as Lt. Gen.). MajS.K. Sinha of 5 GR was another outstanding officer, with tremendous military and history knowledge. These officers became my role models. Sinha took voluntary retirement from the post of Vice Chief of Army Staff, being passed over for the appointment of Chief of the Army Staff. However, later he did magnificent work as our Ambassador to Nepal, followed by Governor of Assam and then J&K. Chiman, Hari Kulkarni, Mohan Tuli, Jasbir Khurana and Ganju Rawat with their wives and children became our close friends; this association continued even after retirement. Col Sagat (later Lt. Gen.) was from erstwhile ex-Rajasthan State Forces, tall with an impressive personality. As junior officers, we found him dynamic and full of new ideas. Later, in the 1971 Indo-Pak war, Col Sagat as Corps Commander used brilliant tactics in bypassing centres of resistance and making a dash to capture Dacca.

There were two major highlights of my tenure at Mhow. Col. Sujan Singh Uban was our neighbour. He mentioned to us that he had taken *diksha* (initiation) from a Bengali Saint, (Sri Sri Sitaram Das Omkar Nath) who was a self-realised soul. Neeru had always been interested in finding a suitable guru and, therefore, requested him to inform us, if Guruji came to Omkareshwar (a religious town in Madhya Pradesh on the banks of the river Narbada). One

Saturday evening, Col Uban informed us that Guruji had arrived in Omkareshwar and if we were interested, he would be glad to take us to him. Thereafter, he along with his boss Col Lachhman Singh started off for Omkareshwar in his car. With difficulty, we found a tonga (horse driven carriage) who agreed to take us to the railway station next morning, which happened to be a Sunday, to catch a train to Omkareshwar. Those days there was no bridge over river Narbada at Omkareshwar and we had to cross the river by boat. Now there are two suspension bridges. Somehow we reached the Ashram and found that Uban and Lachhman Singh were already there. It was 19 July, 1959, which happened to be Neeru's birthday. We were introduced to the great divine soul and while touching his feet I was overcome with emotion and tears started flowing involuntarily. It was a strange phenomenon. Baba, as he was popularly known, agreed to initiate us into Mantra Diksha, though we had already taken tea. This was an important event in my life. Then onwards the course of my future career, I feel, was largely guided by Baba.

Sometime in the latter part of 1960 I got a letter from my old instructor Lt. Col. Tappy Raina, AMS (Assistant Military Secretary) in Army HQ, to inform me that I was being considered for an appointment which would benefit me financially, socially and professionally but advised me not to talk about it till I received official intimation. This was very intriguing. I had already been out of the regiment for 5 years and was expecting to return to my battalion 5/11 Gorkhas. I waited anxiously for an official order. It was during the Infantry School Fete that Brig Dunn came to me and informed me that I had been posted to London as GSO2 (General Staff Officer Grade 2) to Military Adviser of High Commission for India. My wife and I were really surprised and delighted. All my friends congratulated us and some remarked that I probably had some powerful contacts at

Army HQ. I replied that God and my Guru were the only powerful contacts we had. In retrospect, I feel that this posting had more than made up for the injustice done to me during the selection for a foreign staff college course in 1956 and this could be attributed to Guruji's grace and blessings.

Assignment in the UK

We stayed in Bombay for a week, with our Guru Bhai Brig Lachhman Singh, the NCC Commander, before boarding SS Corfu in December 1960.We made some good friends on the voyage. Wing Comdr Latif was going to Paris to take over as Air Adviser to our Ambassador; he later became the Air Chief and subsequently Governor of Maharashtra. Sqn Ldr Nehru was going to Cairo to join Indian Training Team; he later did the NDC (National Defence College) course with me. Mr N.N. Gupta was going as Second Secretary to our High Commission UK. He, his wife Saroj and children became family friends for life. Maj Sharma of AMC was going on study leave. The voyage was most enjoyable and we had great fun, specially while crossing the equator and on New Year's Eve. During the New Year's party, all passengers were required to be in fancy attire. I put on a priest's dress while Neeru dressed up as a gardener's wife. Pravin, my eldest son, got a prize for putting on a dress of 'ready to rest and work' (He wore a shirt and trousers and a sleeping suit underneath and was this ready to rest work, at a moment's notice.) While going through the Suez Canal we saw the famous Guli Guli magic show and also experienced sea sickness while crossing the Bay of Biscay.

At London we and the Guptas were put up at a hotel near Hyde Park and were much impressed by the egalitarian society, where no distinction appeared to be made between different levels of society. After some time I was shifted to a flat in the Councilor's office in South Audley Street. After office hours, Neeru and I would hunt for a house. Though the British always boasted that there was no racial discrimination in UK, we discovered that every time we approached a house owner he was frank enough to reply that he could not give the house to Asians! It was a frustrating experience. After a long and exhausting search we found a house in East Finchley, whose owner, one Mr Hughe, was shifting to South Cornwall.

We quickly settled down at 13 Summerlee Gardens, East Finchley. Pravin, my elder son was now 11 years old and was admitted to Tollington Grimshaw Grammer School; my daughter Ranjana and younger son Ashutosh were admitted to Tetherdown School, which was close by. We had a very helpful and friendly neighbours in Francis and Rona Wood and our friendship continued even after we returned to India.

The Military Adviser was Brig D.G.R. Rajwade, who was known to me from Kargil days, when he was Able Garrison Commander. GSO I was Lt Col Sahukar ASC. My colleagues were Maj Patnaik of Artillery and Capt. Shankar Barua. Except Rajwade and me, all the other officers at the Indian High Commission were there on compassionate grounds. We had a British peon, one Mr Purse, who was quite efficient and willing to carry out errands. He also made coffee for the staff at 11:00 hrs and during lunch. When I arrived in London, Mrs Vijay Laxmi Pandit was the High Commissioner. After some time, she left and Mr Kaul officiated for sometime before Jivaji Rao Mehta took over. The Indian High Commission had a large staff and offices were spread over four places, India House, South Audley Street, Germyn Street and Acton. Virtually every ministry of the Government of India had representation there. My contact in the War Office was Col Steal (retd), who had served in the IMA as instructor and we became good friends. Col Mains of 9 GR was Secretary of Gorkha

Association in the UK. He kept track of all Indian Officers from Gorkhas, who came to the UK. He was extremely friendly and we enjoyed his hospitality at his house in the countryside.

My main task was to prepare a monthly intelligence report to be submitted by the MA to the Director Military Intelligence, Army HQ. It included information on developments in the British Army, future trends regarding modernisation and any other information of general interest. The information was collected from open public sources e.g. newspaper reports, magazines, and friends and I often wondered, why it was known as intelligence report! Our regimental friend Maj Rajender Nath (11 GR) , his wife Krishna and son Danny who was born in Canada stayed with us on their return journey from Canada during their enforced halt before boarding another ship. Rajender Nath was returning after completing a two-year Defence Services Staff College. We had a wonderful get together. Rocky Hira (Col. R. D. Hira) and Sajni came from Cairo, where Rocky was Defence Adviser to our Ambassador there. They were staying with Sajni's brother, but often came to see us. Rocky along with one of his friends spent an evening with us on Diwali. We had great fun playing cards and later drove down to London Bridge. We ended up at Rocky's residence and had breakfast, before returning to our place. This was yet another memorable regimental get together.

Gyan Khosla of the Second Course (IMA) from Dogras and Anand Swaroop from 8 GR had gone to USA for a commando course and on their return passed through London. We asked them to come over and had a wonderful time together. Maj S.K. Sinha (Manne Sinha) also came to attend the Joint Services Staff College Course and often used to visit our office. He got an outstanding report from the Course. He had come with his family, including three children. The son was too young. They were keen to visit

Paris, but did not wish to go with the children. I persuaded them to visit Paris and Neeru offered to look after their children for a week. The Guptas who had travelled with us from India became our close friends and we often went out to various beaches for a picnic on weekends. Sahi, an IPS officer from Bihar cadre was the security officer of the High Commission; he and his wife Neelam also became our good friends. This friendship continued after we returned to India and even after retirement. Neelam, after the death of Sahi, joined the Congress Party and became a Minister of State at the Centre. She continued to represent her constituency in Parliament till Laloo came on the scene and wiped off the Congress influence in Bihar.

During the Edinburgh festival, India sent a big contingent for participation, which included the Band of the Sikh Regiment and 61 Cavalry, with horses. I along with my family travelled to Edinburgh to witness this. Memories of the British empire were still fresh and the Indian Contingent got the biggest ovation. From there we moved North and visited 1st Black and Watch, who were having their Regimental sports. The particular item of interest was the inter-company competition of Scottish dances. We went round the Lock Ness, popular as the home of a legendary monster. In fact we visited all the important places of tourist interest in Scotland. In retrospect I regret that I did not play golf those days, otherwise I would have certainly visited the St. Andrews Golf Course from where the game of golf had originated.

We also visited Devon and Cornwall and stayed in a farm house. We visited the southernmost tip of the British Isles facing the Atlantic Ocean which was famously known as 'Land's End' as if nothing existed beyond it!

In 1962, we got the news about the Chinese attack in Ladakh and Northeast India. There was tremendous interest in the UK and considering their past association with India and Indian Army, they expected us to put up stiff resistance. They were surprised by the debacle and so were we at the High Commission. It was most embarrassing and difficult to explain to our friends,the reasons for this defeat. Perhaps this was a blessing in disguise. This gave an impetus to our defence preparedness and paved way for expansion of the Army and modernisation of weapon systems. We were thus able to face the onslaught of Pakistan, against our country in 1965.

During the last year of our stay in 1964, we visited Europe by camping, as we could not afford to stay in hotels. It was a month long trip. We made a round trip starting from Paris, visited Lourdes, which has the Basilica of St Bernadotte, San Sebastian, Madrid, Barcelona, Tower of Pisa, Rome, Mt Vesuvius, Pompeii, Island of Capri, Florence, Venice, Innsbruck, then on to Switzerland, Heidelberg, Cologne, and Brussels and back to UK. This was the most enjoyable trip. Camping sites were well organised and we had a fixed routine. On arrival at a camp site, while I with the help of kids pitched the tent, Neeru did the cooking. After a quick meal we went out sightseeing. However, we made it a point to have meals of the country/town we visited in a local restaurant. It must be remembered that in the sixties, there were not many Indians abroad and often we were the object of curiosity for the locals whom we found very friendly. We particularly visited the site of the famous Battle of Monte Cassino fought fiercely between the British and the Germans, during 1939-45 war, in which Indian troops had taken part and demonstrated their valour.

Dr Satish Chandra (subsequently Chairman UGC) was on study leave and so was Mr Rajeshwar Prashad IAS. Both were accompanied by their wives. Rajesh was the Secretary to the Prime Minister, Mr Lal Bahadur Shashtri. We met them through N.N. Gupta and they became our lifelong friends.

It was nearly nine years since I was away from the Regiment and expected my posting any day. Meanwhile, I did a two week's winter warfare course at St. Andreasberg (erstwhile West Germany) under the British Army of the Rhine and also a week's course of Civil Defence at Sunningdale. The Winter Warfare Course was a physically demanding course, structured around imparting basic skiing skills and their application in war. It entailed cross country skiing in full battle gear as well as basic winter survival skills (A very useful course for officers posted in J&K and other high altitude areas, where Indian Army operates). The Civil Defence Course imparted measures to be taken during natural disasters and ariel bombing of urban areas during war. It was an added qualification for an officer though not of much practical use to me during my service years.

I made full use of my stay to visit all the important British institutions, especially Royal Military Academy at Sandhurst and Staff College at Camberley. Neeru and I attended the passing out parade at Sandhurst at which salute was taken by FM Slim. I also witnessed the Queen's Birthday parade and felt that we could have done much better! On the whole we had enjoyed our stay in the UK and I enhanced my professional knowledge. The children went to the best schools and Neeru did a Montessori course and also attended a number of short courses at Stanhope Institute. How prophetic were the words of Col. Raina, who had said that this posting would immensely benefit me socially, economically and professionally.

There was a shortage of manpower in UK to provide various services and run factories due to enormous casualties in World War II. Immigration was therefore very easy and I found that even the semi-skilled were being allowed to come to UK, where they easily found employment. A large number of Indian students were able to pay for their studies through part time employment. Rudra, one of our relatives and his friend Sushil Kanwar, often visited us. As luck would have it, Sushil's younger brother Yadu Kumar, later married my elder daughter Ranjana. Neeru's cousin Dr Atam Dev Sharma, from Bulandshahr, was working in a hospital and was a frequent visitor to our house. He saw us off at Glasgow, when we departed for India. I also thought of getting some one from our family to the UK and examined various options. I found that only Daya, my brother-in-law, and Gopal, my younger brother, were the right choice to be sponsored for immigration. I wrote to them about my proposal. Gopal was a matriculate and a trained tool maker working in the Dunlop Factory, Faridabad while Daya was a graduate and could easily adapt himself to the English way of life. My elder brother-in-law Bal Krishen promised to arrange Daya's air ticket. I sponsored his passport, which was delivered to his address, but he never made use of it and thus missed a great opportunity. As regards Gopal, he ran around and obtained a passport, while I sent him an air ticket. Consequently, he arrived in the UK. He stayed for some time with us and later got a job in a factory in Finchley and shifted to his own apartment. After our return to India, we learnt he got married to a charming Scottish girl and settled in Aylesbury, as a British citizen.

In mid-1964 I was informed that I would be posted to 5/11 GR, which was in field area at Binaguri (West Bengal). However, I was first posted to 11 GRRC at Clement Town, Dehradun for 3 months to enable me to move my baggage to a peace station. I took the decision to send the children by Air India and decided to have a last fling at adventure travelling by sea, with my wife. On arrival at Delhi the children were looked after by my cousin Manne and Neeru's younger sister Usha. On our arrival at Bombay, by ship, we again stayed with Brig Lachhman Singh, our Guru Bhai. It took some time to have the baggage and car cleared through customs. Prem, my cousin from Delhi joined us at Bombay and we drove from Bombay to Delhi in our new imported Ford Classic.

7

Back to the Regiment

I landed in Bombay and had the baggage and our Fond Classic Car custom cleared. I had no difficulty as it was a transfer of residence. From Bombay I drove to Dehradun via Mhow and Delhi. I reached 11 GRRC Officers Mess located in Clement Town about 1400 hrs and saw a man having a dip in the Gardner's Pond. Coming closer, I discovered it was Maj Brahm Bali, my old friend of 5/11 GR. He hugged me without bothering about his wet clothes. It was obvious that after a good drink on Sunday afternoon, he was cooling himself off in the pond. I thought it was a great homecoming!

Rocky (Col R.D. Hira) was commanding the Centre. I was immediately given family quarters. In a few days my baggage arrived and I sorted it out and also completed the formalities with the Marine Insurance. I stayed at the Centre for three months and then moved to Binaguri to report to 5/11 GR. My family was settled at Delhi. I faced a lot of difficulty getting my children admitted in various schools. I finally managed to get my elder son Pravin admitted in Sherwood, Nainital. My younger son Ashu got admitted to St Xavier's Delhi with the help of our friend Rajesh, who was Private Secretary to the Prime Minister, Lal Bahadur Shastri. Mayo at Ajmer and Doon School had refused admission bacause children did not know Hindi. My daughter Ranjana was admitted to Queen Mary Convent, Kashmere Gate, but only after Neeru had presented the Principal with an imported cardigan! There was no provision for separated family quarters for officers posted in the field and we had to hire a two room apartment at Rohtak Road area close to our relatives, Manne, Usha and Manne's uncle Hukum Chand ji. They were of great help in looking after my family when I was away in the field area and during 1965 Indo-Pak war.

Gorkha Rifles

The Battalion, 5/11, was being commanded by Col Kamal Bhalla and Maj. G.S. Harika was the Second in Command. It was part of 165 Inf. Bde commanded by Brig Maitra 1 GR, a diehard Gorkha. The accommodation was in bamboo barracks and tents. My colleagues had already picked up rank of Lt. Colonel. However, I was informed that I was earmarked to command the battalion, but I had to earn a satisfactory regimental report before I could be promoted. I therefore had to work hard to prove my ability for the command. The atmosphere in the Battalion was rather gloomy due to a tragic incident in Sikkim, where a sweeper who was suspected of stealing a pistol had died due to alleged torture by some officers; an enquiry was in progress. The officers concerned, conducted themselves with exemplary dignity and fortitude. Neverthless, the CO was a worried man. Nothing of significance was happening in the Unit, except normal training. A fairly good number of subalterns were in the Unit, who were commissioned after 1962. In the evening, there was lot of drinking in the Mess, while Bhalla generally remained aloof in a contemplative mood.

Binaguri was located in the midst of tea plantation area and we officers of the battalion had good interaction with many planters, among whom there were many a British. We were made honorary members of their club, which had a golf course and other sport facilities. Major Tilak Prasher was instrumental in initiating me into golf here. One evening the youngsters*after a few drinks, behaved rowdily in the Mess; I decided to discipline them, with the permission of Bhalla. After dinner I took them out for a road walk and run for 5 kilometres in pouring rain and many of them had problems in keeping pace. This was a forerunner to even tougher training which was to follow on my taking command.

One of the lessons of Indo-China war 1962 was lack of battle inoculation training of men which made them shy of facing battle noise. Bhalla instructed me to lay on a demonstration of company attack supported by Battalion mortars and medium machine guns. We were equipped with 81 mm mortars provided as US military aid. The demonstration was witnessed by all officers of the Brigade. Our troops were able to close in with their objective within 150 yards, before the mortar and machine gun fire was

---

* The battalion had 8 Lieutenants and some young Captains with 3 to 4 years service who were referred to as youngsters. This was in 1965. After 1962 sino-India war the intake of officers in various training schools had been increased to make up the deficiency of officers in the units. Hence, all units had a good number of Lieutenants at that time. My own Second in Command, when I became the Commanding Officer had only 6 years service!

lifted to assault the objective, with their war cry of 'Ayo Gorkhali'. The demonstration was well appreciated by all officers. After some time I was interviewed by the Brigade Commander who informed me that he was happy with my performance and was recommending me, on advice of my CO, for promotion and command of the Battalion. By July 1965, Bhalla and Harika were posted out and I became the Officiating Commanding Officer of the Battalion on 13 July, 1965 pending final orders for my promotion from Army HQ. My Second in Command was Maj Sachinder Singh, who was junior to me by about 10 years. He was young, a public school product, popular with officers and men and enthusiastic in implementing tasks given to him. He provided sterling support to me throughout the 1965 Indo-Pak war. Later, Maj H.S. Mamik was posted as my deputy. Capt Abjeet Mamik was my Adjutant and and Capt Bhasin was the QM. The four company commanders were, Maj B.S. Negi B Company, Maj Tilak Prasher C Company, Capt M.S. Negi A Company and Sub Chanderpal Limbu D Company (Officiating OC–Maj. Barua was away on temporary duty and joined only after operations). Support Company was being looked after by Sub. Karm Kumar Chhetri. My Subalterns were, J.B.S. Yadav (retired as Lt. Gen, DCOAS and Col 11 GR), Bopanna (retired as Lt. Gen DG NCC), Khanna, Joshi, Talwar, Tiwari, Ghosh, Bannerji and Capt M. M. Marakose, the Regimental Medical Officer. They were all very enthusiastic and dependable. Bhalla was unmarried and a thorough gentleman, who had no other love in life but the Regiment and 5/11 GR in particular. He expired while staying with the Battalion in Lucknow, during Regimental Reunion in 2003 and was given the unique honour of carriage of his mortal remains by two Lieutenant Generals and two Major Generals, who had served under him.

I put the troops under a rigorous training schedule. Companies were sent out on a camp for a month to be trained, under their company commanders. These camps ended up with two sided exercises, set and conducted by me. Long marches through thick jungle were undertaken. During these marches, everyone was 'self contained' for three days which included the Commanding Officer. Obstacle courses in the unit were made more difficult as were weapons training and short range firing. All officers had to undergo that. This had a favorable impact on troops. At the end of this training the Battalion developed enormous self-confidence to attain any task assigned to it. We also had our lighter moments and we invariably went out as a group on Sundays to either Binaguri Club or Mishamari Club and enjoyed ourselves.

By mid-1965 the Battalion had already done three years in field and was due for a peace station. We were ordered to move to Lucknow but this was changed in quick succession to Fatehgarh, Ambala and then finally, Nahan. We were to be relieved by 5 Madras. Throughout August 1965 the Battalion remained packed and ready to depart but our peace station was in a flux. Finally, we were informed that we were moving to Nahan and the special train arrived on 31 August, after a long wait at the station. Col Bedi the CO 5 Madras requested that since the train was taking time to arrive, the troops could finish their dinner. I agreed; the result was that some of the JCOs and men were rather high after consuming rum, but I had to ignore this. Binaguri was a small station and there was no lighting at the station. The train arrived after 10 pm. Loading became a problem and I had to innovate by lining up all the trucks with their head lamps on, to facilitate loading. Ultimately, we left after midnight.

Gen Bewoor, our Col. of the Regiment was GOC 33 Corps and we were expecting him to be with us for sometime at Siliguri station. However, he was in an important conference and could not make it. Col Vishnu Sharma, Commanding

7/11 GR in Sikkim was there with his officers and some men and so were Col. Daljeet Singh Commanding 107 TA Battalion, with a detachment, who hosted a sumptuous breakfast for the entire Battalion. Maj B.S. Negi, being the senior major was made the OC Train. I instructed him not to let the train leave Siliguri till the railways provided us with lights in the compartments. There was a flurry of activity and railways provided temporary lights by laying special electric cable connecting each compartment with a bulb, before we left Siliguri. We had to change into broad gauge at Barauni.

Here I must relate an incident, which had a salutary effect on the discipline of the Unit. One of the JCOs had behaved rudely with Sub Major Narjit Rai at the time of loading the train at Binaguri. I had witnessed this incident and made a mental note. I had a pending vacancy for NCC. During the running train I held an orderly room and ordered this JCO to be taken off the train at Barauni and dispatched to the NCC! On 2 and 3 September the movement of the train was slow as is customary with military specials and we had long halts at wayside stations for breakfast and lunch. During these breaks I took out the whole Battalion for road walk and run till the meals were ready! The locals found this very amusing. On 4 September we suddenly discovered that the train was moving very fast and leaving mail trains detained at wayside stations to give us way. On enquiry from the guard, we were informed that we had been placed on White Hot Priority to enable us to reach Ambala as early as possible. Another interesting incident in the journey was the train moving in reverse for a couple of kilometres to retrieve the paybook of one of our men who had inadvertently dropped it outside the running train!

Neeru met me at Moradabad station where we had a lunch break and she travelled with us a few stations before returning in a train coming from Ambala to Moradabad.

Dada Ghosh was commanding the 11 GRRC at Dehradun. He had earlier commanded the battalion during 1960-62. He received us with the Centre Brass Band and complete Mess Detachment with his officers, JCOs and some men at Saharanpur station. As the train steamed into the station they gave us the most enthusiastic welcome with full fanfare of the regimental buglers. The dinner was sumptuous and hospitality unmatched. The Station Master was pestering us to leave early as the train was on White Hot Priority and he had no power to detain it. However, he also became a victim of Ghosh's usual charm and hospitality and after a few drinks he did not press us for early departure. I placed two of our pipers in the Guards Compartment and we left Saharanpur with Centre Band playing and officers and men waving to us, while our pipers played *Auld Lang Saine,* as the train departed.

We were to detrain at Brara for Nahan. However, on arrival at Brara station we were met by a staff officer from 4 Mountain Division (4 Mtn. Div.) who informed us that the orders had changed and we were to detrain at Ambala Cantt. He further informed us that 4 Mtn Div had moved out to the border and that on detraining we were to move to 1 Sikh lines and await further orders. I took a jeep from 1 Sikh and came to Advance HQ of Western Command. where I met the Brigadier General Staff (BGS) by the name Sirkar. He instructed me that 50 civilian trucks were being provided and we would move to Kaluchak, near Jammu and report to GOC 6 Mtn Div. In Binaguri we had been equipped with USA aided weapons (81 mm mortars, 7.62 mm rifles, light machine guns, pistols, medium machine guns and radio sets) which we had not been allowed to bring with us. We had thus no weapons. I was given release order for all Battalion weapons to be collected from nearby Ordnance Depots. I was also instructed to take over all vehicles of 1 Sikh batallion, as it had moved to Srinagar by air. I immediately returned to the Unit and dispatched various officers for collection of weapons and equipment. By evening, the Battalion was equipped with necessary weapons and ready to move in civilian trucks. It was 6 September 1965 and we departed for Ambala in the evening. The night journey through Punjab was most exciting. We were stopped after every few kilometres by local patriotic people who thrust packets of snacks and sweets into our vehicles. We were indeed overcome by this show of patriotism. With such people supporting the troops, we could achieve the impossible in battle.

We arrived at Pathankot early morning even as the Pak Air Force air strike on our airfield was in progress. We had been caught napping and they were able to inflict considerable damage to our aircrafts and the airfield. Then the truck drivers informed me that they had run out of diesel and they could not move further without replenishment. I toured entire Pathankot Cantonment but could not find any source from where I could get diesel. Our convoy was parked on the Pathankot-Jammu road where there was one civilian petrol pump being run by a Sikh gentleman. To my pleasant surprise he offered to top up all our vehicles merely on my signature. On my part, I promised that after the war he would be fully reimbursed (after the war, the gentleman was paid by Pathankot Sub. Area). By mid-day, I was heading my convoy on a cart track, towards HQ 6 Mtn Div. located in a Rest House. Maj Gen Shrikant Korla DSO of 1 GR was the GOC. He had been my instructor in the Junior Command Course, Mhow. The entire track was jammed with 6 Mtn Div vehicles which were on way to their assembly Area for launching an attack on Pakistan on the morning of 8 September.

I was too excited that the Battalion would soon get the opportunity to go into battle. However, Maj Gen Korla honestly informed me that his Division was made up and he did not need me. He was a gallant soldier, highly decorated and even FM Slim had once proudly announced that Korla was the best Company Commander East of Suez during the last World War. In such a situation any General would have welcomed additional troops, but not Korla. I was naturally disappointed. He spoke to BGS HQ 1 Corps located at Kaluchak, who happened to be Brig P. Chowdhury 5 GR my old instructor of Staff College. He requested Korla to instruct me to report with my Unit to Corps HQ. I turned about the convoy with considerable difficulty and reached Corps HQ, before dusk. I was met by Maj Dick Dias of my battalion, who was Staff Officer to Corps Commander (Lt Gen P.O. Dunn 3 GR, who was Commandant Infantry School, when I was posted there). He guided me to Chowdhury who was delighted to meet me, offered me a cup of tea and informed me that he had found a place for us under 19 Inf Bde part of 26 Inf Div. The Brigade was commanded by yet another 11 GR officer, Brig Aban Naidu, at Ranbir Singh Pura. As it was getting dark we hastened to move to 19 Inf Bde.

Brig Aban Naidu welcomed me and briefed me on the operation aspects. 19 Inf Brigade comprised 14 Dogras, 9 Mahar and 5/11 Gorkha Rifles. We were under 26 Inf Div commanded by Maj Gen M. L. Thapan. The other two brigades of the Division were 162 and 168 Inf Brigades. Task of 26 Inf Div was to contain enemy in Sialkot Sector and protect the right flank of Main Offensive, which was being launched by 1 Corps with 1 Armd Div, 6 Inf. Div and 14 Inf Div in area Maharajke-Charwa. 162 and 168 Inf Bdes had already moved to Concentration areas, with a view to launch an attack on the night of 7/8 September. Their objectives were Niwe Wains, Unche Wains, Anula and Bajra Garhi.

We reached Miransahib about 8 pm on 7 September and in the dark took over defended area vacated by 9 Mahar which had already moved forward. A Company commanded by M.S. Negi was placed under command of 168 Inf Bde and was given the task of guarding the gap between 168 and 162 Bdes, while they went into attack. B Company commanded by B.S. Negi was placed under command of 14 Dogras. On 8 September, we were strafed by two Sabre jets of Pak Air Force. Our brave soldiers fired away at them with LMGs and MMGs, but without result. Some men were found missing from the Battalion after the air raid, which gave me some very anxious moments. I was hesitant to report the matter to the Bde HQ. However, they returned the next morning. It turned out they felt they were safer in the sugarcane field, rather than in the trenches. No action was taken against them for the innocent act.

On 9 September we were ordered to occupy a defended area at Mahute village to prevent infiltration along Sialkot Jammu Road and from the West. Border outposts at Karotna, Khatmarian and 32 r, were earlier vacated by Punjab Armed Police. We sent out patrols under Yadav, Mamik and Khanna to these places. Yadav and Khanna were fired upon but returned safely in the evening. On 11 September a platoon of D Company occupied Khatmarian and Yadav in command of a platoon from B Company occupied Karotna without a fight. In the evening B.S. Negi in command of B company, with a platoon of D Company with Maj Bajwa from 69 Lt Bty as FOO (Forward Observation Officer), moved to 32 r after completing an approach march of 6 km and occupied it without a mishap. There was intermittent shelling by the enemy on Battalion defended area and we suffered two casualties who were evacuated to 305 Med Battalion. The enemy had a post opposite 32r at Badulian. We had earlier sent patrols to ascertain its strength. Later, on 16 September, Yadav led a strong raiding party to Badulian and after closing in, lobbed grenades in their position. Enemy opened fire and one Indian jawan was injured and another did not return. Later, it transpired that he was taken prisoner by the enemy. He was subsequently released and received a mention-in-despatches.

On 17 September, the Battalion was placed under command of 52 Mountain Brigade commanded by Brig. R.D. Hira (Rocky), former CO 1/11 GR and 3/11 GR. I attended orders at Brigade HQ, which was planning an attack by the Brigade on Tilakpur and Muhadipur. This task was assigned to 1 Madras and 10 Mahar, which were an integral part of the Brigade. I was given the task of establishing a firm base at Nandpur, Dhure and Malane for the above battalions to launch their attack on Tilakpur and Muhadpur. Both attacks were to be silent by night, with Divisional Artillery on call. My only regret was that Rocky did not give the main task of attack to us. Perhaps, he had more confidence on the other two battalions, as they had been under him for some time.

The Battalion HQ, with A Company moved up to Chanduchak behind 32r and took up defences, while C Company under Tilak Prasher passed through Karotna and established a firm base in Dhure and Malane. B Company under B.S. Negi ex 32r established firm base in Nandpur. It was replaced by D Company at 32r under of command of Sub Chandra Pal Limbu. The mortar platoon, under Sub. Karma Kumar Chhetri was also established at 32r. These operations were completed by 0300 hrs on 18 September. The Brigade attack was launched during the night 18/19 from the firm base established at Dhure, Malane and Nandpur. The mortar platoon was given the task to engage Badulian and Surgpur to divert enemy attention and prevent them from interfering in the attack. During the attack, Rocky asked me to come to his HQ. He was calm and collected and in full control. No enemy was encountered and 1 Madras and 10 Mahar dug in on their objectives. Our line communications laid on ground to companies were often disrupted due to enemy shelling. Lt Talwar as Signals Officer and Sub Chandra Bahadur as his deputy did a commendable work in restoring these lines, even during shelling. Our baggage truck was also strafed by Pak Sabres and my personal baggage including my video camera was burnt. However, according to rules I claimed compensation and the CDA (O) Pune surprisingly paid without any fuss.

On 20 September, the enemy attacked 1 Madras position. Rocky had asked me over to share a glass of beer and I was witness to the manner in which he handled this situation. He was absolutely calm and collected and directed support of Divisional Artillery to 1 Madras with superb self confidence. CO of 1 Madras was at times jittery but regained his confidence after Rocky assured him full support. The counterattack was beaten back. Our forward companies were on stand by to reinforce the position if the need arose.

The capture of Tilakpur by 52 Brigade and Mahadipur by 1st Madras and 10 Mahar had threatened the Pakistani Chhaprar-Sialkot axis. Pakistan 9 and 10 Baluch battalions, supported by their 20 Lancers (Chaffee Tanks) and Divisional artillery, attacked the 10 Mahar position on 21 September. 10 Mahar, under the command of Lt. Col. R. H. Bajina fought with grit and great determination repulsing the attack. Seven Chaffee Tanks had penetrated the Battalion area and one of them even penetrated deep into the Battalion Headquarters. These tanks were destroyed by the brave Mahars with hand held anti tank launchers. Our mortar platoon also joined battle by firing on the flanks of Mahar position. In the morning, 92 Pakistani bodies and 7 Chaffee Tanks were found in the Battalion area. One JCO and one Other Rank of Pak army were taken prisioner.

During the entire operation Col Bajina, the CO demonstrated excellent leadershilp qualities, and personal example of bravery and grit which rallied the men. By early hours on 22 September, the counterattack had petered out and the enemy withdrew, leaving behind large number of dead bodies and a tank, within the defences of Mahars.

Rocky, as Brigade Commander displayed rare leadership qualities and at no time did he lose his usual self-confidence. Our A and C Companies were on standby to reinforce the Mahars at any time, if the need arose. On 22 September, after the attack was beaten back I was the first to visit 10 Mahar and see the aftermath of the battle, which made me proud of the Mahars and I conveyed this to Col Bajina. A Company now moved forward and occupied a defended locality at Ghug and the platoon of D Company moved from Karotana to Bidipur. Battalion HQ moved from Mahute to Karotana.

I had protested to Rocky that he had not given us a chance to fight the enemy. He asked me to get ready to capture Palaura Nikka opposite 1 Madras position. I carried out the reconnaissance and issued orders to the Battalion but to our great disappointment, the operation had to be called off as India and Pakistan had agreed on a ceasefire to be effective from 0300 hrs on 23 September 1965. During the operations our defended areas were heavily shelled and we suffered one JCO and two jawans dead, while Lt Prosanto Ghosh was injured. To honour the brave soldiers we constructed a small memorial at Karotana, whose picture was published in *The Times of India*. We now reverted under command of 19 Inf Bde and Rocky, with his 52 Mtn Bde moved out of the area. A large number of anti-personnel mines had been laid to block certain likely infiltration routes. These had to be lifted. I found that men were hesitant. To set a personal example I along with all officers first lifted some mines and the men followed. Dhure, Malani, Nandpur, Ghug and Bidipur were all Pakistani villages. After the ceasefire we stayed in the area till May 1966 when we moved to Damana camp on the Jammu-Akhnoor road. Before withdrawing from Pakistan area, our men repaired some damage caused to their mosques in the villages occupied by us. We marched the whole distance of 35.5 kms from R.S. Pura to our camp, entering ceremoniously to the tune of our regimental march past, played by our pipes and drums! The families, children and civilians cheered us. I left for Mhow to attend the Senior Officers Course, after leaving the battalion at Damana. On return from Mhow, we were ordered to move to Nahan, our original peace station.

While on Senior Officers Course at Mhow,I got a call from Pravin that he had cleared the entrance test to National Defence Academy but could not clear the medical due to poor eyesight. He was to appear before a Medical Board and wanted to know if I could use my influence to help him clear this hurdle. I advised him that I would be unable to help him and that he should take this as a blessing in disguise as God had obviously some better plan for his future!

I must relate some interesting episodes, which occurred during war. On reaching RS Pura we discovered that one Shaktiman truck driven by Rifleman Kungyal Tamang was missing. To our pleasant surprise he resurfaced on 25 September. On interrogation, he informed us that his truck had broken down and thus could not join our convoy. By mistake he joined a convoy of 1 Armoured Division and since then he had been performing duties with them.

We also made an interesting visit to our sister battalion 3/11 GR, commanded by Shabegh Singh, located at Jindra as part of 68 Inf Brigade commanded by Brig Zoru Bakshi of 5 GR. Shabegh had earlier done Staff College with me before being posted to 11 GR. After lunch with Shabeg's boys, we departed in a joyous mood. Shabeg with his officers and the unit's pipes and drums marched ahead of our jeep up to the gate. Here, we were surprised to meet Brig. Bakshi and his officers, who thanked us for visiting their Brigade. Later, Shabegh did a commendable job while commanding Shakti Bahini in Bangladesh in 1971 and was awarded PVSM, as a Brigadier. Unfortunately, as GOC Madhya Pradesh

Area Jabalpur, he got caught in a corruption case and was discharged from the Army. This completely alienated him from the Army and embittered him against the Force. He later joined Bhindaranwale as his military adviser and died with him in the Golden Temple during Operation Blue Star in 1984.

We relieved 1/9 GR at Nahan and became part of 4 Mtn Div under 7 Mtn Bde which was commanded by Brig Harminder Kochar. 1/9 GR handed over considerable quantity of .303 empties, which we took innocently. These were not accounted for and were subsequently a source of great worry till I met a friend, Satish Caroli, the General Manager of Nahan Foundry, who offered to convert them to make a bell for the Quarter Guard. He did a good job and later he and his charming wife Maya came all the way to Dharamshala to present the bell to us. However, he did not pay attention to the regimental badge and affixed it inside out on the bell.

While at Nahan, we did plenty of training, including short notice moves. There was no accommodation for men and by drawing tents from Ordnance we created a small tent colony by ourselves. No entertainment facilities existed except a civil cinema, which was far away from our camp. We created a tented cinema and bought a machine from Cine Sales, which provided some entertainment to our men. We permitted civilians to see the shows by paying for tickets, which generated income for the Battalion fund. The officer's accommodation was not adequate and some officers had to be accommodated in the Officers Mess. Maj H.S. Mamik had joined us at Damana, as Second in Command and he along with his family had to be accommodated in the Mess. Capt Shah was our new Regimental Medical Officer (RMO), a soft spoken officer and a gentleman. He informed us that he was in love with a Punjabi girl who was a nurse in Army Medical Corps (AMC). One day the girl (Saroj) landed up at the Battalion without prior notice. Shah wished to accommodate her in his single quarters in the Mess, which I flatly refused. However, my wife came forward to help and accommodated her in our residence. They were duly married in the Regimental Temple by the Battalion priest and we acted as Saroj's parents. They could now live together as a married couple in the Mess. Saroj was a great help to Neeru when she was ill during the birth of our daughter Reena. Many years later in 2009, we met both Shah and Saroj in Jalandhar while returning from Amritsar. They were both critically ill and expired soon thereafter.

The Brigade HQ with 4 and 7 Grenadiers were located in Ambala and we often used to drive to Ambala with families either to attend some social function or professional meetings and on return, we invariably had meals at the Ambala dhabas, famous for their Punjabi and Mughlai cuisines. This did not last long and the entire division was ordered to move to Yol, Dharamshala, Palampur. While at Nahan, a Bollywood movie 'Gunahon ka Devta' was shot in the local palace and we were invited by the director to witness the shooting of a dance scene and when the picture was released we were amused to see ourselves sitting there as part of a barat! (Marriage attendees)

We set up a camp at Pathankot where our men and families could stop for the night before proceeding further. We were allotted Dharamshala cantonment. It had enough accommodation to accommodate Brigade HQ and two battalions. The second battalion was 5 Garhwal commanded by Lt Col Virender Grover, while the third battalion was located at Yol-this was 7 Grenadiers commanded by Lt Col Raj Singh. Dharamshala used to be 1 Gorkha Rifles Training Centre and we often used to visit them in 1948 when posted at our Centre at Palampur before both the centres moved out. Accommodation for officers was good and life was peaceful except for a lot of collective training, including long self-contained marches over hilly terrain.

There were also lot of social activities and morale was high under Gen Harish Rai, GOC 4 Mountain Division. He gave lot of respect to his commanding officers. I still remember an exercise, without troops. This was an exercise at a division level. Officers were to consider various factors related to an attack by a division on an enemy position in the mountains. It lasted for three days. The final day was attended by the Army Commander, Lt Gen Harbaksh Singh in Kasauli area in which all commanding officers of the Division participated and he permitted their wives to accompany in Army transport. In fact it was a pleasure-cum-work trip to a well known hill station. There were also many social evenings, as Brig Kochar, the Brigade Commander was very fond of them and we developed a close friendship with him, which continued after my retirement. We also developed a close friendship with Grover, CO 5 Garhwal, which also continues post-retirement.

In one of the Brigade exercises, the Battalion was to make an approach march by night, along a ridge running parallel to Pathankot-Kulu Road. It was pitch dark and we were progressing well when we suddenly heard a cry from behind, 'Bhasin Sahib Gayo' (gone). I stopped the column and on enquiry found that Major Bhasin had slipped down into a deep ditch, but luckily his haversack was entangled in a tree and his fall was stopped, which otherwise would have been fatal. I left his company behind with instructions to rescue him from the ditch and bring him down to the road. With considerable difficulty he was brought down early morning and was immediately evacuated by helicopter to Command Hospital, Chandigarh. He subsequently recovered fully from his injuries. Those were some of the hazards which we had to face in night marches in the mountains. There were two major Divisional exercises, in which the Battalion, participated. The Battalion was given the task of establishing a road block behind the enemy Brigade to prevent his withdrawal while the division launched the attack. We were self-contained for 4 days and made a wide outflanking move without the enemy having an inkling. We used to march by night and lie low by day. On the 5th early morning our road block was in position. I as CO used to carry my own big pack, while my batman carried one or two live chickens. At halt, all men including officers would do their own cooking or survive on shakarparas. When the enemy started withdrawing, his entire artillery and vehicle column was in our bag. The operation was much appreciated by the Army and Divisional Commanders (Lt Gen Harbaksh Singh and Maj Gen. Harish Rai). In the second exercise we were to attack an enemy position from the flank involving a night march. Unfortunately, our route was leaked out by an umpire to the enemy and the column got ambushed. Perhaps the intention was to bring out a lesson. After some time, we were allowed to proceed further and the exercise continued. These two exercises enhanced the reputation of the Battalion and the officers and men developed confidence of attainning even the most difficult objective, in operations. Obviously, our hard training in Binaguri, Nahan and Dharamshala paid good dividends and paved the way for the Battalions' outstanding performance later in 1971.

Before leaving Nahan, Neeru was admitted to Military Hospital at Ambala and she delivered a baby girl through caesarean operation. She needed blood transfusion. Blood was voluntarily donated by many jawans of the Battalion, for which Neeru and I felt very grateful. This further strengthened our ties with the Battalion, as my youngest daughter Reena has an element of Rai and Limbu blood. Neeru had not fully recovered when she was discharged from the hospital. Our residence at Dharamshala was located on a hill top and was connected by a narrow footpath to the main road. When I returned from Ambala with Neeru lying down in the backseat of the car, to my surprise I discovered that the Battalion had widened the footpath so that the car could go upto my residence! How can I and my family ever forget such affection which we enjoyed from officers and men of the Battalion?

All my children were in hostels and they invariably came to meet us during the holidays. Pravin came to meet us during winter holidays in 1966. I wanted him to go to Vrindavan and meet his grand parents before returning to Sherwood. He decided to 'hitch-hike' in the manner he had seen in the UK. The environment in India was not favourable for such an adventure, but I agreed, as I wanted him to learn through experience. On the Grand Trunk Road, National Highway 1, between Pathankot and Delhi, he got a lift in a truck driven by a Sikh driver. The driver deprived him of his wrist watch when Pravin dozed off; this was his first and last experience of this mode of travel.

It is not that we only did training; there were lighter moments too. Holi was one occasion, when the Brigade Headquarters' Officers joined us in the Mess for festivities. After some time, we all decided to move to Dal Lake, located in the upper region of the Battalion area. The lake was partially frozen. DAAQMG Maj Brara declared that he would gift a bottle of Scotch to any officer having a dip in the lake.. There were many volunteers and some of them quickly jumped into the lake. The prize went to Capt (later Lt Gen) J.B. Yadava. After this we all moved to our residence and sent for the Battalion pipes and drums while Neeru rigged up a dinner quickly for all officers and their families. Battalion Raising Day and Dussehra were celebrated with usual pomp and show. A fete was organised on the Raising Day and the most popular stall was that of officers' wives under supervision of Neeru for Delhi chaat (Delhi spicy snacks). On Dussehra, we had a variety programme, which was attended by some Divisional and Brigade officers, notably Maj Gen Harish Rai GOC 4 Mtn Div accompanied by

Asst. Military Attache from US Embassy and Brig Kochhar, the Brigade Commander. The make-up and costumes of our boys were superb, to the extent that the GOC and others were made to believe that dancer Prem Bahadur was an actress from Bombay, who had specially been invited for the function!

In January 1968, I got my posting as GSO I of 17 Mountain Division located in Sikkim and departed on 2 February, 1968. I received a very memorable and affectionate send off from my officers, JCOs and men. As FM Slim once said, "the best command in the Army was that of a platoon, a battalion and a division." I had enjoyed every moment of my command and learnt a lot from my men, JCOs and officers, who gave me hundred percent loyalty and cooperation and I still feel that what I am today is, in a large measure, due to my command of 5/11 GR.

8

Tenure as Col GS of 17 Mountain Division And Command Of 163 Infantry Brigade

My relief had moved out before I arrived at the Division Headquarters located at Gangtok. GSO 2 (ops) was Maj Sabharwal of Engineers, professionally efficient and a gentleman. He briefed me and after some time he was also posted out. I met him later in Nigeria, where he had gone as our Defence Attaché. I was Director Staff Duties at Army HQ and I was invited to lecture at their Command and Staff College at Kaduna. Sabharwal was instrumental in organising this function. Nigeria was under military rule and Sabharwal had excellent relations with their General heading the Government.

GOC of 17 Mtn Div was Soamy Gupta from Artillery, a soft spoken and thorough gentleman. Soon after I took over as GSO 1, the appointment was upgraded to Col. GS and I was promoted to the rank of Colonel. One day, when Gen Gupta was proceeding to Mess for lunch, he wished to visit the divisional canteen, which was located in an old motor garage. Unfortunately, the inspection bay behind the counter was not closed and Gen Gupta inadvertently fell into it and broke his leg. He was evacuated to Military Hospital Siliguri. He never returned to the Division and was replaced by Maj Gen I.S. Gill of Parachute Regiment. Inder, as he was known, was a down-to-earth soldier. During World War II he was in the British Army. He was also my instructor at the IMA. The first thing he did was to move the Main Division Headquarters to Kyangnosla; 'the pass of the braying donkeys' while Rear Headquarters stayed at Gangtok. The two forward Brigade Commanders were Brig Kundan Singh 63 Bde and Brig Kataria 64 Bde. The reserve Brigade 112 Bde was in Gangtok on the approach road to north Sikkim, commanded by Brig Bakshi of Armoured Corps. Inder now undertook to visit all the posts, which involved tough high altitude climbing. I accompanied him to most of the posts. Brigade Commanders found it difficult to keep pace with his climbing. Some of the Brigade Commanders had not visited all the posts and therefore, found it difficult to identify visible mountain features from these posts, causing much embarrassment to themselves in the presence of their GOC.

The Sikkim Guards, responsible for the close protection of the Chogyal, comprised Rais and Limbus from 11 GR and was always commanded by an officer from 11 GR. The Commandant was one Lt Col Knigger Ajit Singh from 1/11

GR, who was from third Course IMA and had joined the Regiment at Palampur, some time end of 1948.

I now must relate some of the highlights of Gen Inder Gill's command of the Division. He wrote a sand model exercise which he conducted personally, except the last problem related to load tables, which I was asked to conduct. Officers from all the divisions of the Corps attended this. Interestingly the name of the exercise was *khota* (donkey).In north Sikkim, the road was only up to Chumathang, where 17 Assam rifles Battalion Headquarters was located. There onwards all movement was by foot. However, the northern part of the area was open and flat. While the Chinese always drove in their vehicles up to the border, our Assam Rifles men always trudged along on foot. Inder had a brilliant idea of bringing in jeeps in knock down condition by helicopters to north Sikkim and re-assembled them on location. Thus, our men also became mobile while patrolling the border.

Inder faced another major challenge during his tenure. There were heavy rains, causing unprecedented floods which washed away the main bridge on Tista River connecting Sikkim with West Bengal. Many roads and bridges on rivulets within Sikkim were washed away. Sikkim was completely isolated from the rest of India for a couple of weeks. Rations for civilians became scarce. Vehicle movement within Sikkim was severely restricted. Inder rose to the occasion. He personally walked to all major road block sites along with divisional engineers and started repair work on a war footing. The Division was put on half rations and from our reserve rations the Division spared substantial quantity for the Sikkim Government for distribution among the civilians. There were no dropping zones in Sikkim due to narrowness of the ridge tops. However, Inder was able to select a DZ (dropping zone) and with his influence with the Air Force, he persuaded them to carry out supply drops on these difficult DZs. Within a week the road to Kalimpong was opened and a link with the rest of India established. A new bridge on Tista came up much later. The Chogyal and the Government of Sikkim were quite grateful to the GOC personally and to the Division for their efforts.

Inder was very fond of drinks. While, he always had lunch in the Mess with officers, he never came to the Mess in the evening. His mind functioned better after a few drinks. He always wrote in long hand and did not normally give dictation to his PA. Occasionally, he had one too many, but always maintained decorum. Only on one occasion I remember when I personally had to persuade him to retire to his room and put him to bed. I also had a mishap that restricted my movements for some time. While coming down to the office from my room I slipped and broke my leg. I was in plaster for 6 weeks. My batman, Sepoy Bagga Singh from Sikh Light Infantry Regiment used to carry me on his back from the room, located on a hillock, to the office. I used to have my lunch in the office and in the evening Bagga would carry me to my room. AA&QMG (Assistant Adjutant and Quarter Master General) was Lt Col Yespal Dev from Artillery who had done Staff College with me and we formed a good team, with complete understanding.

Once when Gen Inder Gill was on leave he informed me that Maj Gen Munshi, who was Chief of Staff HQ 33 Corps would be visiting Gangtok and that he was his good friend and must be looked after well. We did look after Gen Munshi when he visited us. One evening after a few drinks Gen Munshi was rather high and after dinner insisted that I drive him to the Chogyal's Palace. I did not succeed in persuading him to postpone this visit to next morning. It was almost midnight. On reaching the Palace we found that the Chogyal had retired to his bedroom but on Munshi's insistence he came down and offered us a drink. He took the whole episode in good humour and was very gracious during our meeting. A number of VIPs visited the area while the GOC was away on leave and Brig Kataraia Officiating GOC and I received them. The first to visit was Chief of the Naval Staff, followed by Lt Gen Manekshaw the GOC-in-C Eastern Command.

I soon got my posting as a Brigadier to command 163 Inf Bde in Ladakh. Families were not allowed in Sikkim. After I got my posting I requested that my wife be allowed to visit Gangtok before my departure. Lt Gen Jagjit Arora, the Corps Commander, gave his permission for her visit. Neeru, along with Ashu and Reena, my daughter, spent holidays in Darjeeling and stayed with the family of Maj Sikand, Corps of Signals. Mrs Sikand (Pem) was a superb host and we were grateful for the hospitality. Neeru, Ashu and Reena came to Gangtok and stayed as guests of Knigger Ajit for a couple of days and later moved to Border Road Guest House, closer to Rear Headquarters of the Division.

Meanwhile, General Manekshaw had moved to Army HQ as COAS and Jagjit Singh Arora was posted as GOC-in-C Eastern Command. Maj Gen Zorawar Singh of 20 Mtn Div was retiring. The Chogyal threw a farewell party in honour of these VIPs in which we were also invited. During the party, Zorawar Singh came to Neeru and questioned her presence in Gangtok, as families were not allowed. She merely answered that she was there on permission of Gen Jagjit Singh Arora. She mentioned this to Gen Arora, who replied that she should ignore this and that as he was now moving as Army Commander, he would take care of this. There was a Jat Battalion in Gangtok, commanded by Tahlirmani ex 11 GR. He invited us for dinner in the Mess, which was located on a hill top and could be reached after climbing many steps. Somehow we reached there quite exhausted. After dinner there were heavy rains and on the return journey we discovered that a portion of the road had been washed away and we had to cross a fast flowing stream. The men got some planks, put them across and

Neeru was bodily lifted by the men and taken across the stream. It was a unique experience for her. On the eve of my departure, the Chogyal invited us for a glass of beer and also gave us a silver beer mug as a parting gift. Inder gave me a farewell dinner in the mess where he was most gracious and affectionate. I found Inder a great leader of men, who led from the front and I was fortunate to be associated with him.

During my stay with the Division, the Chogyal of Sikkim conferred the highest State Award on Honorary Capt Ganju Lama, VC of my Regiment and I being the senior officer of the Regiment on the spot, the Chogyal invited me to attend the function at the Palace. I considered it a great honour to the Regiment.

During 1967-71, while I was Col GS HQ 17 Mtn Div and Commanding 163 Inf Bde, my family stayed in Partap Chowk, Delhi Cantt. Neeru had earlier done a course in Montesoorie teaching and had no trouble in getting a job in Salwan Public School, Rajinder Nagar. My younger daughter Reena also got admitted in the same school in Nursery/KG class.

Command of Infantry Brigade

I was to relieve Brig Rex Kharbanda 3 GR but he had already moved out and as in the case of 17 Mtn Div I had to take over 163 Infantry Brigade command on 1 July, 1969, without the benefit of any briefing by my predecessor. This was part of 3 Infantry Division located at Karu, as a reserve brigade. The two forward brigades were 114 Inf Bde at Tangtse, commanded by Brig. Harish Dutta 8 GR my colleague of Second Course IMA and 70 Inf Bde by Brig Ranjit Dayal, PARA, from Third Course IMA. Div HQ was located at Leh and General Officer Commanding (GOC) was Maj. Gen. P Choudhry 5 GR, my old instructor from Defence Services Staff College and ex-Brigadier General

Staff 1 Corps, during the 65 Indo-Pak war. All these people were known to me. There was no acclimatization for induction to Leh as was the case in 1953, when 5/11 had moved from Barrackpore to Kargil and 7 days were given at lower heights.

I moved from Chandigarh Airfield by an Indian Air Force AN 12 and on landing at Leh was placed on Lasix tablets (known as piss tablets) for 3 days and rest; thereafter normal work could be resumed. Three battalions were 2/4 Gorkha Rifles, 3 Grenadiers and 5 Rajput. Artillery Regiment affiliated to me was commanded by Tannon. A Company of Ladakh Scouts was also under my command. There were no active operations and focus was on collective training at high altitude. I conducted exercises for my own battalions and the GOC asked me to set and direct an exercise for 114 Inf Bde. These exercises did a lot of good and the phobia of high altitude operations was overcome. I particularly recollect an exercise conducted for 3 Grenadiers commanded by Lt. Col. V.P. Airy, envisaging an attack on Polokangkala Pass Manali-Leh Axis (via Lahaul), which was at 17000 ft. Despite my protests, Gen. Choudhury insisted on being present on the Pass when the attack came in. I was hesitant to have the General at 17000 ft and that too past midnight. We were accompanied by our staff officers and wireless links. It was bitterly cold. 3 Grenadiers did a superb operation and were bang on target early morning. Choudhury was so much pleased and complimented Airy and his troops. Major Hoshiar Singh was one of the Company Commanders. However, one of my wireless operators fell sick. We always carried small oxygen gas cylinders and this was immediately given to the operator for use. He felt better and was sent down from the Pass to a lesser height. It later transpired that the cylinder was empty! So, it was not the oxygen but the psychological impact of the cylinder which improved the operator's condition!

During the winter, Div HQ organised baseball and ice skating competitions to keep us busy and avoid boredom. I also learnt ice skating. On Sundays, we played bridge with Brig Shambhu Bhakri, Commanding Artillery Brigade. Life was good except the bitter cold weather. Ashu, my younger son, along with two sons of Gen Choudhury, visited Leh and they thoroughly enjoyed their visit.

Many VIPs visited Ladakh. Some of them were: Prakash Singh Badal, Chief Minister, Punjab accompanied by an entertainment troupe, headed by Deepak and Madhumati. Their shows were immensely liked by the troops. Jagjivan Ram, the then Defence Minister, also visited Leh and I was asked to lay on some troop activity for him. 5 Bihar had replaced 5 Rajput and they were asked to demonstrate rock climbing, which was liked by the Minister. He was happy to meet the troops who were from his State and interacted with some of them in their mother tongue. A Parliamentary delegation also visited Leh but they got stranded due to bad weather and the GOC found it difficult to keep them busy in Leh. They came to my Brigade. I took them to the famous Hemis Gompha, which was across the Indus. Later, they had a *bara khana* (lunch) with the jawans and insisted on squatting on the ground. Their enforced halt made them realise the difficulties under which we were operating in Ladakh. I made some good friends; among them Brijendra Singh, the Maharaj Kumar of Kota was particularly friendly. During my leave in Delhi he invited me to his residence for a drink and later introduced me to his father, the Maharaja of Kota. Later, when I was DSD at Army HQ, I visited Kota and the Maharaja was gracious enough to invite me to the palace for cocktails.

Gen Choudhury was replaced by Maj Gen Smoky Malhotra, who was the Adjutant of the IMA in 1947, during the time I was a Gentleman Cadet as part of the post-war Second Course.. He continued to push the programme of collective training. I was asked to conduct an exercise for 70 Inf Bde, commanded by Brig Ranjit Dayal who was asked to conduct an exercise for my Brigade. I also had an Animal Transport Battalion under my command. I made full use of them and organised a 'Pagal Gymkhana' which included musical rides on mules, races with bets (no income tax sanction taken) for which booths were created. There were special items for officers. Food stalls were also set up. All available officers from the Division attended the event and the programme was a big hit. It was repeated next year. Such events were necessary in the dreary atmosphere of Ladakh. At that time I got selected for the next National Defence College Course, due to commence in December 1971. However, subsequently, due to threat of war with Pakistan, all Army courses including National Defence College Course were suspended and students returned to their respective units.

By the middle of 1971, there were indications that war with Pakistan was imminent. Tension was building up on East Pakistan border. Mujibur Rehman, who had won the Pakistan elections and had the majority, was denied formation of the Government. Consequently, his Awami League declared East Pakistan independent and redesignated it as BanglaDesh. Pakistan came down heavily on the Awami League supporters. A military dictatorship was imposed and a wave of repression let loose on the population. A large number of them fled to India. Their main political leaders established the Provisional Government of Bangla Desh in Calcutta. Refugees from BanglaDesh in India rose to one million. India could not be a passive spectator to these events in its neighborhood. Indira Gandhi, who was the Prime Minister took a whirlwind tour of major nations of the world and explained India's viewpoint. Indian defence forces were deployed on eastern and western borders. It was crystal clear that war with Pakistan could not be avoided.

In the event of War, 3 Inf Div was assigned the task of capturing certain features in possession of Pakistan in Kargil area. For this operation 121 Infantry Brigade and my Brigade were to be used. In early October 1971, I was attending a sand model exercise in Kargil, based on the above task, when the GOC 15 Corps rang up Maj Gen Malhotra to say that my Brigade was to move down to the plains for a new task and that I should immediately return to Leh and prepare for the same. 2/11 GR commanded by Lt Col R.B. Gurung was at that time located in Kargil. Gurung requested me to address the troops before returning to Leh. I was glad that the battalion acquitted themselves extremely well and captured Pt 13620, one of the most difficult objectives during 1971 Indo-Pak war. They won many bravery awards, including Vr C for the Commanding Officer and a Battle and Theatre Honour for the Battalion.

On my return to Brigade HQ, I got my unit commanders and informed them that the Brigade was moving down to Punjab. There was a feeling of euphoria, as we were now certain to be involved in battle, while in Kargil one was not sure. At the end of the war, we felt cheated as there were no active operations in my Brigade Sector, while on the other hand 121 Brigade in Kargil got involved in fierce battle. 5/3 GR my ex-Brigade was left behind and got involved in battle under 121 Brigade in Kargil.

I left for Chandigarh by an IAF plane and was directed to report to GOC Fox Sector Maj Gen Ram Singh at Abhor. On arrival at Abhor I found that Gen Ram Singh was in a conference and I had to wait till the conference was over. Ram Singh informed me that I had to occupy a Brigade Defended Sector at Suratgarh in Rajasthan.

As regards to threat perception, Gen. Ram Singh told me that Pakistan's Strike Force II Corps comprising 1 Armoured Divisin and 33 Inf Div were located in area

Montgomery Okara. The possibility of 7 Inf Div being made available to the Strike Force could not be ruled out. Their possible attack objective could be between Fazilka Ferozepore, with a thrust towards Bhatinda or attack South of Fazilka through Ganganagar-Suratgarh, developing a thrust towards Sirsa. To cover this threat, Ram Singh had 67 Inf Bde with its supporting arms components plus two armoured squadrons, 51 Para Brigade and my truncated Brigade. Ram Singh's defences' plan was based on the 'fortress' concept, with early warning detachments ahead of defences.

On the enemy side, facing the Foxtrot Sector were their 125 and 105 Infantry Brigades, with some rangers deployed from Bhawalnagar to Fort Abbas in south. Terrain on our side had good communication without any natural obstacles. Fazilka was the main communication centre. On the Pakistan side, the area was similar, but communications south of Bhawalnagar towards fort Abbas were not well developed. Pakistan had a 'bridge head' on ourside Sulaimanka Bridge. Sulaimanka Bridge and its Headworks were of vital importance to Pakistan, as numerous canals originate from there for irrigation of the vast fields.

67 Inf Bde commanded by Brig S.S. Chaudhury was to defend Fazilka Sector. He developed Fazilka as a fortress and ahead of it Sabuna distributary (used as ditch-cum-bund) as main defences, with company size strong points between Sabuna and Indo-Pak Border, Troops were also deployed forward for early warning. All bridges from Fazilka to the border were prepared for demolition and manned to ensure that these do not fall in enemy hands intact.

Abhor was defended by a group of three Engineer Regiments. Ganganagar was the responsibility of 51 Para Brigade commanded by Brig Thyagarajan. I was asked to defend Suratgarh Sector. It was indeed a daunting task with inadequate troops, against the threat envisaged.

Then, I moved to Suratgarh via Hanumangarh, where 51 Para Brigade was located. I met Brig Thyagarajan Commander of the Brigade, who briefed me on the local situation and I moved to Suratgarh. I occupied the PWD rest house, which remained my residence-cum-office throughout the war. I discovered that the local population was leaving Suratgarh due to threat of war. I met the District Magistrate and also many civilians and assured them that they were safe and my Brigade would be here soon to defend Suratgarh. Pak intelligence was so good that the same evening their radio during the news bulletin announced the arrival of my Brigade in Suratgarh!

163 Infantry Brigade, comprising the following troops, left Leh in five Air force sorties on 31 October, 1971:

HQ 163 Inf Bde

163 Bde Sig Coy

5 Bihar (CO-Col RC Sharma)

15 Fd Regt less one bty (CO-Col Tannon)

11 pl C Coy 503 ASC Bn

AWD 118 Fd Wksp Coy EME

Pl Fd Coy Engrs 3 Inf Div

They arrived at Chandigarh and moved by train for Suratgarh reaching there the same day. At Suratgarh, 2/8 GR and 92 (Ind) Recce Sqn equipped with PT 76 tanks were placed under my command. I was promised an Inf Bn TA, but it never arrived as it was diverted elsewhere. PT 76 Sqn was commanded by Maj Shamsher Singh. A BSF battalion less three companies, located at Raisinghnagar, was also placed under my command. It was commanded by Dhoom Singh and they had their families with them, who had not been evacuated. Lastly, a medium artillery battery completed my order of battle.

During summer, the Ghaggar river flooded the area West of Suratgargh and the movement of vehicles across country was not possible. In November, we found that even a jeep could be driven cross country anywhere (cross country from Suratgarh to Indo-Pak border). It was a vast area from Bikaner to Ganganagar. The road to Ganganagar and Bikaner was good. There were two roads extending to West up to the Border of Pakistan; one to Anupgarh and other to Raisinghnagar. Bikaner lift canal was ready, but this was far away from the border. Indira Gandhi Canal was also ready but had no water in it. Further, its alignment was from East to West and, therefore, could not be used as a tank obstacle. Gang Canal had a number of channels, which came up to Suratgarh, but these were no better than big drains and could not be used as obstacles. There was a railway track running parallel to the International Border from Anupgarh to Raisinghnagar and from there to Suratgarh. It was a meter gauge line. Vijaynagar was a prosperous farming village and the habitants there were quite friendly. Opposite us the Pakistan area was much less developed and the border posts were manned by their rangers. Fort Abbas was a major landmark, which was being defended by their rangers. There were no troops south of Fort Abbas. It was obvious that the Pakistanis could not mount a major thrust through our area, due to under developed infrastructure and their focus would be either to make a thrust through Ganganagar or Fazilka. To counter this threat Western Command had positioned 1 Armd Div at Kot Kapura.

Anupgarh approach was made the responsibility of Armd Sqn, supported by a medium battery. 2/8 GR was allotted the task of covering troops and deployed along Suratgarh-Raisingnagar approach, while 5 Bihar was given the task of close defence of Suratgarh, as also defending the Suratgarh-Raisinghnagar approach. The local school building next to the Rest House was used to accommodate Brigade HQ troops and its playing field served the purpose of an airfield, for Air Observation Post light aircraft and for helicopters. Since we came from high altitude, 5 Bihar was not equipped with anti tank weapons. We sent a party to Bombay to collect 106 rcl (recoilless) guns, just imported, while rocket launchers were collected from the nearest ordnance depot.

I carried out extensive reconnaissance of the area and assured the local population of our full support in their defence. We laid many anti-tank and anti-personnel mines to cover the likely approaches, which could not be fully covered by troops. The Chief Minister of Rajasthan Mr Barktulla Khan and Mrs Usha Khan visited us and instructed local administration to provide us with all the help. They also presented us with a case of choicest drinks. Gen Manekshaw (Sam), the COAS accompanied by the Principal Defence Secretary Mr Lal also visited us and addressed the troops. He was full of confidence and his talk to the troops was most inspiring. Sam had been Colonel of 8 GR and was delighted to see troops of 2/8 GR in good spirits. GOC 11 Corps Lt Gen Rawlley and Maj Gen Ram Singh the GOC Fox Sector also visited us to take stock of the situation.

On 3 December, 1971, the Pakistan Army launched their attack in Fazilka Sector supported by tanks, after heavy prepatory bombardment. In fact, the entire Western Front had become active. In Fazilka Sector Pakistan had still retained a sizeable enclave on our side of the River Sutluj and Sulaimanke Bridge, which was in their possession and was capable of taking heavy tanks. It appeared that our out posts sent greatly exaggerated reports, about enemy concentration opposite them and withdrew in haste. 3 Assam which had a role of covering troops discovered that the enemy had reached behind their position. This greatly alarmed them and in panic they withdrew to Sabuna Bund. The enemy advanced close behind and occupied a portion of the Sabuna Bund. A quick counterattack by a company of 4 Jat supported by tanks of 18 CAV failed. Tanks had bogged down and could not provide intimate fire support. The enemy hung onto a part of Sabuna Bund tenaciously. The Brigade Commander apprehending outflanking movement by Pak forces wanted to withdraw to inner defences of Fazilka but this was countermanded by the Army Commander Lt Gen Candeth. The Brigade Commander was replaced. Repeated attacks on the enemy position in Fazilka did not yield success and we suffered heavy casualties. There was no change in the position of both the sides when the ceasefire took place. Gen Candeth attributed this debacle to overestimating the enemy strength, Commander's lack of determination and keenness to withdraw, and poor planning for counter attack. Finally, it was a complete failure of our leadership in battle. However, it must be said that after the initial shock our troops fought tenaciously and hung on to their positions despite repeated counter-attacks by the enemy. Gen Ram Singh, the GOC, was wounded, but refused to be evacuated. He had already lost his son in Bangladesh operations. He got admitted to hospital after the war was over. This gallant officer met with a tragic end, when after retirement he was living in Delhi Gymkhana and his body was found in the deer park close by. Presumably, he died of a heart attack.

After the ceasefire, I visited Fazilka and found 3/11 GR commanded by Peter Aswal. They were in fine spirits. They were moving to take over border posts captured by 15 Rajput. Peter requested me to meet the troops and address them, which I was happy to do.

Throughout the war, I was instructed not to do anything which might activate our sector of the border as their hands were full in Fazilka. Gen Rawlly and Gen Ram Singh made several trips to my sector during the war perhaps to snatch few moments of relaxation. During the second week of

December, when our troops were knocking at the doors of Dhaka, some formations from the East were transferred to the Western Front. HQ 2 Corps under Lt Gen Raina was such a formation. Gen Raina visited our sector to familiarise himself with the area and take stock of the situation. It was only when the war was about to end that I was told that we could capture a few of Pak outposts opposite us. A battery of Fd Regt was moved forward to provide support and the task was assigned to 5 Bihar, but the same night the ceasefire was declared. This was the second time in my career that destiny had cheated me from launching my troops in active operations; earlier it was in 1965 in RS Pura, under Brig Rocky Hira.

After the ceasefire, Army's training institutions, which had earlier suspended courses, reverted to their normal schedule. I was informed that I had to report to the National Defence College, New Delhi in the end of Feb 1972 and that the course would commence on 6 March, 1972. However, we could not afford to lower our guard and continued to be vigilant. Ashu my younger son visited me and thoroughly enjoyed himself. Maj Shamsher took him on a ride on a PT 76 tank and also on a few partridge shoots along the border. Capt. K.Y. Kumar of Armd Corps visited me a couple of times. His squadron had moved from the Eastern Front. I liked him and later he became my son-in-law. My Brigade Major (Maj Surjit Singh) and Deputy Assistant Adjutant and Quarter Master (Maj. B.R. Shah) provided commendable support to me, during the war period.

During the period of preparation for war, the COAS Sam Manekshaw had ordered that all combatants used as batmen and attached to separated families must return to their respective units so that the unit's strength is made up. He had also issued instructions that any family, living in separated family accommodation not allotted to them, must be made to vacate this. In Delhi, the rule was that if an officer got posted out to a field area from Delhi his family was provided separated family accommodation in Partap Chowk. But outstation officers posted to field area were asked to hire accommodation on reimbursement basis. In my case I had moved from 17 Mtn Div to 3 Inf Div, from field to field and therefore accommodation could not be allotted in Partap Chowk. However, my Signals Officer, Capt Kahlon had an accommodation in Partap Chowk, which was not being used by his wife, as she was living with her parents in the village; so he offered the accommodation for use of my family. The accommodation was below my entitlement but my wife was very happy as the area provided good security. After the war, I joined the National Defence College and my family shifted to Raksha Bhawan, where we were allotted accommodation for the duration of the course.

9

National Defence College and Posting at HQ Central Command, Lucknow

National Defence College (NDC) is the highest Defence Institute of learning, which was attended by selected officers from Defence Services, Foreign Service, Administrative Service, Accounts and Audit Service, Postal Service, and many foreign countries e.g. USA, UK, Australia, Canada, Nepal, Sri Lanka, Egypt and so on. Air Marshal Moolgavkar was its Commandant (he was Wing Commander in Halwara in 1951, when I was a GLO). Maj Gen M.N. Batra, ex-Director Military Intelligence, was my Directing Staff. Many of my batchmates from IMA, notably Brig Chiman Singh, Brig

Mohan Tuli and Brig Farhat Bhatti were there too. The focus in the course was on subjects concerning national interest. This was done through lectures by eminent persons from all walks of life followed by Q&A sessions. We were also made to write a thesis on an important current issue (I wrote on Nepal) and also visit major defence and civil establishments to gain knowledge about the progress made by the country. An important programme, most popular among the students was foreign visits to selected nations and the interaction with their defence and government officials, as also visiting their important institutions to judge for ourselves the progress made by them compared to our own. As I had stayed in UK and visited Europe, I opted for the Eastern Leg. I thus went to visit Thailand, Malaya, Singapore and Indonesia, including Bali Island. We also visited selected important industrial units and national institutions and had interaction with their chief executives. The course was most educative and I made many friends, with whom I interacted throughout my active career. It was a matter of great pride for me personally, when I as Director Staff Duties in Army Headquarters, along with Air Marshal Gole (from my NDC batch), were requested to address the NDC students in 1980 on manpower problems of our respective services. At the end of the course in December 1972, I was posted as BGS (Brigadier General Staff) HQ Central Command, Lucknow.

In the Land of Nawabs

GOC-in-C Central Command was Lt Gen P.K. Sibal of 5 Gorkha Rifles and the person I was to relieve was Brig Jassi Nair. The Chief of Staff was Maj Gen Munshi whom I had earlier met at Gangtok. Sibal was extremely fond of Jassi, who was keen to continue at Lucknow. Jassi continued to function as BGS and showed no desire to hand over charge to me. I spent my time, sitting in his office and acquainted myself with current problems of the Command. Zoru Bakshi was the Military Secretary at Army HQ and I had to ring him up to apprise him of the problems. By this time Gen G.G. Bewoor, Colonel of my Regiment, had taken over charge as the Chief of Army Staff and firm instructions were given to Command HQ for Jassi to hand over to me and move to his new appointment of Sub Area Commander, Bangalore. After some time Gen Sibal retired and Lt Gen K.K. Singh of Armd Corps took over. Munshi also retired and Maj Gen Reddy took over as the new Chief of Staff. Both of them were thorough professionals and gentlemen. On retirement of Reddy, Maj Gen Harish Bakshi 5 GR took over as Chief of Staff. Central Command had no operational responsibility of defending national borders. However, there was a contingency plan to move into Nepal to defend her from external aggression from the North, if the situation so demanded, as per understanding of Indo-Nepal agreement. Besides, a large number of Central instructional institutions, training centres and administrative depots were located within the Command jurisdiction. By and large, life was peaceful and enjoyable.

One of the major events organised by the Command was the Civil Military Liaison Conference. It took place during the command of Gen Sibal. Participants were Chief Secretaries from UP, MP, Bihar and Orissa. For their entertainment, an evening programme was organised 'Shaane Awadh' by Mrs Sibal, assisted by my wife and other station ladies. This was a grand affair and went off very well. During this function, the Home Secretary of Orissa (now Odisha) became my friend and invited me to visit Bhubaneswar, as his guest.

Facing Troubled Times in UP

After Indo-Pak war-1971, the country went through some law and order problems and disorders, created by trade unions, especially in the Railway and Power sectors. The Police in UP was also affected. Mrs Gandhi was the Prime Minister. The first problem, which we confronted was the strike by junior power engineers of various power generating units in UP. This greatly affected the supply of power and the army engineers were asked to help. Army had no expertise in the field of handling power generation equipment. However, our army engineers accepted the challenge and took over various units and made them partially operational, restoring power supply to some extent. In some units, civil engineers tried to indulge in sabotage which was prevented due to vigilance of our men. Soon the civil engineers realised the futility of their strike and an agreement with the State Government was reached and the situation restored to normalcy. The other strike which we faced was by Railway unions, headed by George Fernandez, who later became Defence Minister in the Vajpayee government. Here again the Army was asked to run a limited number of trains. We had some Railway Territorial Army Units, which were embodied and called to run these trains assisted by army engineers. The trade unions were not successful in completely paralysing the train services. As BGS, I had a key role in organising this assistance. Soon the strike was called off. The biggest challenge was the strike by UP Provincial Armed Constabulary, which subsequently spread to the entire police force, including their Intelligence Branch.

During the summer of 1973, I had planned a holiday with my family in Nainital. Maj. Gen. Kaul the GOC, UP Area, very kindly offered the use of his official apartment at Hogsdale at Nainital. Hogsdale was located next to Military Engineer Service Inspection Bungalow (MES IB), overlooking the Naini Lake and had two portions; one for use by the GOC UP Area and the other by the Central Army Commander. It was well furnished. My cousin Mahender Joshi (Manne) and his wife Usha who is my wife's younger sister also joined us. We travelled from Lucknow to Nainital by road in our Fiat car. After a week I got an emergency call from my GSO I (Operations) Col. Suresh Gupta (later Maj. Gen.) that the Army Commander wanted me to be in Lucknow by the next morning. It was already evening and we quickly packed and hit the road. Half way, we stopped at Shahjaanpur, where Brigadier Virender Grover (ex 5 Garhwal) was commanding a Brigade, and had a quick dinner. I discovered that since we were travelling in a private vehicle, the police would not allow us to travel alone. Night travel was considered unsafe and the police would let vehicles move only in a convoy, escorted by a few constables. However, Virender provided a military escort to us and we arrived in Lucknow safely by the morning. I quickly got ready and reported to Lt Gen K.K. Singh the Army Commander, who directed me to attend a meeting in the office of the Chief Secretary Mr Sanwal. The meeting was attended by the Director General Police Mr. Das and Inspector General Police (Intelligence) Mr Jain as also the Home Secretary and various other senior officials of the UP Government. Mr. Sanwal mentioned that the strike by UP Police Armed Constabulary had spread to Civil Police and lately, even the Police Intelligence and the Police Wireless personnel were also reported to be affected. He felt that even the telephone lines were not secure for administration to pass any orders to their officers at district level. This was a very serious situation and the entire UP administration was critically affected and consequently brought to a standstill. He requested for the Army's immediate help to restore the situation. My only comment was that we should have been kept in the picture when the strike threat was developing and by telling us at this late stage, the Administration had made the Army's task difficult.

I returned to Command Headquarters and briefed Gen K.K.Singh, who spoke to the Chief of the Army Staff, Gen Bewoor and gave me the green signal to organise the aid to the UP government. There was not enough time to call the formation commanders to Lucknow for instructions as UP Government wanted stern action against the striking police units by next morning. It was generally agreed that the main threat was from the armed constabulary. If they were disarmed, the civil police, intelligence and wireless personnel would fall in line. Major trouble spots were Sitapur, Kanpur, Barabanki and Varanasi.

Brig Grover at Shahjahanpur was given the task to disarm the police personnel at the Training Centre at Sitapur. Grover mentioned that his Brigade was out on training, but he had two infantry companies at his disposal and was confident he could carry out the task with that much force. He reached Sitapur before dawn at the head of the two companies and took possession of the armoury, without any resistance from the guard. He posted his men at vantage points around the campus. When the men woke up they found the Army in possession of their weapons. Grover and all his men then had tea with the police personnel. There were about two battalions. They seemed to be happy and there was no grudge against the Army. In fact some of them remarked that if they had officers like the Army there would have been no trouble.

At Kanpur Brig Mahipat Singh Ji was in command of a Brigade. Kanpur also had a Training Institution of the PAC and their strength was sizeable. Police personnel refused to surrender their arms despite repeated warnings from the Brigade Commander, who was compelled to use his 81 mm mortars, which clinched the issue.

At Varanasi we had only an Artillery Regiment. They were armed with their personal weapons and instructed to proceed to the PAC lines (without their guns!) and carry out the task of securing their surrender. It was dark and when they approached their camp through a narrow road, with buildings on either side, they were fired upon by police personnel, who had taken up positions on roof tops. A Major commanding the artillery column suffered fatal injuries. However, the Army after the mishap surrounded the campus. Police personnel, realising that their game was up, came down from roof tops and surrendered.

There were no Army troops at Barabanki. The PAC battalion was inside an old fort. However, it was not far from Lucknow and troops were moved from there to Barabanki to surround the Fort. The Battalion refused to give in till a couple of tanks and field guns from Jhansi were moved up as a show of force. There was no violence and the police gave in soon. With this the operation came to an end and normalcy was restored. The army was worried that this might result in tension between the Army and the Police, but it did not happen.

Gen G.G. Bewoor, the COAS made an official visit to Lucknow. He had also been Colonel of the Regiment 11 Gorkha Rifles. His Military Assistant, Brig Umesh Saxena informed me that the Chief desired to call on me. We were delighted. Gen Bewoor and his wife Mrs Radhika Bewoor graced our residence for cocktails in the evening and thereafter had dinner at the Command House, where we were also invited.

Uttar Pradesh, Bihar and Odisha have some famous holy places. We took the opportunity to visit most of them, particularly Uttarkashi (where we met our Guru Shri Sitaram Das Omkar Nath Ji Maharaj), Kedarnath, Badrinath, Prayag (Allahabad), Varanasi, Bodh Gaya and Jagannath Puri. At Bhubaneshwar we were treated as State guests, by kind courtesy of State Home Secretary, who had earlier attended the Civil-Military Liaison Conference at Lucknow.

Our elder daughter Ranjana got married to Capt K.Y. Kumar of 63 CAV while we were at Lucknow. There was a guest control order in force and we could not entertain any of my colleagues of the Command Headquarters. Gen K.K. Singh appreciated this and directed that only the barat would be served food. All my colleagues and staff helped me in this social event. Col. Omkar Dikshit of 11 GR had just retired and settled at Lucknow. One morning he walked in and offered me a cheque of Rs 20,000.00 and said that it was a daughter's wedding and I would need additional cash. It was a token help, he added, and I could return the amount to him when convenient. My wife and I were overwhelmed by his gesture. What a regimental sprit!

Neeru was a great source of encouragement, as she with her foresight had already collected ornaments, clothes, sarees, etc required for the wedding, over a long period. Yet, being the first wedding in the family, I was worried about overall expenditure. However, Pravin who was now working with the Sahu Jain Group, relieved us of this worry by providing necessary support. Ashu's friends from St Xavier's, Bharat, Rahul, Love, Sameer and Sunil from Delhi also attended the wedding and helped in arrangements. Later, I organised a trip for them to Kedarnath and Badrinath, which was a memorable experience for them.

I must relate an interesting incident. On one Sunday morning I got a call from Command Duty Officer that there was a politician from Jamshedpur, who called himself a Member of Parliament. He was thoroughly drunk and was insisting that I should be called to be present in the office. I asked him to send the alleged M P to my residence, along with a guide. The time was about 11 am. He wanted to be served whiskey. Since he was already drunk I was reluctant to serve him any more alcohol and pretended that I had none at my residence. He threatened me with dire consequences. I rang up Gen Bakshi the Chief of Staff and explained my dilemma. He asked me to send him to his residence. Gen Bakshi handled him tactfully and after serving him with a couple of drinks, got rid of him. Next morning I reported the matter to Gen

KK, who assured me that I should not worry about this. He mentioned it to the Chief and both had a good laugh.

Posting to Mizoram

I had now completed two years at Lucknow and I was posted on promotion as GOC 57 Mtn Div in Mizoram. The Army Chief Gen. G.G. Bewoor was aware that my wife Neeru was not well. I had even approached Saxena, his MA (Military Assistant) to ask if my posting could be reconsidered a peace station. But, the Chief thought otherwise and felt that my posting to Mizoram would be good for my future. So it was to be. Some time in 1976 Gen Zoru Bakshi the Military Secretary visited Mizoram when I was commanding 57 Mtn Div and I asked him frankly, why my request for another posting was not considered. He informed me that it was Bewoor himself who insisted that I must go to Mizoram and command 57 Mtn Div. I settled my family initially in a hired accommodation in Anand Niketan, New Delhi but later they shifted to Partap Chowk. Mizoram was in the news due to active insurgency and activities of Brig T. Sailo, ex Assam Regiment, who was trying to enter politics. He was taking great pains to publicise alleged atrocities by Army against civilians during insurgency operations. He had formed an organisation 'Human Rights Committee', which he was using as a forum to project his own image as a crusader against the Army's so-called inhuman approach to civilians and launch himself in Mizoram politics. It was obvious that command of that division was not going to be an easy task. I moved to Mizoram in the last week of April 1975.

10

High Drama in Mizoram

Command of Mountain Division

On my way to Mizoram, I was asked to stop at Calcutta and meet Lt Gen Jacob GOC-in-C Eastern Command. I landed at Dum Dum airport on 28 April 1975 and was met by an officer from Command HQ. Maj Gen Hari Shingal was the Chief of Staff. I knew Hari well as he was my GSO2, when I was GSO3 in Army HQ in 1955. He advised me that while talking to Jacob I must be sure of my facts. He had a tendency to flare up even on small issues but at heart he was a wonderful man. In such a situation I should allow him to cool down. I was to see such traits very often, during my next two years in Mizoram. Jacob briefed me on the situation in Mizoram. It was just a superb briefing and he had everything on his fingertips. My old colleague from UK, Brig Chatterji from Ordnance was there in Command HQ.

Gen Jacob was very informal and immediately put his visitor at ease. While speaking he did not look you in the eye. He spoke softly and fast–and sometimes it was difficult to grasp his words. He felt that the situation in Mizoram was deteriorating. Civil administration had nearly collapsed, due to widespread infiltration of the hostiles at all levels of the administration. He told me that Mizos avoided confrontation with the security forces, unlike the Nagas. Gen Jacob had some solid advice for me:

"– Take personal security measures, without making it too obvious.

– Chief Minister Mr Ch. Chunga has a vacillating nature and was weak.

– Be careful and make no firm commitment, till a problem was examined and cleared by Command HQ.

– Do not allow yourself to be pushed around.

– The division of responsibility is clear and there would be no orders to the security forces, from the Civil Administration."

Notwithstanding all this, Gen Jacob asked me to develop rapport with the civil administration. About the Mizos, he mentioned that it was a closed society and the Mizos were devout Christians and it was difficult to break into their society. Jacob asked me to study the tribes of Mizoram in detail and added that anything in print had an enduring impact and could be exploited. He pointed out that the Mizo rebels were generally crafty and devious and had to be handled carefully. He added the following points as advice:

"– Atrocities must be stopped; whatever good work was done by security forces, was being undone.

- If there is anything important, do not hesitate to ring up the Army Commander.
- There is a problem in Tripura also but this could be taken care of by the Artillery Brigade Commander located there but a watch has to be kept on the situation.
- Mainly focus on Mizoram."

On the whole, the briefing and guidelines were most comprehensive and focused. On 30 April, I met Hari Shingal to have a session with him. I had always been impressed by his honesty and integrity. He was a crusader against irregularities and corruption. What was refreshing was that he set a personal example, though at times he went to absurd limits. He returned Re 1 to me which I had sometime paid for a coolie used by his wife; the occasion I did not really remember! I met Gen Choudhury my former GOC 3 Infantry Division in Ladakh earlier. He and his wife were very happy and were most hospitable. He specially brought out a rare Scotch bottle for the occasion. He had since retired. He was particularly critical of Sam Manekshaw and Gen K.K. Singh. Maj Gen Chowdhury felt that he was far more capable an officer and had deserved a much higher rank/ command. He felt he had been let down by Manekshaw and KK, due to some inexplicable bias.

On 1 May, I took the flight to Silchar. It was a great feeling to put on the rank. At the Airport I was met by Brig Amar Singh Cheema, the Artillery Brigade Commander (my Second Course IMA batch mate), who was officiating as GOC, GSO I Lt Col Basant Mahapatra, and Lt Col Surinder Kumar, the AA&QMG. I met the Division HQ's officers at tea. Amar, GI and AQ briefed me on Divisional responsibilities and the current situation. There was a party at the Officer's Institute, with a local live band in attendance. However, I did not enjoy the evening, as my mind was on Mizoram. While the entire Division HQ was at Masimpur, Div Tactical HQ was at Aizawl with GSO I (Int) Lt. Col. Verghese and GSO2 (Ops) Maj Sagar. With a meagre staff the GOC was required to carry out counter-insurgency operations in Mizoram. I took Capt Hardev Singh from 2/11 GR as my ADC. He served me well and was popular among officers, as well as civilians, due to his friendly nature. 5/11 GR, the Battalion I commanded could not find a suitable officer as my ADC.

Mizoram covers an area of 21,067 sq km. Its population was 3.3 lakh (in 2005 it increased to 8.9). The dominant and majority tribe was Mizo but, there were others, like Lakhers, Chakmas, Pawis Baites, Hmaars and Riangs. They did not play a major part in Mizoram and remained rather subdued. Christianity was and still is the main religion and literacy is nearly 90%, second highest after Kerala. Its international border with Myanmar on the East is 404 km and with Bangladesh (erstwhile East Pakistan) in its West is 318 km. It has Manipur in its north and in north-west are the states of Assam and Tripura. Mountains run from north to south and its highest mountain is Blue Mountain at 2065 m. A main road also ran from North to South but road communications were not well developed at that time. Main towns were and still are Champai in the East, Lunglei in the South, Turiel near Aizawl, where a small airstrip existed for use of Dakotas and helicopters.

Brief History of Mizos

It is pertinent to briefly recall the history of Mizos, to understand the causes of insurgency in Mizoram. Historically, origin of Mizos is shrouded in mystery. It is believed that the Mizo tribe was part of the great wave of immigration from China, through Myanamar into India, during the middle of 16th century. During 18th and 19th centuries there were many instances of Mizo's raids into the plains of Assam and consequent retaliatory action by British security forces. As part of consolidation process in the North-east, North and South Mizo Hills were united and declared as Lushai District with Aizawl as its headquarters in 1898. The Government of India Act 1935 declared this area as "Exclusive". As the time for independence of India approached, there was gradual political awakening amongst the Mizos. They formed political parties and started discussing amongst them about their political options. Many of them wanted complete independence.

After independence of India, the Constituent Assembly appointed a committee to go into the problems of the North-east and recommend steps to meet their aspirations. As per their recommendations, Lushai Hills Autonomous Council came into being in 1952. That also abolished the system of 'chieftainship' in Mizo society. However, this only partially met the aspirations of Mizos. In 1954 various political organisations in Mizoram represented to the States Reorganization Commission that Mizo inhabitated areas of Manipur and Tripura be merged with Lushai Hill Council, but this was not accepted by the Government of India. This resulted in discontentment amongst the Mizos, which kept on simmering for some time.

Mizo National Front, the organisation behind the insurgency, had a strange beginning. A famine called, Mautam, occurred in Mizoram in 1959. The word Mautam (not much different from its Hindustani meaning 'mourning') means death of the bamboos. The bamboos in Mizoram have a life of 30 years, after which they flower and die. The death of the bamboos is usually followed by a multiplication of rodents who attack the standing crops. This results in scarcity of food supplies. The Mautam occurred in 1959. It was believed by the people that the Government did not help them much, which caused frustration, despondency and hatred towards the plains people. They formed a citizen's organisation called Mizo National Famine Front. Laldenga, then an accountant in the office of the Mizo District Council and an ex-havildar of the Army Ordnance Corps, became head of the organisation. Later, the word 'famine' was dropped and this got converted into a political organisation as Mizo National Front (MNF) in 1960, with Laldenga as President.

MNF took six years to prepare for an armed rebellion and finally, the fuse was lit on the night of 28 Feb/1 March, 1966; they declared independence at 0001 hrs on 1 March, 1966. 61 Infantry Brigade was in Agartala. They were rushed to Silchar and commenced advancing into Mizoram on 3 March, 1966. In a five-week operation, despite underdeveloped road communications, they had relieved Assam Rifles and BSF (Border Security Force) posts besieged by the rebels. This is the only case in the history of counter insurgency operations in India that Indian Air Force fighters were used to strike at insurgents, besieging 1 Assam Rifles Headquarters at Aizawl. By 15 April the MNF had gone underground. 2/11 Gorkha Rifles was one of the first battalions of 61 Brigade, used to make a push towards Champai and re-establish Government control in that area. MNF was outlawed in 1967. The demand for statehood for Mizoram gained further momentum. In 1971, the Government of India offered to Mizos the status of Union Territory, with two seats in Parliament (one each in Lok Sabha and Rajya Sabha). This was accepted and Mizoram became a Union Territory on 21 January, 1972.

Taking on the Mizo Insurgents

An insurgent always exploits the sympathy and association with the local population; the latter provides him with food and shelter and other kind of support. He also must have a cause to fight for. In Mizoram the local population never refused food and shelter to the rebels, as it was part of the Mizo social custom. It was so much ingrained in the society that even Ministers of the Union Territory were reported to have given shelter to insurgents for days. Son of the Chief Minister Ch. Chunga had also joined the insurgents. On the pattern of anti-insurgency operations in Malaya, the Army, under direction of Gen Manekshaw, the then GOC-in-C Eastern Command, moved in to most of the remote villages which were not connected by road, near the main roads, radiating from Aizawl towards Lunglei, Champai and Masimpur. These villages were grouped for convenience of administration and security. A military post was established at each group of villages to prevent their contact with insurgents. It did cause a lot of hardship to the villagers as their fields were now far away and they had to trudge daily to till them and take care of the crops. Main centres of populations were Aizawl, Lunglei, Champai, Saitual, Serchip, Kolosib and Demagiri. The local administration was under threat and insurgents would collect taxes from the population with impunity. As is common in an insurgency, two factors helped it sustain; a helpful local population and hostile neighbours with common borders, who could provide weapons, training facilities, safe sanctuaries and some financial support. This was readily forthcoming from East Pakistan and China. So far as Myanmar was concerned, they did not have effective control over the area adjoining Indian border and consequently safe sanctuaries were available to Mizo insurgents, just across the international border.

As a result of Indo-Pak war of 1971 and creation of Bangladesh, which was friendly to India, the Mizo insurgents had lost their sanctuaries in Chittagong Hill Tracts and other support e.g. supply of weapons and funds. Their headquarters was now located in Arakan South of PARVA, (south end of Mizoram). They still had about 1000 men with arms, who moved about freely in Mizoram, with the help of the locals. They had a good intelligence network and an ingenious system of signaling their messages from one hill top to another by lamps/flags. Their organisation had two wings; Political and Military. The political set up had Laldenga as President, Zoramthanga (later Chief Minister of Mizoram) as General Secretary and Tlangchhuaka as Vice President. They were reported to have all the departments of a sovereign nation e.g. Defence, Foreign, Finance, and Health and so on. Laldenga was in UK while Zoramthanga was looking after the affairs related to insurgency in Mizoram from the Arakan Base.

The Mizo National Army had self-styled Brig Biakchhunga as Chief of the Army, with two brigades; Lion Brigade and Dagger Brigade. Each brigade had four battalions, with very limited strength. Dagger Brigade had responsibility of North Mizoram, while Lion Brigade was to look after South Mizoram. It is interesting to note that during the period 1965 -1975, when security forces conducted operations, the insurgents suffered approximately 600 dead, 6000 apprehended and 4000 of them surrendered. Approximately 4500 weapons were recovered from them. During this period, the security forces suffered 11 officers, 6 Junior Commissioned Officers and 310 Jawans killed and, 15 Officers, 13 Junior Commissioned Officers, and 392 Jawans wounded. During 1971, Army was withdrawn from Mizoram for operations in East Pakistan and Assam Rifles with some police forces left there. This gave the Mizo insurgents the opportunity to reorganise and re-establish themselves. In March 1974, Lt. Governor S. P. Mukherjee, IAS (retd) was ambushed on the Aizawl-Masimpur road. He was evacuated to Calcutta and never returned to Aizawl. His replacement was Mr S K Chhiber IAS (Retd), a thorough gentleman and experienced officer. Chief Secretary was Surinder Nath IPS, a brilliant officer–the only police officer to hold the postion of a Chief Secretary of a Union Territory.

Surinder Nath later became Governor of Punjab but met a tragic end when he died with his family in an air crash while traveling from Chandigarh to Kulu.

The Army was now re-inducted to take charge of counter-insurgency operations. In January 1975, the insurgents carried out a spectacular assassination of Mr. G.S. Arya Inspector General Police, Deputy Inspector General Police and Superintendent Police in broad daylight in their office in Aizawl, while they were in a conference. IGP Mr Arya was known to me personally, as he was the Police Liaison Officer with the Army during our operations to quell the police revolt in UP. He was an energetic and a dynamic officer. The incident sent shock waves through the Mizoram Government and the Central Government in Delhi. The insurgents had planned this bold action in the house of IGP's PA Miss Vanlalzari. The insurgents had hoped that the action would trigger off an exodus of civilian officers from Mizoram, but they were disappointed.

The new IGP was Brig Randhawa on deputation from the Army. Randhawa was a professional and go-getter, who instituted some tough measures. One Mizo police battalion, which was heavily compromised by the insurgents, was moved to Hazaribagh for training and refit. Randhawa was able to infuse new life into the Mizo police. All the insurgents involved in the January episode had been accounted for. On the Army front, additional troops were moved in and GOC 57 Mtn Div located his Tactical HQ at Aizawl to plan and control counter-insurgency operations. Aizawl was put under curfew for nearly 5 months and relentless operations carried out against insurgents.

Confidence-Building Strategy

I found that I could not be effective with a skeleton staff. I decided to move the entire General Staff Branch of the Div HQ from Masimpur to Aizawl; this was approved by the Army Commander. I had two brigades; 301 at Lunglei commanded by Minwala and 73 at Aizawl commanded by V. N. Sharma (Tich) of Armored Corps (later he retired as Chief of the Army Staff). In addition, there were two Assam Rifles Battalions, one UP PAC battalion and elements of BSF looking after the Mizoram-Bangladesh border. Later, two more brigades were inducted to enable me to mount greater pressure on the insurgents. These were 24 Inf Bde commanded by P.E.M. Menon (retd as Lt. Gen. DG Assam Rifles) and 40 Inf Bde commanded by Bhushan Sehgal (retd as Lt Gen–Military Secretary Army HQ). My predecessor used to move around with a strong armed escort comprising pilot jeep, a section of infantry in a jeep with mounted LMG, GOC vehicle, Signal rover, another section of infantry with mounted LMG. I stopped this practice and always moved by road with a pilot jeep, with all personnel fully armed, followed by GOC vehicle in which my self, ADC and driver were armed, followed by the Signals rover, in which Signals personnel were armed. All of them were trained in anti-ambush drill. This was to demonstrate to the public that the GOC was not jittery and was ready personally to face any eventuality. I also got a labrador dog and had it trained by the dog unit. This was for personal safety at my residence. The dog (Panzer) was so well trained that it would not allow even my ADC to enter my cottage without my permission!

My own strategy was to mount relentless pressure on insurgents by continuous operations, based on local intelligence, discourage encounter killing and avoid harassment of civilians by troops. Any complaint of torture of civilian detainees would be investigated and if necessary, action taken against the culprits and a friendly approach to civilians was deliberately adopted. I developed a close rapport with the Lt. Governor Mr Chhibber and Chief Secretary Mr Surinder Nath. However, I found some difficulty in close cooperation with the IGP Brig. Randhawa, who was always so secretive about his plans and at times even avoided presenting insurgents arrested by his police to the Army for joint interrogation. In fact it appeared that once he complained to the Army Commander, during his visit to Calcutta that he was not getting support from the Army! The Army Commander spoke to me about this and I informed him that it was the other way round. However, on advice of the Army Commander, I met Randhawa and cleared the matter. The Lt. Governor held periodical coordinating conferences, attended by Chief Minister, Chief Secretary and IGP, where general matters were discussed, but no Army plans were talked about. I found that points raised by the Army were quite often soft pedalled, as implementation might have been opposed by the State Administration. Nevertheless, my personal equation with the LG remained excellent.

Some time in June 1975 Gen. Jacob visited us primarily to attend the wedding of the son of the Chief Minister and also take stock of the insurgency situation. This was my first encounter with him in Mizoram and as Hari had warned me, he had a volatile temper and thought that he had all the answers to all the problems. My first meeting with him was not a pleasant one. In the evening there was a conference at Raj Bhawan with LG, CS, and IG. Jacob launched his broadside against the politicians and civil administration, causing a flutter and embarrassment among the audience, but soon after he quickly and very tactfully retrieved the situation. His aim was to bring home to the civil administration that unless the Mizo problem was solved early, the bulk of the troops might be withdrawn from Mizoram for tasks elsewhere. We had lunch with 1/5 GR. Gen Jacob had joined the unit 33 years ago as a 2/Lt in Iraq. He enjoyed the visit and was particularly pleased, when the Gorkhas produced a silver kukri as a present for him. At the helipad, prior to take off, he met Brig Sailo. The meeting turned acrimonious and had to be abruptly called off. Brig Sialo later called on me and put across his views about Mizo insurgency. He specially mentioned about certain alleged atrocities by security forces on the civilians. I assured him that in future if any such case was brought to my notice, I would take severe action against the persons concerned. Brig Vankunga, who was with me as instructor in the Infantry School, also called on me along with his wife and we generally discussed the Mizoram situation. He did not appear to have any political ambitions, like Brigadier T. Sailo. An interesting visitor was Mr Lalwanga–a foreign service officer, who had been on the staff of Indian Embassy at Kathmandu. He had visited Mizoram after a long time and was now under posting to Mauritius.

Maj Gen Hari Kulkarni, a close friend from Infantry School days was commanding 101 Area at Shillong. Maj Gen Chiman Singh was Inspector General Assam Rifles in Shillong. I visited Shillong to meet them and was a guest of Gen. Chiman. I called on the Governor L.P. Singh and a lively discussion on insurgency in the North-east followed. Later, I visited 5/11 GR (my old battalion) under 23 Inf Div and found it most exhilarating. I also visited the field firing of my Arty Brigade, which was being commanded by Brig Sukhchain. Later, I visited Jorhat at the request of my old Second Course friend Brig Govind Sharma VrC, DIG Assam Rifles. There I also met Rajendra Narain Gaur, who had been RMO of 5/11 GR in 1951-52. He was now with the Air Force. This was a good break from hectic activities of Mizoram.

In August 1975, the MNF was declared an illegal organisation. It helped deter civilians, particularly officials from collaborating with the insurgents. Army's relentless pressure was to have an effect on insurgents. There were rumours of surrenders. Lal Denga had expressed a desire to have a settlement within the Constituion. He was brought to Delhi and negotiations were in progress. Biakvela had taken a gang to China and was on return, after training with weapons and some money. He was asked by MNF HQ not to enter Mizoram but park himself in Churachandpur (Manipur) till the final settlement. However, I was due for annual leave and the Army Commander had approved it. Chhibber and the civil administration were not in favour of my proceeding on leave as they were expecting the final settlement and surrenders. I was not so optimistic. I therefore proceeded on leave via Calcutta. At Calcutta, I took the opportunity to visit 2/11 GR commanded by V.K. Jain in Barrackpur. Viren gave me a red carpet treatment and I was happy to visit the unit and meet the troops. Viren had a vigorous and compulsive personality and I thought the battalion was in safe hands. He continues to serve the cause of ex-servicemen, mostly Gorkhas, in Darjeeling-Siliguri area, even now. I also met the Army Commander and briefed him about the situation in Mizoram before proceeding to Delhi.

During September newspapers were full about the news of agreement with Laldenga and likely surrender of insurgents. Gen Raina, Chief of Army Staff wished to meet me. I met him on 25 September and briefed him about the situation in Mizoram. On return from leave on 7 November 1975, I met Gen Jacob in Calcutta, who briefed me about the latest developments in Mizoram. Laldenga had agreed for a settlement within the Indian Constitution and had also agreed that rebels would surrender arms, unconditionally. On return to Masimpur, I flew directly to Lungle and then to Aizawl to brief my Brigade Commanders about the fresh developments. Offensive operations against the insurgents were to stop during the negotiations but patrolling of the areas of responsibility were to continue. Troops of two Brigades (24 & 40 Brigades), inducted into Mizoram from outside, were also to be gradually de-inducted. Gen. Raina, the Chief of the Army Staff visited on 26 November, 2005. accompanied by Gen Jacob. The visit went off extremely well.

Many VIPs visited Mizoram and Gen Zoru Bakshi, the Military Secretary, was one of them. We were good friends from Infantry School days. He himself touched on the subject of my posting to Mizoram during lunch and clarified that it was Bewoor who had insisted that I must move to Mizoram. Bewoor felt that it would be good for me. The atmosphere was full of expectancy, as the negotiations with Laldenga dragged on. On New Years Eve a dance party was organised in the Aizwal club. The crowning feature was a fashion show put up by Mizo girls, with grace and elegance. A girl by the name of Boite was among the best. She was a lower division clerk in Chief Secretary's office. However, the first prize eluded her. She was thrilled to learn that the GOC's special prize of Rs. 300/- was awarded to her.

In March 1976, I visited my Arty Bde carrying out field firing; the regiments involved were 194 and 5 Mtn. I also met Maj Gen M C Gupta, GOC 23 Mtn Div a chronic bachelor and my batchmate from Second Course IMA. I got the impression that he was unduly harsh on officers and was not running a happy team. I was informed that one officer felt so harassed that he committed suicide by jumping off the Brahmputra bridge into Brahmaputra river! I also met Lt Gen Stan Menezes, GOC 4 Corps, who was on a visit to the Division. I knew him when I was in MO Directorate and he was in the Chief's Secretariat. A thorough professional and intellectual, but with a sarcastic sense of humour, he always ended every sentence with 'HUM'.

The Defence Minister Bansi Lal visited us in April 1976. There was some confusion about his programme and at the last minute I was informed that he would leave Shillong one hour earlier than scheduled. I informed Gen Jacob, who blew up and remarked that he could not change his programme. He also used some foul language, which I did not appreciate and disconnected the phone. He realised that it was not my fault if the Defence Minister changed his programme. So he rang me up soon and put me in good humour. Bansi Lal's visit went off well. Jacob was present. He stayed at the helipad due to shortage of time and met every one there. He also addressed the troops and had tea with them. Chhibber (the LG) told Bansi Lal that the Army had done excellent work, while his police had done equally well if not better. This infuriated Gen. Jacob and he left in a huff for Div HQ, after Bansi Lal had left. We met Bansi Lal again at Kumbhigram, as his helicopter was diverted there, due to bad weather. Maj Gen G.S. Rawat (Ganju) GOC 8 Mtn Div was also there. The Army Commander informed Bansi Lal that the two generals (G.S. Rawat and me) had done extremely well and the Defence Minister was also full of praise. Gen G.S. Rawat was unhappy with the Army Commander due to his mercurial temper and felt that he had been awarded the PVSM, because of pressure from Civil Administration and L.P. Singh the Governor (of Nagaland and Manipur) and not because of Gen Jacob. On the other hand, Gen. Jacob did not seem to be happy with the performance of Gen Rawat. He mentioned to me in confidence that 8 Div had always performed well, during the period Gen Rawat was on leave!

Lt Governor S.K. Chhibber and his wife were very friendly and informal with me. They often dropped in at my cottage for a drink and chat and never went back without a meal. On 6 May we had a long discussion on various matters. He felt that Laldenga was being ambivalent about the accord, which was yet to be signed. Laldenga had reservations about surrender of arms. My view was that it would take a long time for them to come around and give up violence, as a method for solving their problems. Ajit

Kumar Doval (who later retired as Director Intelligence Bureau) was a shrewd and extremely efficient intelligence officer. He was the main representative of the Government in contact with insurgents in Mizoram. We often met and discussed the situation. I always had a feeling that he was always shielding them as was evident from the information he used to pass on to us. The information, was so timed that we could never catch the insurgents based on his information as by the time troops moved into action the insurgents had already disappeared! However, at this crucial time, during negotiations, he was keeping us informed as there was no active operations though we were free to nab insurgents indulging in illegal activities e.g. tax collection, ration collection, recruitment, etc. Earlier, he had informed us that Biakvela's gang, which had returned from China was camping in Chura Chandpur (Manipur) awaiting the outcome of negotiations. We continued to patrol and remain vigilant during this period. Chhibber felt that the Army was not doing even patrolling, which I denied strongly. Apparently, while going to Delhi he conveyed this to the Army Commander and Gen Jacob was unhappy with me for not doing enough. I told him that he was misnformed. I took the matter up with Chhibber on his return and told him that it was unfair to complain to Jacob when we had already discussed the matter. He denied this and said that he would write to Jacob and set the matter right. I never got to know whether he kept his promise or not. The additional brigades inducted into Mizoram were disengaged during this period and were free to be de-inducted.

In May 1976, Maj Gen Harish Dutta, the Commandant of College of Combat and Maj Gen Chiman Singh, Inspector General Assam Rifles visited us. Both of them were my IMA batchmates. Harish invited me to deliver a lecture at College of Combat, on insurgency in Mizoram, which I accepted. Chiman had four of his battalions under my operational command and we generally discussed about their problems. At the end of May, Neeru with daughter Reena came to Calcutta, where I received them. Gen. Jacob invited us for a drink in the evening. During the conversation Neeru inquired from him if she was allowed to visit Aizawl. Jacob told her that if she could organise an entertainment troupe and was willing to perform in Mizoram for the troops, she could be given special permission. I returned to Agartala, where we visited Tripureshwari Devi. Gents were allowed in the temple only clad with one piece dhoti. A daily sacrifice of a goat is still performed. I visited 1/9 GR commanded by Lt Col Puri. He was having serious problems with his officers. I addressed the officers and pointed out the consequences of their indiscipline and ganging up against the CO. However, the tactless handling of officers by Puri in a rigid and harsh manner could not be ignored, when I found that without exception all officers were against Puri. I decided to apprise their Col. of the Regiment Gen. Eric Vas, about the situation. Later, I found a similar situation in 2/9 GR, located at Aizawl, commanded by Col. Khatri. In this case Subebar Major of the unit wished to meet me on a Gorkha net. The Subedar Major felt that I, being from a Gorkha Regiment would give him a sympathetic hearing; however I proceeded to give him a dressing down in the presence of his Brigade Commander, Brig K.D. Issar, for by passing his Commanding Officer. I made it clear this was an act of gross indiscipline. I addressed the unit and reminded them of their fine tradition and implored them to be disciplined and not to do anything which might bring a bad name to the unit and the Regiment. Perhaps these episodes of 9 GR could be one of the reasons that alienated Gen Eric Vas and he showed his displeasure in various ways, when he was GOC-in-C Eastern Command and I was Director General Assam Rifles from 1979 to 1981!

In, June 1976, Neeru, Ashu, Reena and I, alongwith ADC Capt. Hardev Singh visited Shillong and stayed with

Maj Gen Chiman Singh, Inspecter General Assam Rifles in the Assam Rifles House, little realising that I would be the next official occupant of this place. We met Maj Gen Kulkarni and his wife Suman, friends from Infantry School days and also called on L.P. Singh, the Governor. We could spend only 2-3 days, when we got the news that Barak river was overflowing the banks and threatening Silchar and I should immediately return to Masimpur. We travelled by road, which had many road blocks, due to heavy rains. We had to stop short of Masimpur at a BSF battalion area as the entire route to my headquarters was flooded. Mahapatra my GSO I sent two boats fitted with outboard motors, under Maj Khanna to BSF location to fetch my party. We had difficulty in persuading Neeru to put on a life jacket and I had to tell her that Khanna was in command and she had to obey him. Barak's flow was menacing and very fast. On our way back the propeller of one of our motor boats got entangled in a fisherman's net under water and the boat started drifting. Khanna had the good sense of carrying a spare motor which he fitted quickly and retrieved the situation. On reaching Masimpur, we found that it was under 4 to 7 ft water and we had to disembark directly onto a Shaktiman truck. The Officers' Mess was located on a high ground and was not affected. After leaving the family at the mess, I rushed to Silchar to take stock of the situation. A bund was breached and Silchar was threatened. The Army provided the necessary assistance with men and material to close the breach and thus saved the situation. Our effort was much appreciated by Assam Government and as a token of their appreciation, the Chief Minister of Assam presented a trophy to the Division.

Rain was continuing and I had to travel by road to reach Aizawl. The Lt Governor of Mizoram, Mr S.K. Chhibber was in our field hospital, due to a heart attack. This was the day, when the news came about an agreement having been signed, between Laldenga and the Central Government. Everyone was congratulating Doval the SIB man for his contribution towards this agreement, forgetting the efforts of the security forces in exerting pressure on the insurgents and thereby making negotiations possible! There were no facilities available to take care of cardiac patients in Mizoram. I had to get cardiologist, Maj Bhawal, along with ECG machine, from Army Field Hospital Masimpur. Mr Chhibber was evacuated to Calcutta for treatment. Before leaving, he suggested that in view of the agreement, we should go easy on all the insurgents involved in 'tax collection' except those indulging in illegal activities! We wanted to know from the Mizoram Government as to what constituted 'illegal activity by insurgents', but their answer was ambiguous.

Flood relief operations continued in Silchar and the Mizoram Government also wanted some rice to be air dropped in villages bordering Kachar district of Assam, which was done. During my various visits to posts and villages I met with locals. I found them politically conscious and all in favour of Laldenga. They felt that it was due to insurgency organised by Laldenga that the Central Government had carried out development of Mizoram. Doval, the local IB Chief, confirmed that Biakvela's gang was still in a camp at Churachandpur. Insurgents were now still moving around in the villages, openly with arms. Doval and the Chief Secretary were not happy and conveyed to me that insurgents seemed to have reservations about surrendering arms. Insurgents had a conclave at Calcutta. Some of them had come from Arakan and assembled at Parva (in Myanmar southern tip of Mizoram) from where Doval arranged their airlift to Calcutta, while others came from Delhi.

Neeru organised an entertainment troupe, from amongst the officers' wives at Masimpur. They all came to Aizawl and gave two shows for officers, men and civilians, which were well appreciated. They were treated as State guests. This gesture by the Army ladies was very much appreciated by all.

On 5 October, about midnight I was rung up by Doval informing me that the ceasefire was not being extended. He seemed to be in an agitated state of mind and asked me to do something about it. I replied that I had no official information from Command HQ, about resumption of operations, though we were already prepared for this eventuality. Two additional Brigades (24 and 40) had again come into Mizoram, which was an indication that we might resume large scale operations, if the agreement was revoked. Insurgents who were roaming around freely had gone underground. I wished we were informed well in time. I spoke to the Army Commander, who confirmed that ceasefire was unlikely to be extended but operations by us were only to be resumed on his orders. However, we were asked to take a tough line on tax collection, ration collection, recruitment and collaborators.

Information came that Biakvela had broken out from Churachandpur camp despite close vigil by the Army. It was reported that the Biakvela gang comprised nine officers and 111 men. China had given them 216 small arms, 543000 rounds of ammunition, 214 rockets, 5 radio sets and some cash. Doval told me that Biakvela was instructed by MNF HQ not to enter Mizoram and move directly to MNF HQ in Arakan (Parva). He was to follow a route, parallel to Indo-Myanmar border, upto Parva. I visited Champai, along with Brig. Menon, Commander of 24 Bde. I could not take chances and instructed him to establish blocks on the likely route of Biakvela, across the border in Myanmar. I felt that it would be a disgrace if the gang went through Mizoram unscathed. On 12 May, Doval informed me that Biakchunga, their self-styled military Chief had sent a message to Biakvela at Vialethlang that if Army pressure was too much, lie low otherwise move to MNF HQ, which was safest. This meant he was already in Mizoram in 73 Bde area. An intensive combing up operation was carried out by our troops. Later, Doval informed me that MNF courier had returned without delivering the letter as Biakvela was not found. He felt that he was still in Myanmar. This was obviously to deflect us from trapping the Biakvela gang.

On 25 October Gen Jacob arrived from Calcutta on a visit. He visited HQ 24 Bde and Champai. Later in the evening he attended a conference at Raj Niwas, and next day, he visited Lunglei, HQ 311 Bde and 40 Bde. During this visit he had a long discussion with Doval. He also visited Agartala and later I travelled with him to Calcutta. He was in a jovial mood, a rarity. S.K. Chhibber after being discharged from hospital came to Command HQ (in Calcutta) and finally on 27 October, we got the green signal from the Army Commander to resume operations.

We had already planned and targets were assigned to Brigades. So not to lose time, I instructed the GSO I, on phone to go ahead without waiting for my arrival. On arrival at Aizawl I was informed by Brig K.D. Issar, Commander 73 Bde that he had definite information about a camp near Turiel and was given a go ahead in coordination with 24 Bde, to raid the camp. The camp was found deserted in a hurry, with warm food and burning fire. Some Chinese literature was also recovered. 3 Grenadiers raided the supposed location of MNF Military HQ but could only catch three men with a radio set and a Chinese pistol.

Doval still insisted that Biakvela, with his gang was in Myanmar but indications were that he was in Mizoram. Information came in that Biakvela had met his wife and presented her with a Chinese shawl. Also, some locals were asked to collect 100 kilogram of rice for delivery to his gang.

It had been a daring performance by Biakvela to cut across Mizoram right under our nose. I was much disappointed and felt that I should ask Jacob to relieve me of command, as I had failed to intercept Biakvela. However, on 1 November, a ray of hope suddenly appeared. Brig Issar reported noticing flares fired at Zopui (in Bangladesh)–obvious signals to strayed insurgents, who were possibly scattered after our raid on their camp. We airlifted a commando platoon of 6 Raj Rif under Capt Lal Chand to lay ambush south of Zopui, across Indo-Bangladesh border. They discovered the gang entering Bangladesh towards Zopui and followed them closely. Doval now informed us that the gang was indeed in Mizoram and was given a feast by locals at Sherzawl. 311 Bde was also ordered to heli-lift some troops to Darangaon and establish some ambushes across the border on the likely route down south from Zopui. Some hostiles were caught by our troops who confirmed the presence of Biakvela in Mizoram. It was on 3 November that we got the information that Capt Lal Chand had an encounter with the gang at Longtain. They had attacked the gang in real infantry style while they were resting and inflicted some casualties on them. They recovered 2 rocket launchers, 2 self loading rifles, 2 pistols and some ammunition, with magazines, all of Chinese origin. We lost a jawan and a JCO was wounded. The casualties were carried back to our side of the border. The Army Commander was not so happy initially and wanted me to rush reinforcements. I explained the difficulties of terrain and assured him that everything possible was being done. He commented that we had come out EVEN! I thought my Guru Ji had answered my prayers and now there was no need to offer myself to be relieved of command.

Jacob rang me several times; apparently, he doubted the success of Capt Lal Chand's platoon. He even doubted whether the gang ambushed was that of Baikvela and the weapons were Chinese. For this reason perhaps Maj Gen M.L. Chhibber, the Director Military Operations (DMO) from Army HQ visited Mizoram. Maj Gen Chhiber was my course mate from the IMA. He saw the recovered weapons and was fully satisfied of their Chinese origin. The Army Commander was generating tremendous pressure on me to show better, almost spectacular results. In an insurgency unless one has reliable intelligence it is not possible to get results. Special Intelligence Bureau (SIB) was presently working towards the peace process and was more interested in protecting MNF than giving us real intelligence. In view of this, only some hostiles were being caught instead of the really big catches. By this time Lt. Governor S.K. Chhibber was a sick man and a cardiologist had to be flown from Calcutta for his treatment. We were asked to suspend operations, during Christmas from 24 December to 1 January, 1977, as a goodwill gesture. This was further extended as the negotiations were still continuing. There were further delays, due to elections to the Parliament.

In the first week of January 1977, S.K. Chhibber and his wife came down to Masimpur for some rest. They were our guests in the Mess in the evening and were thoroughly relaxed. Next day, we visited a big lake–Son Bil and went for duck shooting. It was a most relaxing and enjoyable outing. Chhibber celebrated the evening with a rare scotch bottle. On the way back to Mizoram, I visited Bilkawthlir Post commanded by Capt Girish Tiwari of 5/11 GR. Girish was not on the ball and I was very unhappy with his performance and I reflected this in his Annual Confidential Report when it came to me for review. An officer from the Engineer Regt. Lt Gill, meanwhile, complained to Army HQ that I had misused my position as GOC to provide transport to my son Pravin in Mizoram. This came down to me through Command HQ for comments. Mizoram was an insurgency area and there was no public transport.

The Army usually would give lift to needy civilians. I saw nothing wrong in it. A suitable reply was given, but I was very upset that a complaint of this nature was entertained by the Army. Later the Army Commander apologised to me and mentioned that he would speak to the Chief about it.

The ceasefire was further extended, as negotiations were continuing. Once again the MNF delegation from Arakan had arrived at Parva, and their air lift was being organised by Doval to Calcutta for their meeting. On Army Day, a number of our officers were awarded COAS commendation cards; this included my GSO I Col Mahapatra. The Army Commander arrived on 24 January for a visit. I mentioned to him that I was training a guerilla platoon for covert operations. He blew his top and ordered that this must stop and men returned to their units. Later, he cooled down. This is not the first time when he lost his cool. It was a small consolation that he later felt sorry and apologised for his behaviour.

There was a coordinating conference at Raj Bhavan. This was a tame affair. Gen. Jacob stressed the need to de-induct troops, while the Lt Governor and Chief Minister insisted that there should be no thinning out of troops. I pointed out that prolonged ceasefire was likely to work against the security forces, as the insurgents would get time to regroup and strengthen themselves. The Army Commander once again reiterated that two month's operations by the Army had created a favourable situation for negotiations to re-commence. The LG and CM requested that illegal activities by the insurgents must be stopped by the Army. It was felt that the present stalemate would likely to continue till the elections, tentatively scheduled for March 1977. Gen Jacob was in a good mood in the evening. Next morning, before taking off for Calcutta, he mentioned that I was getting an award of Param Vishisht Sewa Medal (PVSM), for which I thanked him. By the evening of 25 January it was known that I had been awarded PVSM and got many congratulatory calls from friends. It signified recognition of my Division's performance. It naturally gave me tremendous satisfaction, since I had started my Army career from very humble beginnings.

PVSM had a special significance for me as it was awarded to me in service for my leadership and effective counter-insurgency operation, as opposed to award to officers on retirement for their distinguished service.

On my return by road to Aizawl, I was waylaid by 5/11 GR at Kolasib, commanded by Maj Tilak Prasher. It was the battalion I had commanded for nearly 3 years, including the period of Indo-Pak war of 1965. They turned out in full strength with pipes and drums, despite heavy rain and I was forced to have lunch with them. The Unit contractor (who provided the non CSD items for the Battalion) came out with PVSM ribbon, which he was carrying for some time to pin on my chest. It was a memorable occasion and all the trappings of the GOC had to be given up and I felt one of them. At Aizawl on 29 January, the Lt. Governor and his wife called on me personally to congratulate me and I had to open a bottle of champagne. They were both in a happy mood and full of praise for the Division.

On 4 February, S.K. Chhibber, the Lt. Governor informed me that the civilians were planning a civic reception for me. What a transformation of relations, between Army and civilians! I mentioned that this was not traditionally done in the Army and he should discourage this. I visited Jorhat on 12 February on an invitation of Assam Tea Association to attend a special dinner. I met younger sister (Chhutki) of Col. M.L. Barua (ex CO 5/11 GR), who insisted that I should visit her residence for cocktails. It was a gorgeous house with very expensive furnishings. Chhutki had too much ego and airs about her wealth, which appeared vulgar. On return to Masimpur, I along with Chhibber and his wife had dinner with the Bhasins, who owned tea gardens and had become our friends.

On 27 February 1977, Pravin, my elder son, rang up from Delhi that he was informed by Rocky (Lt Gen R D Hira), who was Adjutant General that I was being posted as Director Staff Duties (DSD) at Army HQ. Two days later Gen. Jacob rang up. First he pulled my leg and said that I was posted as DG National Cadet Corps or DG Resettlement, but later corrected himself and said that the Chief Gen T.N. Raina wanted me as DSD and I would have to move in April. I was preparing for my MA examination from Mysore University and had to give it up. The new appointment was very prestigious carrying great responsibility, which allowed hardly any time for relaxation.

On 1 March, during a dinner with Surinder Nath, the Chief Secretary, made a very queer request to me. I was asked if I could take some measures to influence voters in favour of the Congress party! I flatly rejected the suggestion. Amazing how bureaucrats had become committed to the party in power, specially the Congress. On 17 March, the Army Commander Gen Jacob visited Mizoram, this being his last visit, during my tenure. There was a meeting with the Lt Governor and Jacob pointed out that he could not leave additional troops during monsoon. Subsequently, we went to Agartala and during a meeting with the Chief Secretary C.S. Moorthy, the Army Commander lost his cool on the subject of acquisition of land for the Army, but later retrieved the situation tactfully by calling on Mrs Moorthy, a Canadian lady. On 20 March, there was a lot of excitement as the election results poured in. The Janata Party had swept the polls in North and Mrs Gandhi had lost in Rai Bareilly, a constituency which she had nurtured for 11 years. It was a remarkable demonstration of political maturity of the people of India. We could now hold our heads high among the world community. Morarji Desai was to be the new

Prime Minister. The Lt Governor complimented me for forcasting the debacle of Congress in the elections. I again made a forecast that within the next one year, either Sialo or Laldenga would be the new Chief Minister of Mizoram! Negotiations were to restart by the new Government, formed under Morarji Desai.

News came from Delhi that Pravin my elder son had met with a motor accident and was in Army Hospital. Pravin was on a business trip to Delhi, accompanied by his boss. He was using our Fiat car. While trying to avoid a child, he dashed against a boulder. Neeru had tremendous difficulty in tracing him. She went to the police station, but could get no information about his whereabouts. By chance she met one of Pravin's friend who informed her that he was in a nursing home. She ultimately located him and got him shifted to Military Hospital. She got in touch with Maj Gen Aban Naidu, from my Regiment (11 GR), who was GOC Delhi Area and he provided all assistance to her. The car was badly damaged. Mohanka, Pravin's boss, was also severely injured in the accident, but was gracious enough to provide a car for Neeru's use till our own car was repaired. Neeru had to undergo enormous hardship, while running around alone in trying to locate Pravin and shifting him to hospital.

9 April, 1977 was fixed as the day of investiture ceremony for PVSM by the President. I had a 9-hole golf course laid out in Masimpur and after its inauguration on 3 April, I left for Delhi. The Investiture ceremony was attended by Neeru, my mother Krishna Devi, my father-in-law (Mr S.D. Shashtri) and my son-in-law Capt. K.Y. Kumar. During this period, I along with my father-in-law visited Shri Tej Singh, His Highness of Alwar. He was most cordial and affectionate, but so miserly that he did not even offer a glass of water!

3 May 1977 was my last day in Mizoram. I cleared all the backlog, specially some citations for officers and men who had served under me diligently. It was a touching send off in the officers Mess. My heart broke leaving behind Mouli the bear, a hornbill and Mithu the deer, whom I had kept with care and affection. Surinder Nath the Chief Secretary came to bid me good bye and so did Katoch, Staff Officer to L G. Hardev my ADC had a hard time, as he broke down like a child and had to be helped by other officers.

Laldenga subsequently went back on the Agreement. Negotiations were called off in October 1977 and the Army commenced their operations against insurgents. Laldenga returned to London. It was to be another decade before a fresh accord could be signed on 30 June, 1986 and finally peace restored in Mizoram.

Before ending this significant chapter of my career I must relate the measures adopted by us to restore confidence of the public in security forces being fair and just in their dealings with them. I used to travel extensively and whenever I visited a post I always met civilians and listened to their complaints, if any. Gifts were distributed and help rendered in construction of their schools and playfields. A person who had lost his arm in an accident was sent to Pune for fitting of an artificial limb. Several courses were started to train the local youth in radio mechanic trades and motor mechanic, so that they could find useful employment. Better handlooms were installed at a central place to train Mizo girls. During Christmas of 1975, a fair was organised on 1 AR ground, which drew huge crowds. The fair had stalls for food, games and a toy train innovated with jeeps. The Lt Governor released pigeons, as a symbol of peace. A youth expedition was organised to climb the Blue Mountain. All this demonstrated the Army's good intentions and put the local population at ease vis-a-vis the Army. These measures were given wide publicity.

11

Second Tenure in Army HQ-Director Staff Duties

I took over as Director Staff Duties on 5 May, 1977. I had to serve under Lt. Gen Jaswant Singh, Dy Chief of Army Staff, (DCOAS) a dynamic officer, professionally sound, with constructive ideas and quite friendly. He was soon promoted and appointed Vice-Chief of Army Staff. Unfortunately, he suddenly expired, due to a heart attack and the Army lost a fine soldier. He was replaced by Lt Gen K.V. Krishna Rao, as Deputy Chief of Army Staff. Lt Gen Rao was also a dynamic officer, with a vision for the future. COAS was Gen Tappy Raina, who was later succeeded by Gen O.P. Malhotra. Military Secretary was Lt Gen Kundan Singh, Adjutant General was Lt Gen S.K. Sinha, MGO was

Lt Gen Adi Sethna. Most of the Principal Staff Officers (PSOs) and Directors were known to me, which helped me in carrying out my duties smoothly. While the Vice-Chief of the Army Staff was responsible for Directorates of Military Operations, Military Intelligence and Military Training, Deputy Chief of the Army Staff was looking after Directorate of Staff Duties, Directorate of Weapons and Equipment and all Directorates of Arms e.g. Armd Corps, Artillery, Infantry, Engineers, Signals. All PSOs were outstanding officers. The organisation has now undergone a radical change. On the Ministry side I dealt with Mr Harminder Singh and on the finance side I had to deal with Mr Baliga; both became my friends. Mr Sushital Bannerji was Secretary of Defence, one of the best Secretaries, who had a vision and dynamism in implementing defence programmes. Gen. Krishna Rao had an excellent rapport with him. This helped in getting Government sanction for the Five Year Defence Plans and carrying out various recommendations of the Expert Committee. Unfortunately, Bannerji suddenly expired, due to a massive heart attack in 1978. It was a great blow to the Government and specially to the Ministry of Defence, as Bannerji was genuinely interested in improving the security environment of the country, through pushing modernisation and futuristic planning to meet the perceived threats.

Army Re-Organisation Duties

In the year 1975, Gen Krishna Rao headed an Expert Committee, which had Maj Gen Sundarji and Maj Gen M.L. Chhibber as its members. It analysed threat perception for the next 25 years and submitted comprehensive recommendations on a whole range of issues and challenges, including modernisation, new raisings, reorganization, and future planning for the Army. Some of these recommendations were to be processed and implemented by me, under the guidance of Gen Krishna Rao, the new DCOAS. My responsibilities embraced wide ranging subjects, affecting the entire Army. These included financial planning including budgeting, five year Army plan, organisations/establishments, new raisings, identifying appointments for upgradations, relief of units/formations, conferences, which included weekly COAS's PSOs conference, monthly directors conference chaired by the DCOAS, enlarged directors conference, chaired by the COAS, Army Commanders' conference, training teams for foreign countries, Bhutan Army, sanctioning of telephones, work study and so on. Brig Malhotra from Artillery, a very capable officer was looking after financial planning directorate, Brig Kapil Nanda was incharge of other SD sections, except SD1, which dealt with coordination and worked directly under me. Col. Garg headed the Work Study Directorate, under whom Maj Khanduri worked. Khanduri later retired as a Major General, joined politics and became a successful minister in the Vajpayee Government.

There was a major disparity between promotion prospects of Defence officers and IAS officers post 1947. For example, in an Army of 35000 officers there was only one rank of a General; in IAS with a cadre of 3500 officers there were many Secretary level posts. While in IAS, an officer became Joint Secretary after 15 years service, in the Army an officer with similar service was still a Major. Moreover, in order to keep the Army young, officers had to retire much earlier than their civilian counterparts. Most of the officers retired after reaching the rank of Lt Colonel at the age of 50-52.

The IAS lobby was not willing to compensate officers retiring early by enhancement of salaries or pensions. It had caused considerable dissatisfaction among the officers. This was a matter for worry for the top brass in the Defence establishment. After much deliberations and comparative study of officer-structure of other foreign armies it was decided to present to the Government a case of upgradation of certain appointments in the services. Jagjivan Ram made a statement in the Lok Sabha that a cadre review of the officer cadre of defence services would be undertaken. This was taken as a commitment and the three services pushed the case of proportionate higher ranks in relation to the overall strength to provide adequate opportunities to all ranks to attain their potential. A tremendous work was done by the three PSOs; Gen. Krishna Rao, Gen Sinha and Gen. Kundan Singh. A good number of positions in the rank of Lt Generals, Maj Generals, Brigadiers, and full Colonels were sanctioned and service to attain substantive rank of Major and Lt Colonel was reduced. These ranks were then matched with the selected appointments and upgradations approved. In this scheme all unit commanders became Colonel and their Second-in-command Lt Colonel. Though it provided some relief, it had a drawback. Some felt that by such mass scale upgradations, higher ranks had been devalued!

Gen Krishna Rao's focus was on modernisation of the Army through Government's commitment by approving the Five Year Plan, in which he was successful. New raisings and reorganisations were sanctioned, which were implemented by the DSD. Some of the important proposals were the raising of (HQ) 10 Corps, Mechanised Regiments, Mechanised Regimental Centre and a Mechanised Division, reorganisation of infantry battalions and raising of new armored and infantry units.

DSD also dealt with the Royal Bhutan Army and the Indian Military Training Team, headed by a Brigadier in Bhutan. There were certain proposals to reorganise the Bhutan Army, but these were held up in the Ministry. With the help of my friend Harminder, the Joint Secretary and Baliga the AFA these were later cleared. Chief of the Bhutan Army, Lam Ji Dorje always liaisoned with me during his visit to Delhi and we became good friends. Traditionally, the DCOAS had always visited Bhutan but during my tenure I was the first DSD to visit Bhutan at the invitation of His Majesty the King. My wife also accompanied me. I had the opportunity to play bridge with the King and was given special permission to fish in the river next to his palace, which was full of trouts. It was a most enjoyable and educative visit.

Indian training teams to foreign countries were also the responsibility of the DSD. This included Iraq, Egypt and Nigeria. Sabharwal, my old GSO 2 of HQ 17 Mtn Div was our MA in Nigeria, which at that time had a military regime. In 1979, Nigeria extended an invitation to the Indian Army to send a General Officer to lecture in their Command Staff College at Kaduna on Mountain Warfare. There were many officers ready to go on this assignment but Gen Krishna Rao gave me the opportunity to represent the Indian Army and deliver the lecture. I visited Nigeria for a week and watched an execution of an accused punished by the Military Court on the beach being carried out. It was a ghastly sight. Nigeria had discovered oil sometime back and had suddenly become rich. The roads were wide and well constructed and Lagos, its capital, was full of imported cars. The traffic problem was so severe that they had tried to overcome this by ordering that cars with odd numbers would ply on one day and those with even number on the next day. I flew to Kaduna, which is located in the North. I was amused to note that their Command Staff College had a British Training Team, headed by a Brigadier. My lecture lasted for two hours and was well received.

By August 1979, I got the news that I was approved for promotion to the rank of Lt General. This was great news for me, who had started his career as a sepoy havildar. I was posted as Director General Assam Rifles, an upgraded post. My predecessor was Maj Gen Chiman Singh, my old colleague from the Second Course IMA. I along with my wife Neeru and my younger daughter Reena moved to Shillong and took over my new assignment.

12

Taking Command of Assam Rifles

In the matter of promotion to the rank of Lt Gen, M.L. Tuli and I remained to be promoted from the seniority panel of our batch. After vacancies were filled up by those senior to us e.g. Chhibber, Dutta, Chiman and Ganju Rawat, the two vacancies remaining were DG Assam Rifles, an upgraded appointment and GOC 10 Corps, which was newly raised at Bhatinda. Our names were offered to Governor of NE States, L.P. Singh, a very senior ICS officer. After some time I got my posting as Director General Assam Rifles (DGAR). I assumed my appointment at Shillong on 1 September, 1979.

As Director Staff Duties at Army Headquarters, I had dealt with all para military cases, referred to Army

HQ by the Home Ministry and processed our responses. Chiman Singh, my course mate, was the IG Assam Rifles and whenever he came to Delhi to visit the Home Ministry to resolve his Assam Rifles (AR) problems, he invariably dropped into my office to discuss various points concerning AR, under process with Home Ministry. He was unhappy with the way Home Ministry was dealing with AR cases and there were endless delays. As GOC 57 Mtn Div in Mizoram, I had under my command four AR battalions for two years. I was therefore, generally aware of their problems. I felt that the Army was using them operationally to the maximum but was doing little to get them a fair deal from the Home Ministry under whose administrative control they were. Prior to my departure for Shillong, I called on the Home Secretary, Mr T.C.A. Srinivasa Varadan. The Secretary frankly told me that my position as DGAR was like a person between two stools; while the majority of AR battalions were under operational command of the Army, administrative control was exercised by the Home Ministry. This was most unsatisfactory and therefore, the Force tended to suffer, particularly in resolving their problems affecting the personnel. Moreover, the HQ, Directorate General Assam Rifles (DGAR) was located at Shillong, which made it worse with respect to processing the proposals by the Ministry of Home Affairs. The Home Secretary felt that I had a very difficult task ahead of me, working with the two masters and wondered how I would handle the Force, though he pledged full support from his side. The meeting was most demoralising and was not a good beginning for my new command.

Assam Rifles (AR) is the oldest para military force under the Home Ministry; yet they were not given the due they deserved and Border Security Force (BSF) was accorded the status of the Senior Para Military Force, though it was raised only in 1966. There were numerous reasons for neglecting this excellent Force by the ministries of Home and Defence. Hence, many problems got accumulated which needed urgent resolution.

AR is headed by Army officers on deputation to Home Ministry. Its training, arms/equipment, administration, discipline and ethos were akin to Army, so much so that their battalions, prior to Independence, were affiliated to different Gorkha Regiments of the Army for posting of officers; this provided continuity. However, after expansion of Assam Rifles, the requirement of officers increased and also due to shortage of officers in the Army, the scheme became unworkable. Assam Rifles' training, discipline and professional standards were as good as the Army. They had an illustrious history, dating back to 1834/35 and experience of operating in two World Wars as also dealing with many insurgencies in the Northeast. In view of this, the reasons for Home Ministry's action in treating this Force as junior to the BSF is inexplicable.

Of the 21 Assam Rifles battalions, 19 were under Army control for counter-insurgency operations in the North east. Majority of its rank and file were Gorkhas, with a sprinkling of men from other Northeastern states. Its Signal personnel were drawn from all over India with a somewhat greater percentage from Kerala. Administrative personnel were mostly local civilians. AR HQ was located in Shillong. Its dual control and remoteness from the seat of power led to lack of awareness about the Force among the Home Ministry officials and neglect in solving their administrative problems, particularly concerning the welfare of men and their families. On the other hand, the Army considered the Force as Home Ministry's responsibility, though the former took maximum operational work from the Force. It is worthwhile to recapitulate AR's past history briefly.

AR traces its origin to Cachar Levy raised in 1834/35. It comprised 750 ranks in all under a civilian Mr Grange and had police ranks like inspectors, head constable, constable and so on. It was meant to protect the British interests in the plains of Assam from raids of tribals of Naga Hills/Lushai

Hills. Over 140 years, this Force eventually developed into a fine force called the Assam Rifles. Drawing men mainly from the Gorkhas and locals, the Force became popular as 'friends of the Hill people'.

By the time First World War started in 1914, the AR had four battalions. During the war, regular Gorkha battalions of the Indian Army suffered heavy casualties in France, Egypt, Mesopotamia, Gallipoli and North Persia. Since, reinforcements from interior of Nepal and their subsequent training would have taken some time, it was decided to provide the necessary reinforcements from AR. AR provided a total of 23 Indian officers and 3174 men to various Gorkha Regiments; this was equivalent to total sanctioned strength of the Force. Casualties suffered by them were 5 Indian Officers and 237 men killed and 6 Indian Officers and 247 men wounded. Eleven Indian Officers and 69 men earned various gallantry awards including IOM (Indian Order of Merit) and IDSM (Indian Defence Service Medal). Several letters of appreciation from Commanding Officers of Gorkha Regiments, extolling the valour and efficiency of men were received by the Inspector General of the Force. Thereafter, AR played an important role in suppressing the Kuki rebellion in 1917.

During World War II, the role of AR was even more spectacular. After the the capture of Burma (now Myanmar) by the Japanese and withdrawal of 14 Army into India, a V Force was formed from AR personnel, who operated behind enemy lines. Later, during Japanese attack to capture Imphal and Kohima, V Force became the eyes and ears of IV Corps and not only provided information on enemy's advances, but also delayed their advance where ever possible, by disrupting their logistic trail. They also provided a link between the Army and locals as they had lived in the area. Their epic action with 1 Assam in delaying attack by Japanese on Kohima and the defence of Kohima has become a legend and has been written in British War History in golden letters.

As the Japanese attack in Burma progressed in 1942, a large number of refugees came into India through various entry points. Later, the stream of refugees turned into a deluge; they were mostly ill clad and under fed and many were ill after a long trek through thick forests. AR rose to the occasion and organised reception and various refugee camps as also their transit through Imphal-Kohima to Dimapur. In recognition of their outstanding contribution to the cause of refugees, the Government of Burma after the War presented a memento to AR, which has now become their icon.

Yet, another memorable chapter was added to AR history in 1950, when a massive earthquake, the severest in known history, struck Mishmi and Abor Hills of Sadiya Frontier Tract. Rivers were choked, mountain tops rolled down, artificial lakes were formed, which eventually broke their rock barriers causing submerged tracts for miles and fissures appeared on the earth's surface. All inhabitated towns and villages were cut off and so were the 2 and 5 AR including their posts. Roads and tracks in the hills were wiped out. During this calamity, AR personnel, who were themselves affected by the devastation, quickly recovered and provided help to nearby villages in rehabilitating and reconstructing their homes. They restored the land communication by constructing tracks and roads. It was amazing that AR Signals remained intact and continued to provide information to Government agencies, which formed the basis of relief operations. As mentioned in an earlier chapter, I was a Captain working as Liaison Officer with the Indian Air Force and was part of the relief operation based at Jorhat. Bishnu Ram Medhi, the Chief Minister of Assam paid rich tributes to AR for their splendid work during the emergency. However, perhaps the most glorious tribute was paid by the Governor, Jai Ram Dass Daulat Ram, who said, "Probably no event brought out the splendid qualities of the officers and men of AR more prominently, before the outside world than did the great earthquake of 1950. The great earthquake showed that AR were not only an armed force but for civil purposes, they constitute a well disciplined volunteer corps for service of the people at a time of great danger and dire distress".*

An interesting incident, during the earthquake relates to Frank Kingdom Ward, who was a British botanist, famous for his numerous expeditions to China, Tibet and Himalayas in search of various rare plants. He was known to be the 'Doyen of plant hunters'. Ward along with his wife Jean was on an expedition, through Lohit Valley to Rima. At the time of the earthquake he was near the epicenter i.e close to Rima and was subject to the full fury of the devastating earthquake. They were rescued by Assam Rifles personnel. Letters written by them to Col. Friar, Inspector General Assam Rifles, describe the superhuman efforts made by AR personnel, often at great personal risk to rescue and guide them to safety.

Tawang Border Area was south of McMahon Line and yet Tibet had been exercising control and collecting taxes. It was only after Indpendence in 1950, that Government of India decided to establish administrative control and exercise our sovreignity of the Area. Major Bob Kathing (formerly of Assam Rifles) was ordered to lead a column with a protection force of Assam Rifles to Tawang and establish administrative control in the area. Major Kathing acting with determination and astuteness, as also with a

---

* Foreword by the Governor dated 22 Nov 1951 to the 'Review of the work done by men of Assam Rifles during earthquake and floods 15 Aug, 1950', issued by the IGAR Shillong

show of force by Assam Rifles, ousted Tibetan Dzongpens from the area and thus secured the area which belonged to India. Major Kathing has recorded his appreciation of AR personnel who accompanied him thus: "the establishment and consolidation of Indian Administration in the Towang area could be smoothly and successfully carried out only because of Assam Rifles". Over the years, various Governors of Assam and Advisers have appreciated the contribution of AR in administration and assimilation of tribals of the Northeast in the mainstream of Indian society. In fact the most appropriate tribute to AR was paid by famous anthrologist and Indologist, Verrier Elwin, who aptly described AR* as 'The custodians of law and order, the pioneers of every advance into the interior, the guardians of our borders and, above all, the friends of the hill people. Modestly and without fuss, they have faced every possible hardship and difficulty, and thousands of villagers in the wildest area, think of them with affection and gratitude.'

Despite the glorious history and capabilities of AR, its neglect by the Home Ministry and Army was inexplicable. I considered myself privileged to command a Force with such a glorious past. I was determined to campaign for bringing awareness among the main stakeholders and try to resolve the problems of the Force, as best as I could.

In 1948, the responsibility for Northeast was part of External Affairs Ministry and the control was exercised through the Governor of Assam. As part of this historical legacy, the practice continued in a limited manner and Ministry of Home Affairs often took the Assam Governor's advice concerning AR matters and so did the Army Headquarters when the need arose. On arrival at Shillong, I

---

* The remark by Verrier Elwin is quoted by Shri B.K. Nehru, Governor of Assam, 1968-1973, in the foreword to 'Sentinels of the Northeast-Assam Rifles' by Maj Gen D.K. Palit.

called on L.P. Singh, the Governor. He mentioned to me that he had not known me, but had conveyed his preference for me over Tuli, as one of the previous Inspectors General was a "Tuli", who had left behind an unfavourable impression. Like the Home Secretary, L.P. Singh also mentioned the difficulties inherent in my assignment. He gave me a long briefing on the problems of AR and mentioned that Maj Gen Chiman Singh had done his best to resolve them, but had to face many hurdles. He had made some progress to improve the lot of the AR personnel but it was not significant enough to make an impact. He wished me good luck and pledged full support in all my efforts. Subsequently, as my tenure progressed, Mrs. L. P. Singh became friendly with my wife Neeru and treated her like a younger sister.

This relationship also played a crucial part in carrying out my task. LP was an upright man and was always a pillar of strength to me, during my crisis period. After LP retired, he settled down in his house in Vasant Vihar, New Delhi, but remained in touch with us.

Need for Urgent Reforms: Problems and Challenges

The ethos and overall performance of AR has always been different from other para military forces, mainly because it has always been led by Army officers on deputation. Army has always been deficient of officers, yet it has always spared officers for the AR. The system has, however, one drawback. Officers who come on deputation do not generally develop a sense of attachment and commitment to the Force. In their entire career, officers get posted to AR only once for a period of three years, which is not an adequate time for bonding, as in the Army Regiments. An effort was made in the past to find a solution for this by affiliation of infantry regiments to specific AR battalions, thus giving officers an opportunity to develop loyalty to that unit, but the system never worked due to shortage of officers in the Army and expansion of

Assam Rifles, which required an ever increasing number of officers. The Army therefore had to resort to posting of officers to AR from other Arms i.e Armoured Corps, Artillery and Signals. This was certainly not a satisfactory arrangement. Some continuity, however, was provided by AR cadre officers, who were mostly those Army officers, who after expiry of their contract as Emergency Commissioned Officers opted to join AR. They were mostly in the rank of Deputy Commandants (equivalent to Major) and had no scope for promotion. After prolonged discussions, with the Home Ministry, I was able to get a percentage of them promoted to the rank of Commandant (equivalent to Lt. Colonel). However, they were not eligible to command an AR Battalion, though annual confidential reports (ACRs) of these officers were written by Army officers, they attended Army professional courses, and were awarded with Army decorations. I proposed that selected Commandants be given command of some battalions, who were engaged in counter insurgency operations, which required only platoon level operations. The Army was not in favour of this. Consequently we had a discussion in the office of Defence Secretary with Home Secretary, Military Secretary, Deputy Chief of Army Staff. The proposal was strongly opposed by the Army and despite best efforts of Home Secretary and mine, the proposal was not approved. This defied all logic. In BSF, officers of their vintage had already become DIGs. This cadre was ageing and would soon disappear leaving a huge gap in the continuity of officer cadre. I therefore re-introduced appointment of Asst. Comdts., who were selected from rank and file by a Board of Officers. This had the approval of the Home Ministry. This had a tremendous impact on the morale of men as they could now aspire to become officers. A large number of other ranks enrolled themselves in distant education programmes to enhance their educational qualifications, so as to be eligible for becoming officers. The newly appointed Asst. Comdts. were popularly referred to as 'Sushil Commissioned Officers'.

Communications with Range HQs DIGs were generally poor. We were able to get direct dedicated lines from HQ DGAR to HQs DIG and also replace battalion wireless sets by more modern sets.

AR was deployed on Indo-Burma border and Indo Tibet border in Arunachal and Sikkim, with one exception of two BSF battalions, having been deployed along Imphal-Burma Border in 1979. This was not in conformity with the policy of the Government and I had tremendous difficulty in persuading the Ministry to replace them by AR battalions. However, this could not be done till more battalions of AR were raised.

Medical set up was also spruced up. My predecessor had put up a proposal to raise some dental units, which was just approved. Some additional staff was also sanctioned. Each battalion had a mini-hospital, which was improved in terms of availability of medicine and other facilities.

The Army always felt that as AR battalions were located in one station since raising, with families, and owned considerable assets, they had developed vested interests. They acted in counter-insurgency operations, with some restraint, so as not to invite reprisals from insurgents. This, the Army felt, inhibited AR troops from taking aggressive action against insurgents and thus made them less effective, compared to regular Army units. This was not wholly correct. The Assam Rifles battalions had developed good local intelligence about insurgent movements and on ground their performance was definitely praiseworthy and even better than some Army battalions. I seriously considered the rotation of units and felt that as an experiment, a beginning could perhaps be made with the 17 Assam Rifles, located in Sikkim with 7 Assam Rifles, in Jairampur, as this would have created the least disruption. However, due to some reasons this could not be implemented during my tenure and was done later.

Generally performance of AR battalions in counter insurgency operations could be judged by the awards it got. Awards given to them by the Army were appreciable. To further boost the morale, I revived the award of "Governor's Gold Medal" to all ranks for their gallantry and distinguished service.

The staff strength at HQ DGAR was not commensurate with the responsibilities. My Deputy was a Brigadier and there were two Lt Colonels, each heading General Staff and Administrative Branches. On the services side, there was a Lt Colonel as Asst Director Medical Services, a Major for Ordnance and another Major for Electrical and Mechanical Services. I was fully briefed by the staff about the problems and various proposals in process or pending with the Ministry.

At that time Giani Zail Singh was the Home Minister, while Minister of State was Yogendra Makwana, and Additional Secretary was B.G. Deshmukh. Later, Deshmukh became Principal Secretary to Prime Minister Rajiv Gandhi, and retired as the Cabinet Secretary. Joint Secretary (P) was S.S. Jog, an IPS officer of Maharashtra cadre. Jog was the key man to handle all proposals, concerning para military forces. He was most indifferent to the problems of Assam Rifles and my predecessor did not have much success with him, in getting the proposals through. On the Army side, though they had bulk of the Assam Rifles battalions under their operational command and all the battalions commanded by Army officers on deputation, they were not very sympathetic towards AR personnels' problems and felt that it was Home Ministry's baby. The practice was that every AR proposal used to be passed on by JS (P) to Army HQ through Ministry of Defence for comments, before he formulated his own views or recommendations. This tended to delay every proposal and proposals were often dropped due to differences of views of the two ministries.

I strongly felt that since Army was using AR operationally, they should take up AR problems with the Home Ministry strongly and ensure that their men got a fair deal without which they could not give their best in performing their operational tasks.

My first visit was to 16 AR at Ghaspani (Nagaland), where according to a programme, planned by my predecessor, a refresher short course for AR Cadre officers was being run. I addressed these officers and found them thoroughly disgruntled. They were mostly ex-Army officers of the rank of Dy. Comdt. (equivalent to a Major), whose counterparts in other paramilitary forces had already become DIG as mentioned earlier. They told me bluntly that every new IG or DGAR had promised to improve their lot, but nothing had come out of these promises. I assured them that I would do my best to improve their promotion and career prospects. I quickly visited most of the battalions to familiarise myself with their problems. My assessment was that the Force was demoralised, mainly because they were not getting the allowances due to them, their rank structure was far behind the Army and BSF, the living conditions in the posts and Bn HQs were most appalling and even in Shillong living conditions were most unsatisfactory. It was obvious that I had to win over the Home Ministry, as the purse strings were controlled by them and not the Army. I also visited HQ Eastern Command, Calcutta and briefed the GOC-in-C Lt Gen Eric Vas, a Gorkha officer, who was Col of 9 GR and had the bulk of AR battalions under his operational command. I tried to enlist his support to improve the conditions of AR personnel, but regrettably, was disappointed as I did not find him enthusiastic. It is a sad commentary on the Army to neglect the welfare of the men which it operationally commands, contrary to IMA motto: 'The safety, honour and welfare of the country comes first, always and every time, the honour, welfare and comfort of the men you command come next and own ease, comfort and safety come last, always and every time.'

The main difficulty in following cases with the Home Ministry was the distance involved between them and HQ DGAR, tendency of Joint Secretary (P) to pass on every proposal to Army HQ for comments whether it concerned them or not operationally, non-delegation of financial powers and, above all, ignorance in the Ministry about the glorious past and operational capabilities of AR.

Since I was not concerned with operations, I could focus my wholehearted attention on administrative reforms and ameliorating the adverse conditions in which the Force functioned. I gave high priority to instilling self-pride in the Force.

The Long Road: Getting AR a Better Deal

I persuaded Additional Secretary Deshmukh to handle AR cases himself and not leave it to Joint Secretary (P), Mr Jog. I was able to convince him that he should visit some of the AR posts to see the conditions himself. He, therefore accompanied me to HQ DGAR, Shillong and thereafter visited some of the far flung posts on the Burma border. He realised that the conditions under which the Force operated were most unsatisfactory and urgent action was needed to process my proposals. He nominated Mr Bakshi, a Deputy Secretary to handle all AR cases. Mr T.N. Chaturvedi, a Rajasthan Cadre officer, had since taken over as Home Secretary (He later became CAG and on retirement was appointed Governor of Karnatka by the NDA Government). I found in Chaturvedi a sense of understanding and realisation about my problems and willingness to help me to resolve them. Next, I zeroed in on the Ministers.

The Home Minister, Giani Zail Singh, after several meetings and proddings agreed to visit HQ DGAR, but cautioned me not to publicize this. The student agitation in Assam against illegal Bangladeshi immigration was in full swing and he did not wish to give the impression that instead of visiting Assam a problem area, he was giving priority to AR. Next, I was able to convince Mr Yogendra Makwana, the Minister of State, Home, that he should visit AR posts and HQ to familiarise himself with the oldest para military force under the Home Ministry. Giani Zail Singh visited HQ DGAR twice as promised on the occasion of Anniversary Celebrations of the Force and inaugurated the AR Mela (Fair) and presided over the Battalion Commanders Conference, which was rounded off on both the occasions by a variety programme organised by my wife and dinner in the Officers' Institute. This was a historical event, as Giani Ji was the first Union Home Minister to visit the Force HQ. I am glad that my successors continued with this practice.

These events put the AR in the limelight. The fast moving developments in the AR were very prominently carried in the local press as well as the regional stations of All India Radio. However, it was frowned upon by the Army and the Chief (General O. P. Malhotra) questioned me on the wisdom of inviting the Home Minister to DGAR HQ. My response was that this was the only way I could get benefits for my Force which he had sent me to command, specially, when the Army could do nothing to provide relief to the men in terms of financial and material benefits. Eastern Command continued to sulk and became even petty minded to the extent that they stopped supply of fuel to generators to the posts and denial of use of transport and army accommodation for me, while visiting Calcutta and Delhi. When I learnt that posts were not getting the fuel, I informed the respective operational commanders that situation reports could not be sent without charging the batteries for use of wireless sets. Supply was soon restored! In order to spread awareness about Assam Rifles' history and its achievements, I organised production of a film to highlight these aspects. A team was sent to Sikkim to film the activities of 17 AR, the only unit under command of 17 Mtn Div. Its GOC was Maj Gen V.N. Sharma, who had earlier served under me as a Brigade Commander in Mizoram (and later became COAS). I naturally anticipated cooperation and help from him for this small task. To my surprise, I was informed that he had instructions from Command not to allow any shooting of the activities of 17 AR. This is yet another example, to what extent Gen Vas could go to thwart the efforts of Assam Rifles to carry out their awareness programme!

AR personnel are allowed to have families at their posts, many of which involve walking for days. Accommodation for these families was poor. I was keen that my wife should visit these families at far-flung places to boost their morale. This required helicopter facility. My predecessor had applied for sanction to the Home Ministry, but Joint Secretary (P) as usual had taken no action. Air Marshal L.M. (Baba) Katre was the AOC-in-C Eastern Air Command located at Shillong. His father used to be Civil Surgeon at Alwar, during pre-Independence days. This common Alwar connection brought us together and he always used to sign in AR House Visitor's Book as "Katre of Alwar" (Katre later became Chief of the Air Staff, but unfortunately died in harness due to cardiac failure). I mentioned this problem to him. He quoted an old Ministry of Defence letter, which had delegated power to sanction air sorties for Assam Rifles to Governor of Northeast. He suggested that I should get a note approved by L.P. Singh and that he would then provide sorties on 'as required' basis. L.P. Singh had no hesitation in approving the proposal and thereafter, during my entire tenure I had no problem in using either helicopter or Avro aircraft for myself, family and the staff. In fact, Katre often used to spare his own Avro for my use, if the same was available. I then informed the Home Ministry that our letter, requesting for sanction for use of IAF helicopter could be considered as cancelled.

In the Army only GOC-in-C and COAS are allowed to take their wives in Air Force planes. My equivalent status was that of a Corps Commander. This extra facility to AR, which was most essential considering the ground conditions, was one of the causes for indifference on the part of some senior Army officers towards AR and particularly towards me. It is ironical that the Army never grudged such facilities being enjoyed by DGs of other para military forces, e.g BSF, though DG AR was senior to other DGs in protocol, and did not approve similar facility to their own Lt Gen on deputation to Home Ministry!

I asked my Finance Officer, Sarma Roy, as to what were my powers to move troops of the AR. His reply was that I could move them any where. I decided to locate a detachment at Delhi, with a view to using it as a Liaison Office to follow up the cases at the Ministry. I, accompanied by my wife and Dy. Comdt. O.P. Kalra, reconnoitered Vasant Vihar colony in Delhi and hired a house, where I located Kalra as LO and furnished the house. A staff car and a couple of motor cycles and scooters were also sanctioned. This became the nucleus for the AR complex, now located in Delhi Cantonment. The Ministry raised no questions on this move and even provided a room to Kalra in the North Block to be known as 'AR Liaison Office'. This action proved to be a big help in processing the proposals with the Ministry expeditiously. The Vasant Vihar house also provided accommodation for officers of AR, passing through Delhi.

While discussing delays in financial sanctions to my proposals by the Ministry, B.G. Deshmukh suggested that he could make Financial Adviser of Northeast Council (NEC) as the ex officio FA to AR and delegate Ministry's powers to him as an experimental measure. He needed the recommendation of the Governor in this regard. L.P. Singh recommended my proposal and Mr Lall, the FA to NEC, was thereafter made FA to AR. This brought great relief to us and sanction of works and procurement of equipment and other material became easy. Lall was located in Shillong and was aware of the difficult conditions under which AR operated. He gave us full cooperation and credit in large measure goes to him for provision of many facilities to AR.

AR has a very illustrious history, which has been mentioned earlier. Yet, no anniversary was being celebrated as the date of raising was unknown, due to antiquity of the Force. After some research, I fixed 24 March, 1835 as the Raising of the Force, which then onwards was celebrated by the Force as its "Raising Day". This boosted the self esteem of AR personnel, being the seniormost para military force in the country. This subsequently formed the basis for celebrating, 150th anniversary, which was graced by the then President of India Giani Zail Singh, who in his earlier tenure as Home Minister had become quite fond of the Force. All former IGs and DGs were invited for these celebrations. This was a great morale booster for the Force. I am glad that the AR Raising Day is being celebrated with enthusiasm, which also includes a function in Delhi. However, despite our best efforts, we could not gain the first position in the protocol seniority of para military force, due to vested interests and AR contingent continues to march in the Republic Day parade after the BSF contingent.

I also decided to update the history of the AR. The earlier book was written by Col Shakespeare in 1929 and covered only upto 1914-18 war and the Kuki rebellion of 1919. A reputed military historian and a Gorkha officer, Maj Gen D.K. Palit Vr C, was requested to write the history. He was reluctant to undertake this task. However, after much persuasion and cajoling, he was prevailed upon to take up the assignment provided some one from Assam Rifles collected the material. For this task I chose a dedicated retired officer in Col Commissariate, who was to coordinate and collect the material from all battalions. It was an uphill task, as hardly any records were preserved. The material collected was put up to Gen Palit, who transformed it into a beautiful book titled *Sentinels of the East,* which was later released by the President of India, Giani Zail Singh in November 1983. This was a unique occasion as all the living ex-IGAR and DGAR were present on the occasion at Rashtrapati Bhawan. A periodical magazine namely *Custodian* was also launched, which was edited by Col Commissariate. Only with dedicated hard work of Commissariate, an AR history and the custodian became a reality, for which he desereves full praise.

Directorate General Assam Rifles was not authorised an 'Officers Mess' or an 'Officers Institute'. The DG's office was in an old building, which housed DGAR's office and a conference hall. The building belonged to an industrial house. No modifications could be made till we acquired it. Moreover, expenditure on improving the building was opposed by our own finance department. It took considerable effort to acquire the building. As mentioned earlier, by this time financial powers had been delegated to Financial Adviser, Northeast Council for all projects to be sanctioned by the DG. The building was suitably modified to be used as a conference hall and also as an Officers' Institute. We also constructed a hall behind the main building and procured a billiards table for use by officers. A few guest rooms to accommodate visiting officers were also sanctioned to be located next to the Officers' Institute.

In order to improve the pay, allowances and rank structure of the Force, I enlisted the help of two key Intelligence Officers of the Government of India, posted in Shillong. Mr Arvind Dave was the representative of

RAW, who later retired as head of RAW and Governor of Arunachal Pradesh and Mr R.P. Joshi was representing IB, who later retired as Director IB. I briefed both these officers, about the prevailing disgruntlement of the personnel and they, in turn verified through their own sources and reported the matter to the Centre. This imparted some urgency and gave the necessary impetus to the proposals, which I had submitted to the Ministry.

On the pattern of the Army and BSF, Section Commanders were upgraded to the rank of Havildars. Additional ranks of Junior Commissioned Officers (JCOs) were authorised and honorary commissions for the JCOs introduced for the first time. Non-combatants were given the status of combatants and rank structure authorised. A similar reform was carried out in the Signals and Engineers (Construction Companies). Civilian staff, which used to be neglected in the past, were reviewed and higher pay scales authorised. This had a remarkable effect on the morale of the Force.

When I was GOC 57 Mtn Div, I had four AR Batallions under my command in Mizoram. I often used to watch with some dismay the families of AR personnel, travelling perched in precarious positions on top of the baggage in fully loaded trucks! A slight jolt could easily throw them off the moving trucks and lead to serious injuries and even death. I enquired into the matter and learnt that as an economy measure a clause was built in the contractors' agreements to carry the families and jawans in the trucks, which carried stores for the battalions.This was most unsatisfactory as jawans and families were entitled to travel free in comfort either in hired vehicles or Government transport. With the cooperation of FA, I sanctioned buses for each Range Headquarters. This turned out to be a complicated exercise. My Staff Officers from the Ordnance and EME (both Majors) had little experience. However, they rose to the occasion;

truck chassis were acquired directly from the Tatas and body constructed according to our design in Calcutta and the whole contract was examined and cleared by independent Government inspectors at Calcutta. Battalions, which had no electric supply were authorised to have sizeable generators to light up the entire camp to improve the quality of life of the men and their families. Similarly, water trucks were also authorised to the battalions. Permanent accommodation at battalion campus was also sanctioned and in the case of 2 AR, which was located across River Lohit under command of 2 Mtn Div, the Border Roads Organisation was persuaded to construct the accommodation as Central or State PWD services were not available in such remote areas.

In Shillong, there was no accommodation for officers and they were living in hired houses. They had no furniture and many officers were using wooden boxes as make shift chairs/tables. The first thing I did was to sanction furniture, which they were normally authorised in the Army. In Happy Valley, Shillong, there was a small piece of land adjoining Assam Rifles men's accommodation, which belonged to the Army. With the help of my long time friend Maj Gen A.R. Dutt, GOC 101 Area, I acquired that land and constructed officers' accommodation and named it after Capt Jasram Singh of 6 AR, Ashok Chakra winner, which considerably eased the officers' accommodation situation.

One of the problems, which I faced on arrival at Shillong was chronic deficiency of woolen shirts, woolen socks and boots for the men. As far as shirts are concerned, AR personnel traditionally wear 'silver grey'. On enquiry, to my horror, I discovered that the cloth was ordered, but the same was rejected due to low quality and queerly the same rejected cloth used to find its way at a higher cost through local purchase system. Meanwhile, this caused shortage of shirts for the winter. This was an obvious case of corruption. With the help of my friend Lt Gen Sandhu, Director General

Army Ordnance Corps, I was able to procure adequate supply of Angola shirts and woollen socks and boots for the Force, before the winter. This step led to heavy financial loss to the suppliers of silver grey cloth, who came on track and the supply of good cloth became regular from the next year. It may be pertinent to mention here that I was able to get 'terry cotton' uniforms for the personnel of AR, even before the Army. In order to meet this sudden huge demand, the cloth was centrally procured and I asked the respective Range HQs to arrange the cutters. The stitching was to be done by the families of soldiers, through the 'Family Welfare Centres' for which they would be paid. This initiative ensured not only cost effectiveness and timely delivery of the stitched uniforms, but also ensured 'quality' and became a source of additional income for the troops' families. As an incentive, the other ranks' families were presented with sewing machines, if they could stitch a certain number of uniforms. This generated unprecedented enthusiasm. Similar innovative ideas were implemented to make up deficiencies of woollen socks, etc. My wife visited many of these Family Welfare Centres to encourage the jawans' families. By these welfare oriented actions the troops' families also got a sense of belonging.

There was no air courier service to AR battalions or posts. My investigation revealed that the BSF, while submitting their requirement for aircraft used to club the requirement of AR as well. I therefore decided to lay my claim to my share of use of aircrafts (Dakotas) manned by BSF. Home Ministry, on our request, sanctioned use of Dakota as a courier, twice a month from Delhi to Jorhat, Dimapur, Imphal, Tezpur and 2 AR location (Lohitpur). I and my family travelled a couple of times from Delhi to Gauhati and in fact once DCOAS Lt Gen H.C. Dutta and family also accompanied me from Delhi to Gauhati. In this context an interesting episode comes to my mind. When the first courier reached Imphal, I was informed that the DIG Manipur Range had no load for it. I was naturally furious and did not want to lose the facility by default, which I had so assiduously obtained from the Ministry. Brig Jagjit Singh was the DIG and I ordered him to load the aircraft with men, who should be given one day's leave and moved to Dimapur. After landing at Dimapur, they could return to their unit by road! However, the courier to 2 AR across the Lohit River always had adequate load.

Major Atul Dev was the Staff Officer in the 'A' Branch and he briefed me on issues concerning allowances. I discovered that men were not getting the allowances, which all Central Government employees got when posted east of River Bramahaputra. On enquiry for the reason for this anomaly, I was informed by my Finance Department that no Government orders were issued for Assam Rifles, to be eligible for these allowances. I enquired from the BSF and was informed that no separate letter authorising this allowance to them was issued by the Government and the general letter which sanctioned this allowance to Central Government employees was applicable to them. Similar was the case with the troops in Imphal. It was apparent that AR men were being denied this allowance, due to the folly or lackadaisal attitude of their own financial staff. I was on a visit to battalions in Imphal. I instructed my HQ staff to pack up my Finance officer Sarma Roy to Imphal by the next flight. Sarma Roy had never travelled beyond Shillong nor had he ever visited any AR post in the remote areas. Next day, I took Sarma Roy in the helicopter to one of the AR posts perched precariously on a hill top. Sarma Roy was scared to death as this was his first experience of flying in the helicopter! On return to Imphal he admitted that our men were operating in most difficult conditions and deserved all the allowances sanctioned by the Central Government and no separate authorisation was required! I instructed him to go back to Shillong and issue the sanction letter authorising all ranks of AR to these allowances.

However, the Mizoram case was very peculiar. There were approximately 6000 AR troops in Mizoram and since the outbreak of insurgency in 1965, they were denied Mizoram allowance (Field Bhatta), which Army, BSF, CRPF and other police units under Army Command in the Area were getting. Going through the files, I discovered that the Home Ministry had referred the matter to Army HQ, who had replied, under a letter signed by a Major from the AG's Branch that AR in Mizoram were already in receipt of field concessions. This was not true as the only concession they were getting was two free letters a week and free remittance of money orders to their home. This was a glaring case of utter failure of HQ DGAR staff to pursue the case properly to obtain the rightful field allowance for the troops in Mizoram for the last 15 years. I had to contrive a strategy to get it from the Government for my men.

While other paramilitary forces, under the Home Ministry had police associations, the same was not acceptable to us in the AR, on disciplinary grounds. Nevertheess, as a one-time measure, I organised a conference in the Home Ministry in which representatives of all ranks, especially from Mizoram took part after thorough briefing. On the Ministry side, Home Minister, Minister of State, Home Secretary, Addl. Secretary and Joint Secretary (P) attended. The aim was to drive home the concern about denial of Mizoram Field Concessions to men for the last 15 years. It was agreed that immediate sanction for the allowance be issued, but the Finance Ministry was not agreeable to back date it by 15 years. The option was either to go to Court or accept the two years back dated allowance, they offered. I decided to accept the latter not only in the interest of discipline in the Force, but also to avoid the delays one experiences in our courts. As they say 'a bird in hand is better than two in the bush'! This was the first and the last conference of this type that we held. It was criticized by the Army as a derogatory step, without understanding the underlying motive of the conference.

Another serious problem, which AR personnel faced was that of education of their children due to their location in remote areas and non-rotation of units from their fixed locations. Prolonged stay in remote areas with difficult accessibility and inclement weather conditions also posed serious health problems for the men and their families.

A scheme of rotation of units was formulated, but could not be implemented, due to protests from various commanding officers. However, as far as education goes, wherever possible, unit schools were upgraded and officers' wives were allowed to take classes as good teachers were not available locally. Assam Rifles Public School (ARPS) was conceived and started in Laitkor, Shillong, where expenses of children of AR personnel were heavily subsidized. I made a trip to Darjeeling and was able to get Mukut Tankha, the Vice-Principal of St Pauls Darjeeling as the first Principal of the School. Mukut and his wife Asha worked very hard to set up the school from scratch with limited resources. Initially, we started the school in the barracks of our construction company. I had two Assam Rifles construction companies under me (similar to Pioneer companies in the Army), both commanded by Majors. Both companies were located at Laitkor. I had one company vacate its accommodation and squeeze in with the other. Accommodation vacated by the first company was utilised to put up the students of ARPS till suitable accommodation was constructed. Students had to be provided double decker beds due to limited space. A limited number of civilian children were allowed with normal fees. DPS Delhi kindly agreed to send a team to prepare a feasibility report but due to conditions laid down by them for their association, I preferred to go it alone. The governing body had the Governor of the Northeastern States as Patron and DGAR as President. It also included some prominenet local educationists as members, e.g Madam E. N. Shulai ex-Director Public Instruction, Govt of Meghalaya. Initially, we were not able to get adequate students from AR battalions and I had to give an order to Commanding Officers to select boys as per the laid down criteria and send them to the school. I was able to get a grant from the Ministry for ARPS and also raised resources within our own organisation by disposal of fired cases of bullets as approved by the Ministry. Initially, some people commented that it was a 'white elephant' and would soon close down. This did not happen. I am glad that my successors have looked after this Institution and the School has now gained an all India reputation. Its alumni, some of whom are children of Assam Rifles, are Lt Colonels in the Army and senior executives in companies. In fact one alumnus (Col. Shyam Singh). who joined the school in 1980, is a Colonel in my own Regiment.

Each battalion was authorised some mules and ponies. But there was always a shortage. Brig A.K. Dewan from Armoured Corps was DIG Arunachal Range. He being a keen horse rider was selected by me to carry out a procurement drive of good horses from Punjab to make up the deficiency. Some of these horses were made available for the School (ARPS) and also to Brig Dewan at Jorhat to raise an AR equestrian team which has progressed well and taken part in many national and all-India level competitions.

Under the Northeast Council Act, the DGAR is designated as the Security Adviser to the Council and has to attend Council meetings. This made the GOC-in-C Eastern Command unhappy, as he felt that it was his prerogative to nominate a person to act as Security Adviser to any organisation in the Northeast. The Army Commander seemed to hold me personally responsible for the situation. However, I had nothing to do with it, as I was acting only as per the orders of the Governor, who was the Chairman of the Council. The Army should have taken action to get the NEC Act amended.

As mentioned earlier, I was not involved with the counter insurgency operations in the region. However, there is an interesting incident, which is worth recollecting. One evening (in April 1980) there was a dinner in my house and Capt Sumit Chowdhuri 11 GR, ADC to Governor L. P. Singh was also invited. He turned up late and appeared to be in a disturbed state of mind. On enquiry, he mentioned that the Governor had just returned from Tripura, where serious tension had developed between Tribals and Bengalis and it was apprehended that riots could break out any moment. The Governor felt that presence of Army and para military forces at this juncture may restore the confidence among the locals and stabilise the law and order situation.

I spoke to LP, who confirmed what Sumit had related to me. He further mentioned that Lt Gen Eric Vas, GOC-in-C Eastern Command was approached for help and his reaction was that Tripura being a remote area, help from the Army could take a minimum 48 hours. I mentioned to LP that he had two AR battalions under his civil control in Nagaland and if he could accept the risk of thinning them out for a short period, I could position two companies from each of them at Agartala by next morning. This was immediately approved by him.

I spoke to 'Baba' Katre, the AOC-in-C of Eastern Air Command. He acknowledged the seriousness of the situation and readily agreed to position two Dakotas at Dimapur by 0800 hrs the next morning to ferry the AR troops to Agartala. Thereafter, I rang up Brig K.D. Issar the DIG AR at Kohima, who was having dinner in 8 Mtn Div Mess and instructed him to get back to his HQ immediately and await my instructions. By now it was about 2200 hrs. I instructed Issar to send officers to various posts of 3 and 16 AR, wake up jawans and under command of Col Ahluwalia of 16 AR, position them at Dimapur Airport to be airlifted next morning to Agartala to provide support to Tripura

Government. Four Assam Rifles Coys; two from 3 AR and two from 16 AR under command of Lt Col Ahluwalia Comdt 16 AR were moved by Air from Dimapur to Agartala in April 1980 and placed at the disposal of Tripura Government to meet the developing situation. The immediate outbreak of riots was prevented though temporarily, as later in June, Mandi was engulfed in major riots and Army and additional para military forces were called in to restore peace. However, my role was viewed by the Army as one upmanship!

AR has a good football team and also some good boxers. The Army did not permit AR to take part in their tournaments as AR was not part of the Army. AR had to be content only by participating in local civil tournaments. As they needed an outlet to demonstrate their sporting talents, I took a decision to participate in all India Police tournaments and competitions, in which our sport teams, equestrian team, as also shooting team could participate and gain recognition.

In May 1981 Gen. K V Krishna Rao became the COAS and Lt. Gen. Vaidya became the GOC-in-C of Eastern Command. Gen. Krishna Rao was DCOAS, when I was his Deputy as Director Staff Duties at Army HQ in 1977-79. I visited HQ Eastern Command and briefed Gen Vaidya of the problems of Assam Rifles. I also briefed the COAS, about Assam Rifles and my personal difficulties. Gen. Vaidya later visited HQ DGAR at Shillong, the first Army Commander to do so. I was also instructed to organise a sand model discussion on the role of Assam Rifles, which was done at HQ DIG AR Arunachal Range (Brig Dewan) at Jorhat. This discussion was attended by the Army Commander himself and all Corps and Division Commanders of Eastern Command.

Earlier, my wife Neeru, was unwell for sometime and the Chief Medical Officer (CMO) of Meghalaya examined her on the instructions of the Governor. The CMO advised she be evacuated to Delhi and treated at Army Hospital. Capt Suresh Lalla, Army Medical Corps and his wife Capt Vijay Lalla, both of whom were on the staff of HQ DGAR took care of her and literally became part of our family. Later, the COAS visited Shillong and at the dinner hosted by the Governor at Raj Bhawan showed concern about the prolonged sickness of my wife and told her that she needed better medical care, which was not possible at Shillong. He also informed me that he had decided to revert me to the Army and since there was no vacancy at Army HQ, I was to be posted as Chief of Staff, Western Command, whose GOC-in-C Lt Gen S.K. Sinha had consented to accept me. L.P. Singh was reluctant to let me go, but considering my own and my wife's interest allowed me to go. I moved to Western Command at Simla in December 1981. With this an important and very productive phase of my career ended.

Some Current Concerns

At the time of writing this, I have learnt that a review of redeployment of para military forces in the Northeast by a Group of Ministers had decided that ITBP should take over the task of the Assam Rifles in Arunachal Pradesh. I consider this decision not to be in the interest of national security. It seems many important aspects have either not been put up to the GOM or if put up, have not been considered by them.

In 1950, Assam Rifles had assisted the Civil Administration in extending its control over the area and to oust 'dzongpens' of Tibet from Towang, who had been collecting taxes for long. Subsequently, over the years, Assam Rifles had won the affection and respect of the locals and were hailed as their friends. Their service and contribution during the great earthquake of 1950 had further endeared them to the locals and civil administration.

After the 1962 invasion by the Chinese in Arunachal

and consequent intense fighting AR had forged a close relationship with the Army. All Assam Rifles battalions and their sub-units are commanded by Army officers which lends greater strength to their relationship. Assam Rifles have been policing the Arunachal-Tibet border since 1950 and knew the area and its people well. Considering the sensitivities of the area and in the interest of national security, it would have been ideal, if Assam Rifles were allowed to continue to man the border.

In view of the above, it came as a surprise that they should be replaced by ITBP on the pretext that ITBP were already policing the remaining Indo-Tibet border i.e in UP, Himachal, and Ladakh. It is obvious that the decision was taken due to vested interests, with a view to expand the ITBP and provide greater career opportunities for their officer cadre. What surprised me most was that the Ministry of Defence and Army Headquarters accepted the decision. In the above context, I quote Maj Gen D. K. Palit Vrc, FRGS, the reputed military historian and military analyst wrote in the 'Sentinels of the North East-Assam Rifles', published in 1984.

> The unfortunate fact is that Assam Rifles continues to suffer from a feeling of insecurity about its future. Unlike the Army or even bodies of Police Forces, such as the BSF or CRPF, the Assam Rifles can claim no 'Godfather' among the powers that be. And this is because of the curious vicissitudes, which command and control aspect of the Force has experienced.

The second important aspect, which I would like to draw attention to is the composition of Assam Rifles. In the past, emphasis was put on recruiting men from Nepal (Gorkhas), India domiciled Gorkhas, locals from Nagaland and Assam and also other hill people from Garhwal/Kumaon/ Himachal. Signals personnel mainly came from the South while administrative personnel were local civilians. I learn that this had been radically changed to provide employment to men on all-India basis. It must be realised that hill people had over a century found better synergy with the locals, which had helped the Force to earn the sobriquet 'friends of hill people'. Even today, Northeast region is having a problem of assimilation with the mainstream of the nation and they look on the plains people with suspicion. In view of this, to change the character of this Force in our zeal to treat it as a mere source of employment at all India level was unwise, detrimental to national security and needs reconsideration.

ARPS Almuni Association

After my retirement, Lt General M.K. 'Mike' Lahiri of 4 GR, the then DGAR, invited me to visit the ARPS in September 1983 and present a Football Cup, which he named as "SUSHIL CUP". It was a most gratifying visit and I was assured that ARPS had a bright future.

In 2010, the old students formed an old students association, which they named Old Laitkorian Association (OLA) and requested me to attend their first AGM as the founder of the School. The approval from DGAR, which was necessary came too late. However, for their second AGM on 28 May, 2011, Col. Upadhyay commanding 315 Field Artillery Regiment (Kargil), invited me on behalf of OLA and I accepted it with the proviso that this be approved by their DGAR. The DGAR Lt Gen Rameshwar Roy (J&K Rifles) was quick to accord approval and his Asst Military Secretary Maj Pandit rang up to convey that I was most welcome and that they would make all the necessary arrangements. Abhijit, the President of OLA sent me a return air ticket. I along with my grand daughter Bhakti, (who was on summer holidays from her college) arrived in Guwahati on 26 May, 2011 and were received by Dy Comdt Dwivedi of AR, who guided me with a pilot jeep to the AR guest house. The guest house was 40 minutes drive from the airport and was most luxuriously furnished. Next morning on 27 May, we were to visit the famous Kamakhya Temple. At the Guest House, Col GS of HQ DGAR introduced me to his brother-in-law. I did not hear the name. However, I remarked, 'Your face looks very familiar and I seem to have met you'. Later, I was told that the person whom I had met was Rahul Dravid, the famous cricketer. I had a big laugh as even though I often see cricket matches on TV, I could not envisage Rahul being in Guwahati. On reaching the temple I apologised and said that this could be attributed to my old age! Thereafter, we did all the pooja and other religious ceremonies in the temple together. Rahul was with his wife, child and parents. Incidentally, soon thereafter our Indian cricket team visited South Africa, where Dravid played exceptionally well, perhaps due to blessings of 'Kamakhya Devi'! After the visit to the temple, we drove to Shillong. We were received by Maj Pandit and later Brig IC Admin, in the Officers' Mess. The whole set up of HQ DGAR, including the DG's residence had shifted from Laitumukhrah to Laitkor. This is a valley with low surrounding hills outside Shillong, where two Construction Companies and ARPS were located in my time. It is a very picturesque location and the Mess and the DGAR's residence are very tastefully furnished.

I stayed for two nights in the ARPS Mess. I made it a point to call on Madam Shulai, who was one of the members of the Governing Body of ARPS in 1980. She is now 90 years old and although confined to a wheel chair, she is still active and runs a charitable school in Shillong. She was delighted to meet me and called her family members to meet me. In the evening, members of the OLA briefed me about the programme next day. The function was held at the AR auditorium, which was attended by all members of OLA, and staff of DGAR. DGAR joined us later, as he had just returned from Delhi. In my address, I recalled the early days of struggle to build the school. I thanked the organizers for inviting me as their Chief Guest for their AGM. Later, I was conducted through the School premises. In the evening DGAR very kindly hosted a dinner for me. I left Shillong, the next morning, with nostalgic memories. Unfortunately, I could not meet any of my old civilian staff, due to shortage of time, though I did make many enquiries about them.

It is quite satisfying, when men from Assam Rifles even after 30 years of my departure often come and meet me. Similarly many former-students of Assam Rifles Public School, who are doing well in various professions, contact me to convey their appreciation for having started the School.

As a postscript, I must mention about the annual confidential report of DGAR. Prior to Maj Gen Chiman Singh becoming IGAR, annual reports used to be written by the Governor. This appointment was usually a terminal one and the General Officer holding this appointment invariably retired from here. L.P. Singh, the Governor, mentioned to Ministry of Defence and COAS that in future they should consider sending an officer, who had a future and not retire from this appointment. The Army felt that this was possible, if the IGAR was associated with Army exercises and discussions, so that the GOC-in-C Eastern Command could judge his professional capability and reflect this by initiating a manuscript report on the IGAR in addition to report by the Governor. The proposal was accepted by the Home Ministry and the Governor. Consequently, Eric Vas initiated a report on me commenting that I was 'unfit to hold the appointment of DGAR'. This was a bombshell and completely ignored the entire work I had done for the uplift of the AR. I naturally submitted a Statutory Appeal on that, which was backed to the hilt by the Governor. Ultimately, the aforesaid remark was expunged from the report and justice done to me.

13

Colonel 11 Gorkha Rifles

On 22 March, 1981, the First Day Cover for the Assam Rifles was released by the Chief Minister of Meghalaya at Headquarters Director General Assam Rifles, Shillong. On conclusion of the function I flew to Darjeeling to attend 11 GR Re-Union scheduled from 24 March to 27 March 1981 at Jalapahar. On arrival at Darjeeling helipad I was received by the Second-in-Command of 11 GRRC and taken to Jalapahar. I was informed that Col Goswami, the Commandant and Sub Maj had gone to Siliguri to receive Lt. Gen. R.D. Hira, Colonel of the Regiment. Hira was the GOC-in-C Southern Command. It snowed heavily that evening and traffic movement on the roads was extremely slow. Late at night on 23 March, Col Goswami and SM arrived in my room. On meeting me Goswami remarked 'thank God, Sir, at least you are here,' and informed me that Gen Hira was unwell and he was not coming. Therefore, I had to shoulder the responsibility of conducting the Re-Union.

Thus, I presided over the bi-annual conference and the Re-Union in 1981, when I was not Colonel of the Regiment. Strangely enough, when I became Colonel of the Regiment on 1 September, 1981, I had 18 months before retirement and the Centre was on the move from Jalapahar to Lucknow. Despite my best efforts, this move could not be completed prior to my retirement, and therefore, no bi-annual conference could be held in 1983. Very few officers and ex-servicemen attended the 1981 Re-Union due to inclement weather. Apparently March was not the right time to hold this event when the entire area was covered with snow. Brig N. Ghosh was the only senior retired officer who had the distinction of attending all the Re-Unions. Maj D.S. Khatri had come from Dharamshala, Maj M.B. Rai AC, MC, IDSM from Tuensang and Hony Capt Ganju Lama VC, MM, PD, from Sikkim. Army Postal Service released a First Day Cover during this occasion. On conclusion of the Re-Union, I gave a lift to Ganju Lama in my helicopter and dropped him in Gangtok. I also brought Maj Khatri and M.B. Rai with me to Shillong. They stayed as my personal guests in the Assam Rifles House for a week.

Gen Hira (Rocky) was to retire on 31 August 1981 and the new Colonel had to take over on 1 September. Since, the Centre was preparing to move to Lucknow, it was decided to give a farewell to Rocky at 3/11 Gorkha Rifles, located at Alwar (my home town). I was also invited to attend this function. I, accompanied by my staff officer Maj. R P Malhotra of 11 GR, attended this function. During my stay with the Battalion I heard disturbing rumours that Maj Gen Lachhman Rawat was being favoured to take over the Colonelship from Rocky. This would have been against the tradition of the young Regiment, according to which the seniormost officer normally took over as Colonel. However, during the dinner prior to dispersal, Rocky announced that after obtaining the views of all the Commanding Officers and senior officers and in keeping with the Regimental tradition, he had decided to recommend my name to the Army HQ, as the next Colonel of the Regiment. This was followed by congratulations from every one and I had to say a few words in response. It was destiny that I should be conferred this great honour at my home town, after nearly 40 years from the date I joined the Army as a Jawan in the same town.

When I took over as Colonel of 11 Gorkha Rifles on 1 September, 1981 I had just one year and eight months before retirement to work for the Regiment. I was not happy with the Centre administration and I invited Brig Pranab Dutt, who had taken over as Centre Commandant, to Shillong to visit 58 GTC and Assam Regt Trg Centre both of which were well organised and learn from them. Pranab, a dedicated soldier, set to work to reorganise the Centre, and his good work was further carried on by K.N. Nair when the Centre moved to Lucknow.

11 GRRC made four moves, since its raising on 1 January, 1948. It moved from Palampur to Clement Town, Dehradun, Clement Town to Ghanghora within Dehradun, Dehradun to Jalapahar (Darjeeling) and from Jalapahar to Lucknow. As a strategic review of location of strike forces of India and Pakistan, it was revealed that Pakistan reserve forces were located close to Indo-Pak border within easy strike distance, whereas Indian Army reserves were located far away from the border, which would take a few days to reach their battle locations to counter Pak moves. This was obviously an unsatisfactory and hazardous situation. However, various CsOAS (Chiefs of Army Staff) in the past could not displace training centres from Punjab, Himachal Pradesh, Haryana and Western UP to make way for strike forces to be located there, so that they were able to

reach their battle locations on the border swiftly. These training centres having been in their locations for long, had developed vast assets, their large number of ex-servicemen settled in close proximity, and thus had developed vested interests. Their serving and retired senior officers exerted pressure, whenever their move out was discussed.

It was Gen 'Tappy', T.N. Raina, the COAS in 1975, who placed national security interests above all and moved all the above training centres to the hinterland, thus making way for forward posture of field formations. As part of this plan, 11GRRC was moved to Jalapahar. It is not known as to why this was accepted by the Colonel of the Regiment at that time. However, Jalapahar was totally unsuitable for the training centre and there was a hue and cry, from all the old veterans of the Regiment. Due to altitude and inclement weather during most part of the year, recruit training was badly affected so much so that at the firing range, targets were usually not visible due to low clouds. Moreover, close proximity of the recruiting area (Darjeeling) was too uncomfortable and it affected discipline in the Centre. After I took over as Colonel, I explained the Centre's problems, to the then Chief Gen K.V.R. Krishna Rao, who promised to examine the matter. He later visited the Centre, along with Lt Gen Vaidya, GOC-in-C Eastern Command and was convinced that the place was not suitable for a training centre. He approved the move of the Centre from Jalapahar to Lucknow, which was to everybody's satisfaction in the Regiment.

During my tenure as Colonel of the Regiment, I visited all the battalions and tried to solve their problems to the best of my ability. I particularly remember my visit to my old battalion 5/11 GR commanded by Abjeet Mamik, at Uttarkashi. They were celebrating Bogra Day in great style and almost all the ex-COs as also Gen Bewoor attended the function. Abjeet put up a great show and the whole function was well organised. Abjeet used to be my Adjutant during 1965 Indo-Pak war and thereafter was ADC to Gen Bewoor. He had fought a gallant action in Bangladesh, under the dynamic command of Col Dick Dias (later Lt. Gen.) for which he was awarded VrC.There was plenty of liquor flowing as per the tradition of the Battalion, which led to some unsavoury behaviour by some officers during the function; however, this was soon forgotten.

I must mention a word about the history of the Regiment. Several attempts were made in the past to write it and a number of officers were deputed on different occasions to carry out the task, but due to inexplicable reasons it could not be completed. My experience with the recording of history of Assam Rifles had shown that it was better to assign the task to a professional historian. After discussion, with some officers, I approached Col Gautam Sharma, who was a Fellow of the Indian Council of Historical Research and had a number of military history books to his credit and was well respected in literary circles. I found Col Sharma receptive to the idea of writing our regimental history. In case of Assam Rifles, Gen Palit had agreed to write the history only if the material was collected by Assam Rifles and placed before him. However, it was to the credit of Col Sharma that he agreed to meet all senior retired officers and selected senior JCOs and also visited the Centre and Battalions to collect and collate the material and thereafter, put it in proper shape. He put in tremendous efforts for five years and the result was a fine publication *Path of Glory*, which was released by my successor Lt Gen Lachhman Rawat in 1988.

Prior to my retirement, I visited the Centre, which was still at Jalapahar and during Sainik Sammelan ceremonially handed over the Colonel of the Regiment to Lachhman Rawat, who had earlier taken over from me the command of 5/11 GR. I was ceremonially dined out at Officers Mess and given a memorable send off.

14

Chief of Staff Western Command

Western Command is India's Strike Command. The staff was all selected and proficient. I had known Gen Sinha, the Army Commander, for nearly three decades and had an excellent rapport with him. I had one year and four months to retire and this period was enough to make some contribution to the Command. We were housed in Knockdrin, on the Mall, next to Command House. This was a historical bungalow and many VIPs, during the British days had stayed in it.* I was also Colonel of 11 GR and needed some help to look after the problems of the Regiment. I took Capt K.V.S. Lalotra from 2 /11 GR as a staff officer. He proved to be a great asset during my tenure. I also got Col Kashyap of 11 GR as Colonel GS, he provided good support to me, both in regimental matters and in operational matters. Kashyap later retired as Maj. Gen. and Colonel of 11 GR. Gugi Vohra from Armoured Corps was my Maj. Gen. GS, who later became a Lt Gen and retired as GOC-in-C Central Command. Maj Gen J.D. Datta was MG IC Adm, who on retirement became my permanent member in the foursome of Delhi Golf Club. In fact all Arms and Services Advisers picked up their ranks and retired as heads of their respective arms and services, which reflects the high calibre they all possessed. While Gen. Sinha was busy in operational matters and touring a lot, I took on his administrative load.

The top floor of Command Office was burnt some time ago and works were sanctioned to reconstruct it. I discovered that central heating was not included in the works. I found this very strange as the Himachal Pradesh Secretariat and other important buildings in Simla were already centrally heated. The climate of the area warranted this facility for efficient working conditions. I had to work hard to convince the QMG, who was an engineer himself and also the Ministry of Defence that this provision was essential. Ultimately this was sanctioned. I revamped the Command Canteen and organised daily fresh supplies from the DID to entitled officers. A mobile canteen was introduced to tour certain areas adjacent to Simla which had large concentration of ex-servicemen. Lalotra, my staff officer, belonged to Himachal,

* This included people like: Col. H. K. Burne, Military Secretary; Maharaja of Faridkot; Sir Mortimer Durand, Foreign Secretary, after whom the Football tournament is named; and Sir A.U. Fanshawe, Post Master General.

hailing from an Army family. I had attended his wedding. I also attended the wedding of Capt Patial my old ADC, when I was DG Assam Rifles. Both weddings were performed in traditional Himachali style. Capt Lalotra, an outstanding officer, did well in service and was approved to become a Lt. General but had to retire as Maj Gen. unfortunately there were no vacancies to accommodate him as Lt. General before his due date of retirement. Lalotra is currently the Principal of the prestigious Mayo College, Ajmer.

Operational plans and particularly the movement plans for troops to battle locations were continuously updated. It was felt that HQ Western Command was not suitably located to control operations on the Western Front and there was need to create an Advanced HQ, located at Bhatinda, from where the GOC-in-C could visit any active formation he wished and return to his HQ in the evening. This was not possible from Simla due to unpredictability of weather conditions. An underground nucleus of Advance HQ Western Command was developed with all communication facilities at Bhatinda. This was tested by carrying out an exercise of moving the necessary elements of HQ Western Command from Simla to Bhatinda and operating from that location for a few days. Subsequently, HQ Western Command moved from Simla to Chandimandir, thus obviating the necessity of establishing an Advance HQ.

This was the time when Bhindrawale was in the news and he, along with his military adviser Maj Gen (Retd) Shabegh Singh of 11 GR had taken shelter in Akal Takht at Harminder Sahib, Amritsar. I visited Harminder Sahib in 1982 and was welcomed by the Head Granthi and offered a Siropao. The situation in Punjab was tense and conditions were developing for a home made insurgency. At this juncture a DIG Police Mr Atwal was assassinated on the steps of Harminder Sahib. This was an ominous sign. There was lot of sustained propaganda by vested interests, about injustice to the Sikhs by the Congress Government. Some Sikh officers in our HQ also felt that assassination of Atwal was perhaps engineered by the Government to find an excuse to assault their main holy shrine! This was disturbing and Gen Sinha wrote to Army HQ that we should take measures to make the troops aware of the true facts of the situation, in order to avoid disaffection amongst them. In retrospect, it appears that adequate steps were not taken early enough to assure the Sikh troops that nothing would be done to hurt their religious sentiments.

I must relate an interesting incident which occurred three months before I took over as Chief of Staff, which shows how the Civil Administration depends on Armed Forces to pull their chestnuts out of fire in a crisis. During my briefing, I was informed that when Lala Jagat Narain, the founder of the Punjab Kesari was assassinated in September 1981, Bhindranwale was suspected to have planned it and his arrest warrants were issued. Bhindranwale, with his followers heavily armed took shelter in Gurudwara at Mehta Chowk and fortified and barricaded it. Gen. Krishna Rao, the COAS, was out of the country on an official tour while Lt Gen Sinha, the Army Commander, was on tour to Bikaner. In the absence of Gen Sinha from Headquarters, my predecessor Lt. Gen. J.K. Puri was holding the Fort at Simla. Ministry of Defence asked Army Headquarters to issue instructions to HQ Western Command to arrest Bhindranwale and hand him over to Punjab Government. Gen Puri passed these orders to HQ 11 Corps at Jalandhar. Meanwhile, Chief Secretary of Punjab spoke to Gen Sinha who was on his way to Simla and made a similar request. Gen Sinha told the Chief Secretary that it was not the job of the Army, and they had Punjab Police, Punjab Armed Police and CRPF, who should be used for the task. Chief Secretary then asked Sinha if Army could lend them the services of two tanks for this task. Gen Sinha found the request amusing and told the Chief Secretary that use of tank was highly technical needing specialized training and, therefore, it could not be accepted. On reaching his Headquarters at Simla he discussed the matter with Puri and asked him to cancel the orders issued to 11 Corps and also inform the Army Headquarters accordingly. Meanwhile Bhindranwale was persuaded to surrender himself, which he did on 20 September, 1981.

Gen. Krishna Rao, the COAS visited Simla before his retirement. The COAS very graciously accepted my request to have cocktails at our residence 'Knockdrin' which adjoined Command House. Gen Sinha was also present. In my presence, the Chief informed Sinha that he was being moved to Delhi as Vice COAS to enable him to get into broader picture on an All-India basis, which would smoothen his way to the top position. Gen. Sinha moved to Delhi, as VCOAS and Gen Sundarji was appointed as GOC-in-C Western Command. Later, on retirement of Gen Krishna Rao, Sinha was superseded by Gen Vaidya, who was appointed as COAS by the Government. Sinha put in his papers, which later became a political issue. Sinha felt that Krishna Rao, though a very close friend and having clearly mentioned to him that he would succeed him, had stabbed him in the back, as he was interested to secure governorship after retirement. This led to considerable animosity between the two. When I attended the Assam Rifles 150th Anniversary in Shillong in 1984, Krishna Rao was the Governor and sent word to me that I should meet him before departing for Delhi. I always had highest regard for him and met him at the Raj Bhawan, over a cup of tea, before my departure. During our conversation, he particularly mentioned Sinha's supersession, when he was VCOAS. He knew that I was close to Sinha and whatever he mentioned to me would be invariably conveyed to Sinha and might clear some tension, between the two of them. It was of course well known that beauracrats would not favour Sinha as the Chief and would manoeuver to supersede him. According to Krishna Rao, the PM, Mrs Indira Gandhi called him one day and asked him to send her the comparative profiles of Sinha and Vaidya. Vaidya had a good war record having been awarded MVC and bar for having commanded an armoured Regt. in 1965 and an Armoured Bde in 1971 Indo-Pak wars. Sinha did not have war experience, though he had an outstanding record. Krishna Rao made a comparative chart and sent it to Mrs Gandhi. This was enough to justify the appointment of Vaidya as COAS and thus supersede Sinha. They both had the same date of commission. Krishna Rao felt that he had nothing to do with the supersession of Sinha and this was purely a political decision.

Sinha was a keen student of history and came from an illustrious police family of Bihar. He was zealously pushing the case of protocol and pay and allowance of Defence Officers vis-à-vis IAS officers. It was known that the IAS lobby did not want Sinha to become the Chief and manipulated the matter accordingly. In this context I must mention an interesting episode. The Army Commander in Simla used to hold a civil-military liaison conference, in which all Chief Secretaries of the concerned States were invited. States concerned were Himachal Pradesh, Haryana, Punjab, Delhi, Union Territory of Chandigarh and Rajasthan. A major event was a dinner hosted by the Governor on the occasion of the Civil Military Liason conference, during my tenure as COS (1981-1983). According to prevailing protocol, a Lt. General was senior to a Chief Secretary, outside his state. We learnt that the seating arrangement at Governor's dinner was not according to this protocol and all Chief Secretaries, other than the one from Himachal Pradesh were accorded seniority over Lt. Generals (Chief of Staff and Corps Commanders). Gen Sinha sent a message to the Chief Secretary of Himachal that he would not attend the dinner if the situation was not rectified and sure enough the protocol was rectified accordingly! Gen Sinha later became our Ambassador in Nepal, during the Janata Government and then Governor of Assam. He was shifted to J&K as Governor and was only one appointed by NDA who was not asked to leave by the Congress Government, headed by Man Mohan Singh. Sinha did a marvelous job in all his assignments and did the Army and the Gorkhas proud.

During my tenure as Chief of Staff, Western Command, I had the good fortune to meet LP Singh on more than one occasion. One day LP rang up to convey that he and his wife wished to come to Simla and spend a few days with us. His particular interest was a Yogi who had developed reputation for curing heart disease through 'pranayam'. I checked the address he had given me and found the Yogi living in Chhota Simla in a dilapidated house, surrounded by some Europeans. The Yogi indicated some of his disciples, who were bad heart cases but could now go down the steep mountain slope into the valley and return without losing their breath! I conveyed my impression to LP. He and his wife came and stayed with us for 14 days. The Yogi was invited to our house to give a demonstration of some 'Pranayam' (breathing) exercises to LP, who was thoroughly impressed. LP was requested by the Governor of Himachal Pradesh (Bannerji) to be his guest at the Raj Bhavan, which he politely declined, and preferred to stay with us. LP and his wife often waited for my younger daughter Reena to return from her School before sitting down for lunch. During their stay we further strengthened our relationship and personally benefited from his vast knowledge and experience. On the second occasion, he stayed with us in Jaipur, where I was Director of Pratap Rajasthan Special Steel Ltd. After my retirement, he had come to deliver a lecture at Rajasthan University.

Gen Sundarji got married the second time, just before coming to Simla as GOC-in-C Western Command in

January 1983. He and his wife Vani were ceremonially received at Annadale helipad. We hosted a lunch for them at Knockdrin. Vani was so impressed by the quality of food in our house that she often requested Neeru for certain dishes. It appeared, however, that Sundarji was in the mood to have a second honeymoon and for quite some time, he did not visit the office. After much persuation, he agreed to meet the officers of Command HQ and also address them. Prior to his move to Army HQ, Gen Sinha had planned a major exercise with troops named Dig Vijay. Sundarji for the next few months devoted most of the time revising and then conducting the exercise. This formed the basis of his much discussed Operation Brasstacks in 1986-87, when he became the COAS. On my part, I hardly spent time with him (Sundarji) as soon after I retired on 1 May, 1983.

I was replaced by Lt. Gen. R.S. Dayal MVC as Chief of Staff. Operation Bluestar was undertaken about a year, after I retired. Lt Gen Sunderji, as Army Commander and Lt Gen Dayal as his COS planned and carried out the operation, under the orders of Mrs Indra Gandhi, the Prime Minister, which led to far reaching repercussions in the Army and in the entire country.

Alwar Revisited

During one of my visits to Jaipur and while returning from there by Shatabdi Express to Delhi in 1982, I met Mr A.S. Sekon by chance. He was resident of Alwar and was Deputy Superintendent Police. He was also an alumnus of RR College, Alwar. We started discussing about the College as I had spent three years in it from 1939 to 1942. He mentioned that the College had completed its 50 years but was unable to celebrate Golden Jubilee due to various reasons. He requested if I could, as an alumnus of the College, organise this event. He mentioned that the Students Union was strong and potential trouble makers. I promised to consider his proposal if formally requested by the College Principal. On return to Simla, I received a letter from the Principal, Mrs. Sharma, requesting me if I could consider shouldering the responsibility to organise Golden Jubilee of the College. I informed her that I would visit Alwar to discuss the proposal with her and students to asses the possibility of celebrating the Golden Jubilee. I visited Alwar on 13 August, 1982 where Mr Sekon and the College laid a grand reception for me. I was guided to the Circuit House, Sekon personally acting as a pilot. A number of important citizens met me. My relatives were happy and the local papers published lead articles about me with photographs. I visited the College and addressed the students. They were delighted at my initiatives and promised all cooperation. We formed a Steering Committe to chalk out the programme and oversee the arrangements. On return to Simla, I wrote to the Secretary of the President of India requesting the President of India to inaugurate the function. He advised that the request should be routed through the State Government. I met the Chief Secretary of Rajasthan and he agreed to write to the President's Sectt, which he did on 3 November, 1982 requesting the President to inaugurate the function on 18 December and spend time from 1100 hrs to 1430 hrs. and have lunch with the staff and old students. The detailed programme was drawn up for a three day celebration.

I made another visit to Alwar and was advised that there may be some problem from the Art College and also the incumbent MP Mr Ram Singh Yadav, who wanted a prominent role in the celebrations. Mrs Satyavati Sharma the Principal, was keen that Yadav should be given the place of honour in organising the celebrations. I felt that too much politics had crept in and celebrations would not be a smooth affair as too many agencies were involved. On return to Simla I wrote to Sekon and the Principal that due to heavy official commitments I should be excused and Ram Singh

Yadav could handle the event. They were disappointed and protested, but I stuck to my decision. Later, I learnt that the Golden Jubilee was not held at all.

Before my retirement the family got together at 'Knockdrin'. Pravin came from Calcutta, where he had joined his schoolmate Ashok Sen to start a Marketing Company. Ranjana and Col Yadu Kumar came from Delhi as the latter was posted at HQ Delhi Area and Ashutosh came from UK where he was doing CA. My cousin Mahinder Joshi and his wife Usha (Neeru's younger sister) also joined us. We had an enjoyable time together, while I was still in service.

I hung up my uniform on the evening of 30 April, 1983 and joined the fold of 'ex-service men'. I left Knockdrin, my residence on the morning of 1 May 1983. All senior officers of Command HQ and Sunderji and his wife Vani were there to see us off. There were some civilian friends also to bid us good bye. We travelled in our fiat car to Delhi. At Chandigarh, we had lunch with our friend Maj Gen Rajender Nath of our Regiment and his affectionate wife Krishna. They welcomed us to the 'veterans fold'. It was indeed a memorable 41 years tenure in the Army, which I and my family cherished.

15

My First Experience with the Industry

During one of my official visits to Amritsar, I had met Mr Partap Maheshwari, the Managing Director of Partap Steel, on the golf course. I was due to retire soon. He asked me what my plans were after retirement. I admitted I had not given it a thought. He mentioned to me that they were planning to set up a steel mill in Singapore and they were looking for a Chief Executive who could take care of it. They were four brothers and had mills at Amritsar, Mandi Govind Garh, Ballabhgarh, Indore and Hyderabad. None of the brothers could leave India and, therefore, there was a need to find an individual of integrity, on whom they could depend. He asked me whether I would consider joining them and go to Singapore. I agreed to consider the offer.

On return to Simla, I discussed it with Neeru and with Pravin my eldest son, who felt that there was no harm in joining them. I told Partap that I had no experience about steel. He felt that this aspect would be taken care of by engineers and I would be required to oversee the whole venture and as such lack of experience about steel would not be a disadvantage.

Senior Central Government employees cannot join private firms on retirement without permission of the Government. I, therefore, applied to Army HQ. Gen Krishna Rao was the COAS and he quickly approved my request. Prior to retirement, I visited our defence foundry at Muradnagar to acquaint myself with various aspects of Steel Industry. I got a written offer from Partap, who requested me to visit Amritsar after retirement. I retired on 1 May, 1983. After reaching Delhi, I dumped my stuff with Raj Rif Centre and Neeru and Reena stayed with my elder daughter Ranjana and her husband Col Yadu Kumar, who was still posted in HQ Delhi Area. Reena was admitted in DPS, R.K. Puram. I visited Amritsar and stayed there for a month to familiarise myself with Partap Steel. There after, along with P.N. Vijay of Standard Chartered Bank, a merchant banker, I proceeded to Singapore where Partap's proposed company was allotted an industrial plot. We stayed in a five Star Hotel, (Oberoi). Vijay's task was to arrange a Bank loan, while I was required to finalise the formalities of setting up an industry with the Singapore Government.

I called on our High Commissioner Prem Bhatia, the reputed journalist, who infomed me that Singapore was a free market economy and unlike India, there were no controls nor any license required to set up an industry. My meeting with officials of Singapore Government was very fruitful and it took no time to get all the sanctions. Partap and his elder brother Amin Chand visited Singapore to take stock of the situation. Singapore had one National Steel Mill, which was not doing well. The entire steel requirement of Singapore was being met by import from Japan. It was clear that the proposed company would face a fierce competition from the Japanese steel exporters. Indian entreprenuers were used to the license raj and regulated market in India, which thrived on black economy and bribes. The Company had an arrangement with a Swiss firm to get an electric furnace for steel making. The rolling mill was to be exported to Singapore from India, which was made on outdated technology. It was obvious that production in terms of quality and pricing would not be a match with Japanese steel firms. On return to India, Pratap and his elder brother Amin Chand reviewed the project and asked us (Mr P N Vijay and myself) to return to India for consultation. We had stayed in Singapore for nearly three months.

On return to India, I was informed that the Maheshwari brothers had decided not to go ahead with the project in Singapore and I was to return to Singapore and close the project. Since I had joined Partap Steel for the proposed Singapore project, I was now mentally prepared to leave them. They requested me one day to meet them at the Air Force Golf Course. Amin Chand (the eldest brother), Partap, and Prakash (the youngest brother) were present. They conveyed to me that they were not happy about my leaving them. They, therefore, suggested that they had two running projects in Jaipur and I should visit these factories. After my visit and discussion with Prakash Maheshwari, the youngest brother told me that I could join them as their Executive Director there. Since, I had no other plans, I agreed. They provided accommodation, a car with driver and a reasonable salary. Till I got a house, I was to stay in Hotel Ashoka Jaipur, where Neeru also joined me.

I was asked to look after Partap Rajasthan Special Steel Ltd. as Executive Director. Prakash Maheshwari would come to the office for a short time daily while I looked after the entire administration and marketing. The firm had electric furnaces and rolling mill. They were producing ingots and rolled steel. Prakash generally dealt with the General Manager directly, took stock of production and sale. He spent most of the time looking after Partap Copper Foil Ltd. I found that the Company was being run as a family concern and not professionally. I was unhappy, but could not do anything about it. Prakash and his brothers, along with their families were always respectful and treated us like a family. Prakash was mild mannered, soft spoken and a friendly person, with cordial relations with officials in the Rajasthan Government.

Our stay in Jaipur was enjoyable. Jaipur at that time (in 1983-1986) had a small cantonment, with a Sub Area Headquarter and a Brigade. Our 1/11 GR was also located there for some time and we attended all their functions. There were some retired 11 GR officers, who met us frequently and helped us to settle down. Maj. Gen. Dick Dias of 11 GR was commanding 12 Inf Div at Jodhpur and when he visited Jaipur officially, he called on us. Two of our old friends, Lt Gen. Sagat Singh and Lt Gen Kundan Singh were also in Jaipur and we often met them. Some of my relatives were also settled in Jaipur, specially two younger brothers and some cousins. Neeru got a teacher's job in Maharani Gayatri Devi Public School and made friends with the Principal and some other teachers. We occasionaly met Maharaja Bhawani Singh, former ruler and also Maharani Gayatri Devi. We also became quite friendly with Dr S.K. Sharma, Prof of Cardiology in SMS Hospital, a delightful person, who would often drop in at odd hours, unannounced and keep us entertained. One day, L.P. Singh (former Governor of Assam, Meghalaya, Nagaland, Tripura and Manipur) my old mentor rang up that he was being invited to give a lecture in Rajasthan University and would like to stay with us. We were delighted. Governor of Rajasthan Air Chief

Marshal Mehra wanted LP to stay with him in Raj Bhawan, but he politely declined and preferred to stay with us. We went along with him to attend his lecture, and also to Raj Bhawan, to attend the dinner hosted in his honour by the Governor ACM Mehra. Mrs Krishna Sahi, MP, our old friend and a prominent member of the Congress also visited Jaipur and invited us to attend all the functions, connected with her visit, and she introduced us to some important political leaders. Pravin, my eldest son's wedding was celebrated in DSOI Delhi. He got married to Bharati Tawakaley of Delhi, the sister of a very close friend of my younger son Ashu. Their reception was held in Rambagh Palace Hotel Jaipur and was well attended.

Copper Foil Co was not doing well and was suffering losses. After two years with Partap Steel, Prakash Maheswari wanted me to help him in Copper Foil. Technology for this company was taken from East Germany by RFC (Rajasthan Finance Corporation) without market survey and without consultation with Prakash. The Copper Foil project was selected by the Rajasthan Financial Corporation. Prakash Maheswari was requested by the RFC to adopt the project and implement it as his own.He could have declined, but preferred not to do so, as declining it could have negatively impacted his other ventures, supported by the RFC. An agreement was signed with the German company and Prakash was requested to undertake the venture, and was literally forced into it. The technology was outdated and the copper foil produced did not match with the Bakalite product being manufactured in India; consequently, there were serious marketing problems faced by the company. Bakalite continued to import copper foil as the one manufactured by Partap did not match their size. This was because of the failure of RFC in not carrying out a survey before importing new technology. We tried to persuade the Ministry of Electronics to stop the import, but their answer was that we should modify our product to suit the bakelite, before they could impose any ban. Meanwhile, an American gentleman from San Francisco, came to visit the factory and took two rolls of copper foil, with a promise that he would organise its export to USA. Nothing was heard from him for long. A couple of Indian technocrats from USA also visited us and undertook the modification of the machines, to produce the suitable size of foil and also carry out zinc coating. However, this was not wholly satisfactory. All this time the factory's debt was mounting.

Prakash now asked me to visit USA to extract payment of foil, taken by the American gentleman and also visit the original manufacturer of machines in East Berlin to explore if they could do something to modify the machines. I took Neeru and Reena with me at our cost on the trip. The visit to San Francisco was in vain as the gentleman had declared bankruptcy. Our visit to East Berlin also did not produce any result, as that was the time when East and West Germany were about to be merged. I also visited Budapest and Prague to explore markets, but without any success. However, my visit to the Isola factory at Dusseldrof was a success and they showed keen desire to collaborate with us to produce a marketable product. However, by the time I returned, the factory was in heavy debt and Prakash showed no interest in the proposal. I thought that for me time had come to leave the company.

While in Simla, I had been allotted a flat in Som Vihar in south Delhi, a colony developed by Army Welfare Housing Organisation. A deposit of Rs. 35000 was required, which I managed through a loan from UCO Bank. This I paid off only after my retirement from the gratuity money. The remaining cost was paid from a loan from HDFC. While in Jaipur I was informed by one property agent by name Bagga that Ruksana, the mother of Amrita Singh the famous actress and an old friend of Sanjay Gandhi from

Emergency days, was keen to hire my flat in Som Vihar. We were reluctant to give the flat to her. She was living in a flat of DLF Building, near Connaught Place, which was due to be demolished. She insisted on meeting us. During our next visit to Delhi, we met Ruksana, who pleaded with us that she had nowhere to go and DLF wanted to throw her out. Ultimately, we agreed to rent out the flat to her. She never paid rent in time and had to be reminded. At the time of leaving the flat, she did not pay two month's rent. I casually mentioned this to a correspondent of *Filmfare* magazine, who published it in their next issue. Ruksana's daughter Amrita, who had become a film star, sued the magazine. The magazine requested me to come to Mumbai and meet their advocate. Ruksana also made wild charges against the magazine and me, but I had her bounced cheques with me, which could not be refuted. I also filed a case in Tis Hazari Court Delhi to recover the unpaid rent. Ruksana never appeared in court and the judge was furious with her advocate. Subsequently, news came that Ruksana was no more and, thereafter, I considered it prudent not to pursue the case any further.

In 1986, Ashu, my younger son informed me that he would return to India soon. Despite best efforts his work visa was not extended. I had to think of his settlement. As I mentioned earlier, I was unhappy with the way Pratap Steel was being managed and I therefore resigned from Partap Steel in 1986. The parting was quite cordial and they were sorry for me to go.

Since I had acquired some experience in the steel sector, though not in intricacies of marketing, I decided to set up a small factory based on electric furnace at Bhiwadi, where the government was giving a good subsidy. The aim was to start producing ingots immediately and then switch over to foundry. We engaged Mr Varshney, as consultant. Rajasthan State Finance Corporation and also Rajasthan

Industrial Development Corporation went out of their way to help us in completing all the formalities. Similarly electric connection was also obtained, without much difficulty. All this despite the rumours that heavy bribe has to be paid at every step to get various sanctions.

Bhiwadi was just developing and we easily got a good industrial plot. The main equipment was a 1.5 ton electric induction furnace. Mr O.P. Kalra, my old staff officer from Assam Rifles also joined me as a partner. Ashu put in tremendous effort in getting the construction done and the machinery installed. He used to commute from Jaipur to Bhiwadi and back almost every second day. Banks also helped us with required loans. By the time the factory was ready for production, we shifted from Jaipur to our own flat in Som Vihar, Delhi, in 1987.

We were very happy and proud of this venture and were hopeful that it would progress and help the family. Unfortunately, we had not catered to the unforeseen problems. Further, there was no one in the family or friends to advise us. Pravin, my elder son was just beginning to settle down in marketing business in Kolkata. From the time of commencement of production, we faced numerous problems; electricity supply was erratic, there was massive theft of power by all the industries in Bhiwadi and Delhi, Excise and Sales inspectors were encouraging evasion of tax and sharing the gains, and the electric furnace though supplied by General Electric often required repairs and this disrupted production. Due to all this, we started incurring losses. I tried to carry out a campaign with the Lt Governor in Delhi and Chairman, Delhi Electricity Board to stop the power theft but to no avail. There were as many as 60 companies in Delhi, operating with electric furnace, which used to work during night and close down during day. Their production was disposed of before daybreak. Electicity staff connived with power theft and had a share in the profit.

These producers thus sold the product at a low price and still made handsome unaccountable profit. We could not compete with them. Perhaps, we had selected the wrong line. I guess we also alienated some furnace owners as they felt that I was harming their interest.

We were advised by various friends that we had to adopt the business practices followed by others for survival. Somehow, we could not adapt ourselves to these typical unethical practices. As we had no experience, we were taken for a ride by some unscurpulous people on the promise that they would help us get out of the mess. The factory remained closed for some time and as a result the company accumulated further losses. The electricity department also filed a case against our factory for alleged theft of power. We fought the case and after several hearings, over a long period of nearly nine years, we won the case in the year 2000. This was a great relief. We luckily found a buyer for the factory. He was one Mr. Agarwal from Lucknow, who was running a foundry successfully, with some export commitments. We revealed all the debts and problems of the company to him, yet he insisted on making a deal. We found Agarwal a thorough gentleman, in every way, which is unusual in business. After the disposal of the factory our relations with him continued to be close, cordial and friendly. We came to know later that he was able to run the factory quite well.

My elder son Pravin advised that under the prevailing business atmosphere in our country, it was not advisable for senior defence officers to launch themselves into business ventures. I, therefore, decided not to think of any business enterprise hereafter. I had served the country long enough and it was time to relax, do some charity work and follow spiritual pursuits. With this my foray in industry ended.

HMT Enquiry Committee

One day in 1994, I was contacted by Neeru's friend Mrs Krishna Sahi. The Congress veteran, who was then Minister of State for Industries. She asked me if I was free to do an assignment with the Government. She mentioned that Congress MP Malikarjun from Bangalore had been complaining about various problems in HMT and she had decided to constitute an enquiry committee to investigate these allegations. HMT was suffering losses. Mrs Sahi wanted me to become a member of the Enquiry Committee. I agreed. After a few days I got the Government order, constituting this committee with Mr V.K.J. Menon, IAS as Chairman and myself as a member. The other member was the Security Officer of the HMT, an IPS officer. Menon was a retired IAS officer and ex-Chief Secretary of Bihar. The report was to be submitted in three months. I along with Menon made several trips to Bangalore for discussions with HMT officials and also visited various departments of the factory.

At one time, HMT was a leading manufacturer of watches in India, in collaboration with Japan. Many executives and engineers had left and joined Titan of the Tatas. HMT factories were set up to create jobs in certain areas like J&K and Uttarakhand without taking into consideration the location of raw material, markets and availability of skilled labour. This was one of the reasons for increased cost of production. Further, technology and machines imported from Japan were not updated. Inventory management was poor and marketing lacked imagination. The labour unions were strong and production per man-hour was deplorable. Menon asked me to enquire into production problems. During one of the visits to a production unit the manager offered a golden watch with a golden chain as a gift which I declined and mentioned this to Menon. We did a thorough job of it and the report was submitted to Mrs Krishna Sahi in time. As happens with most reports submitted to the Government, no concrete action was taken on this report. However, for me it was on educative assignment and I enjoyed working with Menon.

Earthquake in Maharashtra

While playing golf in the Delhi Golf Club, I met Mr Jagdish Anand from the Anand Group, who manufactured the popular Gabriel Shock Absorbers. We became good friends and often played golf together. Once he casually mentioned that they were running some charitable organizations and asked me, whether I would be interested in helping him. I told him that I would not mind, but I would not be interested in any remuneration. They were keen to start a sports academy at Nasik, where their main factory was located (the factory is still there). I made several trips and also had discussions with the Sports Authority of India, but somehow the idea of the Sports Academy did not work out. I also visited Parwanoo (Himachal Pradesh) with him several times and discussed various projects for Himachal Pradesh, including taking over Golf Course at Annadale. Meanwhile, there was a massive earthquake in Maharashtra on 3 September 1993 at 0356 hours. Primarily, the districts of Latur and Osmanabad were affected. The earthquake measured 7.4 on the Ritcher scale; some 20,000 people died and about 30,000 were reported injured. In Latur alone, 52 villages were razed to ground. Massive aid poured in from all quarters, including foreign countries. The Anands were also keen to make some contribution to the relief operations, after the national calamity. Jagdish asked me to examine the type of aid and the quantum which they should donate.

I met Mr K.S. Sidhu, Secretary, Government of Maharashtra at Mumbai, who advised me to meet the Collector of Osmanabad, for whom he provided the reference. I also met Maj Gen R. Mohan, GOC, M & G Area,

Mumbai, who wrote to Collector Latur (Pravin Pardeshi, IAS). My friend Sushil Gupta, MD Hyatt Regency Hotel, Delhi also provided a reference to Rotarian Dr. Gunjotikar of Solapur, (Rotarian District 3130), who was already doing some relief work in Salegaon. I made several visits to Solapur, Latur, Osmanabad and Omerga and met all the persons concerned. It was a heart rendering sight to see the villages, completely flattened and not a single house being left in the affected area. Mr Sidhu had agreed that Anand could contribute towards construction of a school and a community hall at Salegaon, district Osmanabad. On one of the trips, I also took some students from St. Bedes College and Bishop Cotton School (Simla) to acquaint them with the extent of damage in the area so that they and their institutions could also contribute towards rehabilitation of the area. Subsequently, some contributions did come in. Finally, it was decided to assign the construction of a school and a community hall to Rotary District Governor Dr Gunjotkar, costing about Rs 7 lacs and sponsored by the Anand group. The foundation was laid by Mr Jagdish Anand of the Anand Group in January 1994. This was a very satisfying assignment for which I took only 'out of pocket expenses' from the Anands. I was soon to be involved actively in Gangotri Conservation Project and, therefore, I informed Jagdish that I would not be able to devote any more time for his welfare projects. However, we continued to be friends and met occasionally till his death in February 2014.

Personal Bereavement

My father (Babu Ji) had passed away in 1982, at Mathura, at the age of 82, when I was still in service. Thereafter my mother, (affectionately referred to by everyone as Jiji) stayed at Vrindaban with my younger brother Prakash for a year. After my retirement from the Army in 1983, she joined us at Jaipur, where I had taken up an assignment with Rajasthan Partap Steels. She subsequently moved with us to Delhi in

1988. At 90 plus, she had no major health problems. We shifted in 1991, from Som Vihar to a large and comfortable duplex flat in Vasant Kunj, where my mother had a room to herself on the upper floor. My younger son Ashu and his wife Gauri took good care of her. I used to spend a few hours with her daily. On 2 December, 1996, my mother called me and complained about severe pain in her stomach. I called the family doctor, who gave her medicines and also a pain killer injection but she got no relief. She was then shifted to Army Hospital on the morning of 3 December 1996. She was diagnosed with blockage in the intestine. She expired in the evening the same day and was cremated at Nigam Bodh Ghat on the banks of the Yamuna the next day. She was 92 years old and had been the greatest inspiration, motivator and cheerleader throughout my life. Needless to say, her departure left a void in my life.

16

Involvement with Conservation and other Activities

Gangotri Conservation Project

It is interesting that golf has been instrumental in getting me involved in various charitable activities. Capt M.S. Kohli, my golfing partner, and Chairman Himalayan Environment Trust (HET), who had led the Indian assault on Everest in 1965, requested me if I would be interested in doing some work for improving the environment of the Himalayas. This was in 1994. I was in good health and offered my services to the HET in an honorary capacity. Trustees of HET, who were all legendary mountaineers, like Sir Edmund Hillary, M.S. Kohli, Reinhold Messner, Sir Chris Bonnigton, Junko Tabei and Sushil Gupta of Hyatt

Regency were gravely concerned about the deteriorating ecology of the Himalayan region, specially Gangotri area. They wanted to do something to arrest the deterioration and take steps to improve the ecology of the area.

The Ganga emerges from the snout (Gaumukh) of Gangotri glacier. It is known as Bhagirathi, upto Rudrapryag, where it is joined by River Alaknanda; beyond this point it is known as Ganga. Water from Ganga is considered holy and pure with medicinal properties and retains its purity for long. The river Ganga, its source Gaumukh, the Gangotri temple, its surrounding area and Ganga water itself have been part of India's culture and heritage for centuries. It is the wish of every Hindu to visit Gangotri, at least once in their life time.

The Gangotri basin comprises the Gangotri town with the sacred temple and a large number of Himalayan peaks e.g Kedarnath, Chaukhambha, Bhagirathi, Shivling, and Gangotri. It is, therefore, the most popular area attracting a large number of mountaineers, trekkers and pilgrims. The township of Gangotri is situated at the confluence of rivers Bhagirathi and Kedarganga with an average altitude of 3740m. Before 1985, there were limited visitors to the area due to the difficult journey, which involved crossing river Jhanvi Gorge at Bhairon Ghati. After construction of the bridge over the Gorge and a metalled road upto Gangotri, the number of visitors increased manifold. This has naturally resulted in depletion of natural resources in the area as these were mercilessly exploited to cater to the needs of visitors. Various studies, including one by WWF-India had revealed that Gangotri glacier, which was earlier receeding at the speed of 10 meters annually, was now receeding 23 meters every year. This is alarming as it will impact India's climate and as well as flow of water in the rivers, resulting in an adverse effect on its agriculture.

Himalayan Environment Trust (HET) with Capt. M.S. Kohli as its Chairman, Sushil Gupta as Vice Chairman and the late Sir Edmund Hillary as Patron felt that Gangotri area was the worst polluted and it was necessary to implement measures to improve the ecology of the area. For this purpose, Gangotri Conservation Project was conceptualised after several visits to the area.

Gangotri Conservation Project (GCP) was launched in June 1994 after an International Seminar and an International Trek to Tapovan/Gaumukh, led by world renowned mountaineer Reinhold Messner. My younger son Ashu accompanied the team. The aim was to clean and green the Gangotri basin. I agreed to become the Honorary Director of this project and Col K.S. Mall (Retd) of 11 GR was appointed Chief Warden.

The first Steering Committee meeting was held on 28 June 1994, in which representatives of government of India and Uttar Pradesh Government (now Uttarakhand Government), participated to formulate a strategy. The meeting in which I was present was chaired by Capt. M.S. Kohli, and was attended by Sir Edmund Hillary (Patron), Mr Maurice Herzog, Mr Reinhold Messner, Ms Junko Tabei, Mr Ko Yoshida, Mr Norbu Tenzing Norgay (Rep of Mr Blum), Mr J.C. Kala (Jt Secretary Ministry of Environment and Forests Government of India) Mr AD Moddie, Ms Bachendri Pal, Mr. Sushil Gupta (MD Hyatt Regency) Late Brig Bhopinder Singh, Col K.S. Mall and representative of government of UP. The project was to be administered jointly by HET, Government of India, UP government, some experts and local representatives. Initially 50,000 US dollars were contributed by American Himalayan Foundation, headed by Mr. Blum. An amount of Rs 25 Lakhs each was contributed by the Government India and Uttar Pradesh Government.

During the next 10 years, I was able to create an organisation Gangotri Consarvation Project (GCP) to implement the programme and made innumerable trips to Gangotri and Gaumukh to ensure proper implementation.

During 1994-2004, GCP was able to achieve the following:-

1. Awareness programme was launched through distribution of Himalayan Code of Conduct, sponsored lectures in National Institute of Mountaineering, Uttarkashi, construction of 'obelisk' at vantage points and frequent meetings with local citizens under the chairmanship of District Collector. People are now conscious about the importance of preserving the ecological balance in the area.

2. One lakh trees were planted in Bhatwari Tehsil with the help of local people and students, on degraded land and these were subsequently handed over to Village Van Panchayats. Nurseries were set up at Rowara on land provided by Forest Department, Maneri College and ITBP Mathli.

3. There was widespread cutting of trees in forest areas, and the wood was used as fuel by lodges and ashrams in Gangotri area. At our request, 274 LPG connections were released by Indian Oil Company and District Magistrate was requested to allot them to consumers only in Gangotri. Arrangements were also made to replenish the cylinders frequently. This saved 4700 kg of firewood daily.

4. There was huge accumulated garbage at various base camps—Bhojbas and Gangotri—and this was being pushed into the Bhagirathi. Special expeditions were organised with the help of local mountaineers and youth and the garbage was collected from base

camps and from thre track Gangotri-Bhojbas and backloaded to Gangotri. Garbage at Gangotri was also collected and brought to one central place. From 1996 to 1999, as much as 35,233 kg of garbage was collected.

5. An incinerator was installed at Gangotri to dispose off the biodegradable garbage. This was operated by GCP personnel. Tin and glass was backloaded to Uttarkashi and disposed of through scrap dealers.

6. Fifty garbage bins were placed at various places at Gangotri and enroute to Gaumukh.

7. On request from local people some pre-fabricated toilets were set up at Gangnani, Gangotri, Chirbas and Bhojbas.

8. Gangotri had a 20 kW mini micro hydel plant on Kedar Ganga, which seldom functioned. GCP was able to persuade the National Coordinator and UP government to set up a mini micro hydel with the capacity of 250 kW with the help of UNDP/GEF to provide electricity to Gangotri.

9. Bhojbas—Abode of Bhojpatra (Betula Utelis), had been denuded of bhojpatra as locals had used it as fuel and construction of temporary dhabas. GCP took two steps to rehabilitate this place;

   (a) Started a nursery of bhojpatra at Chirbas, with the approval of Forest Department and started planatation of bhojpatras at Bhojbas on the land allotted by the Forest Department.

   (b) Provided 15 sets of quickly erected lodges to the Forest Department for replacement of dhabas on the route Gangotri-Gaumukh. Each set was also given LPG connection, stove and a garbage bin.

10. With the advice of Dr Iqbal Husnain, GCP persuaded the Technology Department of government of India to set up a weather station at Bhojbas to monitor the weather condition, so that data could be collected about recession of Gangotri glacier.

11. There was no progress on declaration of Gangotri as a National Park, though a notification was issued to invite objections. GCP continued to pressurize the Government to declare the area as a National Park, which has since been done.

12. Several meetings were held under the chairmanship of District Magistrate, Uttarkashi (Mr Venketeshwarlu and Mr Ghosh at different periods were involved) with the important citizens of the area and the press and their feedback was taken to improve the project.

13. The Project was continuously evaluated by the DFO, (Mrs. Ewa Sharma and later Mr. Tiwari) Director Ministry of Environment, Government of India, Dr Kediyal Professor, G.B. Pant University of Agriculture and Technology, Ranichauri and GCP sub, committee comprising Mr D. Moddie and Mr Gurdiyal Singh.

14. An interesting aspect must be mentioned. There was a PIL (Public Interest Litigation:PIL no:23534 of 1995) by Mr O.P. Bhatt, environmental activist and others in Allahabad High Court in 1996, about the pollution of Gangotri area. A judge of the High Court personally visited the area and issued specific instructions about measures to be taken to improve the area. In response, the UP Government quoted the programmes of the GCP, as an example of improvement in the area.

15. GCP in consultation with Uttarkashi district administration selected a boy and a girl to visit

Japan, as part of a team, led by Ms Bechendri Pal on invitation from Ms Junko Tabei (Trustee HET). They took part in operations to clean and save Mount Fiji in Japan.

16 A seminar was held on 30 March, 1996, in collaboration with WWF (World Wide Fund for Nature) and PCED (People's Commission for Environment and Development). It was chaired by Dr Karan Singh, the Chief guest was Mr. Samar Singh, Secretary General of WWF-India and Guest of Honour was Sir Edmund Hillary. I made a presentation on the progress of GCP; this was followed by a lively discussion. Important points brought out were noted for implementation.

17. Another seminar was held on 28 March 1998, on Eco Tourism in Garhwal. There were special invitees from Uttarkashi who actively participated in discussion and presented their viewpoints affecting Gangotri.

18. Dr Iqbal Husnain, Prof in Jawaharlal Nehru University had carried out a comprehensive study of Gangotri Glacier. He was also Adviser of GCP. On his advice, we recommended to Uttarakhand, Government to institute following measures to save the glacier:

    (a) No construction or eating places beyond Bhojbas.

    (b) Restrict number of visitors to Gaumukh.

    (c) Pedestrian traffic over Gangotri Glacier be banned.

    (d) Plying only electric operated vans beyond Bhairon Ghati.

In May 2003, I developed cancer of bladder and was

operated upon in the Army Hospital. My family members, Neeru, Pravin and Ashutosh with their wives, Ranjana and Col. Yadu Kumar as also grand children took affectionate care, which was a source of strength and satisfaction (Reena and Prabal were in USA, but were in telephonic touch). This prevented me from taking any further active part in the GCP activities. My responsibilities were handed over to Mr Malia and I became the Vice Chairman of the GCP. Since then not much has happened in the GCP. However, the Uttarakhand Government has suddenly become aware of the serious situation in Gangotri area and has instituted measures, which the GCP had been recommending for years. Some examples are given below:

- Restriction on number of vehicles from Bhairon Ghati to Gangotri. Earlier, there was no check.
- Number of visitors proceeding beyond Gangotri to Bhojbas/Gaumukh and Tapovan restricted.Check post set up at Gangotri to monitor and restrict visitors.
- Checkpost ensures that disposables carried by visitors are brought back and not left behind as garbage.
- An organisation of safaiwalas set up at Gangotri to clean and collect garbage.

Recent Calamity in Uttarakhand

The June 2013 flash flood in the Char Dham Area of Uttarakhand, as per reports, led to about 1000 dead, and approximately 10,000 missing. Over 100,000 people were rescued by a massive operation involving the Indian Army, Air Force, ITBP (Indo-Tibetan Border Police), NDRF (National Disaster Relief Force), Border Road and the local administration. Unfortunately, the calamity brought into sharp focus the warnings of legendary mountaineers, who regularly visited the area and flagged it repeatedly as extremely polluted and a rapidly developing ecological catastrophe, all 20 years ago. It was to save the fragile ecology of the area that they launched the pilot scheme of GCP in the Gangotri area in 1994.

Since 1994, the number of pilgrims and tourists visiting the area, along with large numbers of vehicles and ponies has increased manifold. A haphazard infrastructure arose to cater to their needs, most of it without any oversight, near the banks of rivers and on deforested hill slopes. Lessons of the CHIPKO movement, which involved women of the area hugging the trees to prevent their cutting by contractors, were forgotten. The eco-system could not cope with this unchecked influx of visitors and consequent developmental activities. The area was a potential catastrophe ready to happen awaiting the right natural trigger.

The Gangotri Conservation Project was conceived to make locals, visitors, and the administration aware of the urgent need to prevent further degradation of the area. The GCP had initially planned to work for 6 years i.e. 1994-2000 but later extended its operations till 2005 on local request.

We should learn from the 2013 tragedy and undertake suitable measures to prevent further deterioration of this sensitive and fragile area to avoid future calamities.

Second Post War IMA Course Association

`During 1939-45 war, Indian Military Academy was converted into an Officers' Training School, which conducted short courses for emergency commission. After the war, IMA reverted to its original role of training regular officers for the Army. As mentioned earlier, the First Course started in February 1946 and Second Course commenced on 8 August, 1946 and got commissioned on 21 December 1947. I was part of this course. By 1987 all of us had retired and settled at various places. Some of our friends had migrated overseas.

Brig A.S. Cheema, my colleague from Second Course IMA (1947 batch) had the brilliant idea to start an Association and maintain a directory of all 1947 commissioned officers including those who went to Pakistan and Bangladesh. We held the first get-together on 21 December 1987. Brig Cheema became the Secretary/Convener, Brig Bhattacharya the Treasurer and I its President. Chapters of the Association were started in Pune and Chandigarh where a substantial number of officers had settled post retirement.

The highlights of the associations activities were an annual luncheon in Delhi on 21 December of every year (still being held as on date), Silver Jubilee, Golden Jubilee and Diamond Jubilee celebrations (25, 50 and 60 years post commissioning) at IMA Dehradun.

The saga of the Second Course will not be complete without mentioning about the invitation from our counter parts from Pakistan to visit them and celebrate jointly Diamond Jubilee of our joining the Second IMA Course on 8 Aug, 2006. This was the period when Indo-Pak dialogue was in full swing to improve mutual relations and the Government was encouraging people to people contacts. By 10 July, 2006 all preparations were complete and we were enthusiastically looking forward to the trip to Pakistan. Then came the bomb blast of 11/7 in Mumbai and the whole edifice so elaborately built up came crashing down. It was felt by both Pakistan course mates and us, that in view of sudden deterioration of political environment in both countries, the time was not conducive the visit of such a large number of retired senior Army officers with families to Pakistan. After mutual consultation and after informing the Ministry of External Affairs and Army Headquarters we regrettably cancelled the visit.

Current Challenges Confronting the Armed Forces

In recent years, I have often reflected on some of the important issues concerning the Armed Forces, which are of vital interest to them and have not yet been resolved. Here I discuss them in the paragraphs that follow.

Higher Defence Structure

Sixty six years ago, at the time of Independence, on advice of Lord Mountbatten and Lord Ismay (Adviser to Mountbatten), Defence Committee of the Cabinet (DCC) was created to take decisions on defence matters at national level. Three Service Chiefs and Defence Secretary were to be in attendance during their meetings. They were supported by Defence Minister's Committee (DMC), Chiefs of Staff Committee (COSC), Joint Planning Committee (JPC) and Joint Intelligence Committee (JIC). After 1948, when operations in J&K ceased, DCC hardly met till 1962 (Chinese attack on India), when DCC was replaced by Emergency Committee of the Cabinet. This was later replaced by Cabinet Committee on Security (CCS); Service Chiefs and Defence Secretary were not required to attend the meetings, unless they were especially invited. Defence Minister's Committee was replaced by Defence Minister's morning prayers, which was attended by Service Chiefs and Defence Secretary; there being no formal agenda for the meeting, the latest developments and events, concerning Armed Forces were discussed and decisions taken.

Prior to 1962, the numerical size of the three Services was small and the nation did not have many security threats. The country has since fought five wars (1947-48, 1962, 1965, 1971 and Kargil) and is surrounded by potentially hostile neighbours. Moreover, the country is also combating insurgency and terrorism. Thus, our national security environment remains a matter of serious concern.

After the Kargil war, government realised flaws in the Higher Defence decision making structure and to review it a committee, under chairmanship of Mr. K. Subrahmanyam was appointed. It submitted its report in 1999. It is worthwhile to quote the serious indictment made by them on our National Security System:

> 'India is perhaps the only major democracy, where Armed Forces Headquarters are outside the Apex Government Structure. The present obsolete system has perpetuated the culture of the British Imperial Theatre system of India Command, whereas what we need is a National Defence Headquarters. The *status quo* is often mistakenly defended as embodying civilian ascendency over the Armed Forces, which is not the real issue. In fact locating the Service Headquarters in the Government will further enhance civilian supremacy.'

The Kargil Review Committee Report was considered by a Group of Ministers who felt that the functions of COSC had revealed serious weaknesses in its ability to provide single point military advice to the Government and the Institution needed to be appropriately revamped. They appointed a Task Force under the chairmanship of Arun Singh, Minister of State for Defence to examine the defence aspects. Their report was submitted in 2000 and *inter alia,* recommended appointment of Chief of Defence Staff (CDS) and Vice Chief of Defence Staff. CDS was to be permanent Chairman of Chiefs of Staff Committee. The appointment was to be held by the Three Services in rotation. They also recommended that Service Headquarters should cease to be 'attached offices' and be integrated with the Ministry of Defence and there should be cross posting of officers so that decision making is speeded up.

It must be mentioned that since Independence Service

Chiefs have been gradually marginalised in decision-making and their order of precedence has been lowered, which further eroded their standing and ability in higher decision-making.

The Government implemented some of the recommendations of Arun Singh Task Force. In 2001 Service Headquarters were redesignated as 'Integrated Army/ Navy/Air Force Headquarters of Ministry of Defence.' This was only window dressing and official procedures continued to be followed as before. Further, Chief of Integrated Defence Staff to Chiefs of Staff Committee. (CISC) was created, to be headed by a three star General. (to be held by Services in rotation). He was to be a non-voting member of Chiefs of Staff Committee. He was supported by various joint committees. However, no decision was taken on the issue of CDS.

In 2012, the Government appointed Naresh Chandra Task Force, which also recommended appointment of a permanent Chairman-Chief of Staff and closer integration of Service Headquarters with Ministry of Defence, through cross posting of officers. These recommendations have not yet been implemented by the Government.

It is reiterated that Services have grown in size, their weapon systems have become complex and nuclear weapons have added a further dimension. A substantial portion of the nation's budget is spent on Armed Forces. There is, therefore, an urgent need to implement reforms in our higher Defence Structure as recommended by various committees, especially those related to Higher Defence set up. Mr Anthony's (Defence Minister) recent statement indicates that there is no move to implement these reforms for the present. National Security Adviser (NSA), who has been either from the Foreign Service or an ex-Police Officer, cannot replace the functions of a CDS. A firm political leadership with a vision and will is required to implement this vital defence reform and not depend on the advice of bureaucracy, who have vested interest in maintaining *status quo* and keep the Services away from higher policy formulation.

Integration of Service Headquarters with Ministry of Defence

Various committees have recommended that Service HQs, which are attached offices to the Ministry of Defence (MOD) should be fully integrated with it. Merely redesignating them as "Integrated HQ of MOD" does not serve the purpose. Many IAS officers in MOD are not fully aware of service organisations, their requirements and their weapon systems. When I was Director Staff Duties at Army HQ during 1977-79, some IAS officers in MOD at Under Secretary and Deputy Secretary levels often approached my staff to seek assistance and guidance in preparation of notings, regarding proposals submitted by Army HQ to be put up to their seniors. Integration of Service HQ and MOD is, therefore, essential and can be achieved by posting of Service Officers to MOD in some posts up to joint secretary level. This will promote better understanding of Services problems, facilitate smooth handling of proposals and cases, and result in early decision-making and save time. A greater necessity exists for such integration in Department of ex-servicemen, as civilian officers are unaware of problems of ex-servicemen. I feel that even Secretary of this Department ought to be from the Services in the rank of Lt General. More recently, ex-servicemen have been holding rallies and voicing their grievances publicly. On the subject of one rank one pension, a large number of ex-service men have even retuned their medals and decorations to the President, which was widely publicised by the media. This is a shame and there is need for the Government to consider their problems sympathetically and resolve them soon. Even the Supreme Court had recently urged the Government to resolve the problems of ex-servicemen, as ultimately it affects the morale of serving soldiers. This has further strained the relationship between Services and the bureaucracy, which is unwarranted.

Shortage of Officers in the Army

Shortage of officers in the Armed Forces is a matter of concern, as it affects their fighting potential. Though Air Force and Navy also face shortage in officer cadre, shortage of officers in the Army is critical. The sanctioned strength of officers in the Army is 47,762, whereas the present strength on ground is 36,790; the deficiency thus works out to 23% of the authorised cadre. The main shortage is at lower levels in the ranks of majors and captains, lieutenants, which gives the fighting edge to the unit. The young officers face the brunt of battle and have always displayed outstanding gallantry in previous wars. The shortage is likely to be further aggravated in future, as the Army has plans to raise a Mountain Corps and additional infantry divisions, in the next few years to meet perceived threats. Some urgent steps are required to overcome this shortage of officers.

It is learnt that the Army is considering measures to meet this situation. A new Officers Training Academy for is already established in Gaya and has started functioning; it will reach its full capacity to train 750 officers by 2015. Efforts are being made to enhance training capacity of IMA Dehradun and OTA Chennai by increasing training facilities e.g accommodation, training areas. However, the process will take a few years. In view of this, the Government should consider taking the following steps:-

(a) Making terms and conditions of Short Service Commissioned officers more attractive including provision for their lateral entry into Para Military Forces to enable them to serve upto 60 years of age.

(b) Raising more Territorial Army units (Infantry)

(c) Making NCC training compulsory for undergraduates and on graduation, they should serve in the Armed Forces for a limited period. This will give relief to units in the junior ranks.

(d) Considering a system of 'reserve' officers, with a liability for active service during any emergency. Presently, a retired officer has a liability to be recalled for active service for upto 2 years from the date of retirement.

Earlier, adequate number of people were not opting for a career in the Army. Since the revision of pay and allowances of officers after the 6th Pay Commission (despite anomalies) response for an officer career in the Armed Forces has improved. But it is far from adequate. Further, allowing families in more field stations and the vast unemployment situation in the country has attracted more people to defence services. But there is still a shortfall in the required number of officers.

Pay and Allowances of Officer Cadre

Prior to Independence of India, pay and allowances of Service officers and officers of Indian Civil Service (ICS) now redesignated as Indian Administrative Service (IAS) were at par. This parity was disturbed after Independence and an IAS officer was given an edge over the Service officer. Successive Pay Commissions, which did not have a Service member (Services made only representation of their case) though Services constitute the largest component of Government Central Services, have further increased this gap. The gap is all the more glaring in the case of Services vis-à-vis Police as the latter is a uniformed Service. In some States, 1981 batch police officers have become Director General (DG) with 3 stars, those of 1987 batch have become

Inspector General (IGP) with 2 stars and the 1994 batch have become Deputy Inspector General (DIG) with one star. In the Army corresponding years are 1972, 1975, and 1979 i.e difference of 10 to 15 yrs. Difference between IAS and the Services is even greater. In the Army, rank structure is pyramidic and promotions can be made only against clear vacancies. In the civil side a post can be upgraded, based on expediency. Top five ranks in the Army constitute 10% of total cadre whereas in Civil a complete batch is promoted to the next rank.

Service conditions and professional requirements in Services are vastly different from IAS and IPS. In IAS and IPS every officer retires at Director/DIG level but in Army an officer retires at the least at Colonel level. Moreover, a Colonel attains this rank after 18-20 yrs of service, while an IAS officer would have already become a Joint Secretary–equivalent to Major General. It is therefore essential and justified that a Colonel's gross salary should be at par with Director/DIG and so on.

The above anomalies have irked the the Armed Forces and several attempts by them to get a satisfactory salary package for officers have been unsuccessful, mainly due to hurdles created by bureaucracy. This has resulted in a strained relationship, between the Services and the bureaucracy. Unfortunately, our political leaders have neither the time nor the will to intervene and resolve this unhealthy state of of affairs. Vacillation has affected the morale of the Armed Forces, who are the only institution available as a last resort in time of crises, as recent events have amply demonstrated.

Leisure and Spiritual Pursuits

As a result of my ailment, I had to make frequent trips to the hospital for check ups and treatment. I was advised complete rest. I therefore decided to take to painting. I had no experience and had to study books to learn the new art. However, I was able to produce one painting a month—mostly copies of prints. I have done about 24 paintings, so far. The subjects covered are lanscapes, flowers, image of Sri Ganesh etc, all in acrylic. This has given me tremendous satisfaction.

Due to service conditions and other occupations after retirement, I was unable to regularly devote time to meditation and Naam Japa as instructed by my Guru. However, for the last ten years or so I have not missed a single day except when indisposed. My wife Neeru has an apartment in our Guru's Ashram at Vrindavan located on the banks of the river Yamuna. She spends most of her time in the Ashram. I also spend atleast 10 days in a month at the Ashram. I also try to find time to play golf, twice a week. Rest of the time I spend with my family members and watch television to keep myself informed of the latest happenings, the world over.

Index